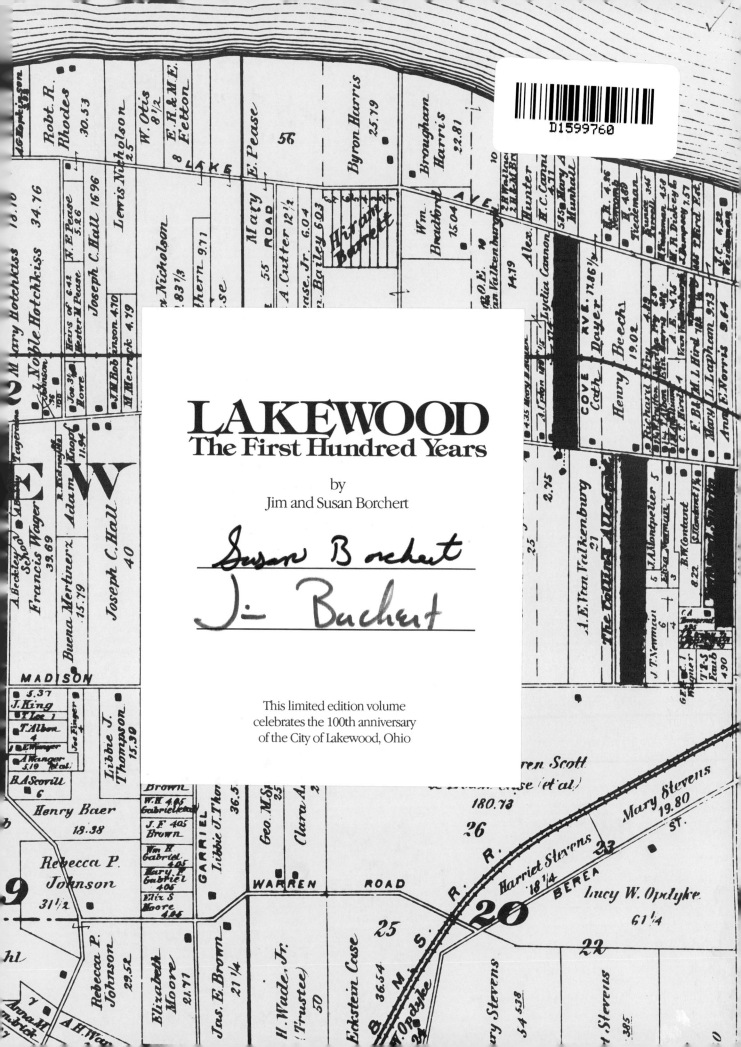

LAKEWOOD
The First Hundred Years

by
Jim and Susan Borchert

Susan Borchert

Jim Borchert

This limited edition volume
celebrates the 100th anniversary
of the City of Lakewood, Ohio

Home Federal Savings Bank, Lakewood's oldest financial institution,
is proud and privileged to sponsor this limited edition of
Lakewood: The First Hundred Years 1889-1989
This book is a reflection upon the past. It is a story of a community
and its people who forged a rich heritage of cultural, educational,
commercial, and charitable enterprises of which we are justly proud.
We dedicate this book to the citizens of Lakewood—
past, present, and future.

HOME
Federal Savings Bank

THE
DONNING COMPANY
PUBLISHERS

NORFOLK/VIRGINIA BEACH

Design by Sharon Varner Moyer

LAKEWOOD
The First Hundred Years

Jim and Susan Borchert

To Our Parents:
Miriam Elson and Frank Roy Borchert, Sr.
Janet Goldberg and Joseph Schwartz

The Donning Company/Publishers
5659 Virginia Beach Boulevard
Norfolk, Virginia 23502

Edited by Christina Cramer
Elizabeth B. Bobbitt, Senior Associate Editor
Richard A. Horwege, Senior Editor

Library of Congress Cataloging-in-Publication Data

Borchert, James, 1941-
    Lakewood : the first hundred years, 1889 to 1989 / by
James Borchert and Susan Borchert.
       p.   cm.
    Bibliography: p.
    Includes index.
    ISBN 0-89865-774-1
    1. Lakewood (Ohio)—History—Pictorial works.
2. Lakewood (Ohio)—Description and travel—Views.
I. Borchert, Susan, 1947-   II. Title.
F499.L17B67   1989   89-7658
977.1'31—dc20   CIP

Printed in the United States of America

CONTENTS

INTRODUCTION

On August 31, 1989, Lakewood officially reached its one hundredth year. One century earlier residents of the eastern portion of Rockport Township decided to form a new community separate from the township. To do so they petitioned the commissioners of Cuyahoga County for permission to form a hamlet named "Lakewood."

So began the story of Lakewood. The next forty years witnessed the rapid transformation of East Rockport vineyards and orchards into a suburban community. The new community moved quickly from hamlet to village, and by 1911 it had become a city. By 1930 Lakewood was the county's second largest city. Although largely a bedroom community for Cleveland workers, Lakewood rivaled the metropolis in density. At the same time residents had constructed a viable community that housed a diverse population and an incredible array of institutions: civic, social, cultural, educational, recreational, and religious. With quiet, tree-lined streets and a wide range of comfortable housing, Lakewood stood out as one of the most desirable communities in the state.

If the first forty years produced monumental changes, the next sixty provided the young community with more than its share of challenges and tribulations. With the rest of the nation Lakewood soon experienced the Great Depression of the 1930s followed by World War II. If Lakewood emerged in the 1950s as an even more impressive and respected community, the mature suburb also began to confront a range of problems previously associated only with urban centers. Moreover, as Cleveland and other industrial cities began to experience sharp changes and dislocations in their economies, Lakewood and other suburbs also began to feel the pinch.

At the same time, other changes began to appear. While remaining a bedroom suburb, the city increasingly combined its traditional role as a suburb with that of a white-collar employment center. In the process high-rise office buildings replaced the once busy commercial center at Warren Road and Detroit. With the development of region-wide cultural programs and institutions such as the Great Lakes Shakespeare Festival and the Beck Center for the Cultural Arts, Lakewood emerged at the end of the first hundred years as a satellite city.

Lakewood: The First Hundred Years is an illustrated history whose publication marks the community's one hundredth anniversary. It is intended to be an impressionistic interpretation of the community's history since its settlement by Americans of European and African descent. Although the story begins with these settlements, the book concentrates on the years that followed the formation of Lakewood as a hamlet in 1889. While Margaret Butler and other local historians have effectively covered the early years, this is the first substantial narrative for the one hundred years since 1889.

We have selected a number of themes that we feel make the Lakewood story especially interesting and unique. Clearly the most central is the transformation of the community from wilderness to garden to suburb to satellite city. In the process Lakewood experienced dramatic changes in institutions, social life, and physical environment.

The ethnic, religious, and social class differences of the peoples of Lakewood help account for the community's distinctive style and makeup. From its founding as a frontier settlement, East Rockport/Lakewood contained peoples with very different backgrounds. Lakewood remains a diverse community as new immigrants from foreign lands continue to make their home in the city.

Perhaps even more remarkable are Lakewood's distinctive environments. As Rockport natives and new suburbanites constructed a new community at the turn of the century, they produced at least five different landscapes. Four of these were residential: a working-class ethnic urban village (the Bird's Nest) in southeast Lakewood; elite communities in Clifton Park and along the lake; a middle-class, "middle" Lakewood of single- and double-family homes; and apartment dwellings. Commercial landscapes along Detroit and Madison make up the fifth. These landscapes have undergone considerable change over time. As the community matured, some virtually disappeared, while others blossomed and grew.

Finally, while we briefly treat the city's political development and institutions, our focus is on its social and cultural life. We have attempted to trace the ways

Lakewood residents lived and the ways their lives have changed over time. *The First Hundred Years* also considers how residents sought to overcome the various challenges of community-building, depression, war, maturation, and discrimination. While not always successful, these efforts demonstrate a vitality and spirit that help mark Lakewood as a vital, unique, and pleasant place in which to live and work.

The book's organization needs some comment. Odd-numbered chapters provide the general narrative history, while even-numbered chapters, called "Vignettes," offer more personal treatments of Lakewood life. Most of these are excerpts from reminiscences by Rockport/Lakewood residents. Each chapter includes one or two "Focus" sections. They are designed to provide an indepth view of Lakewood people and institutions. Some are well known but many others are not known well enough. In many cases the photographs illustrate the text they also provide important supplements in a number of areas.

Several caveats are in order here. While we have been working on Lakewood history since 1980, our research took a different focus. With only six months to research, write, and illustrate this book, we could hardly develop every aspect of community history. The limitations of time and sources cast a long shadow over our work, nevertheless we have struggled to get the story straight and the facts correct. Despite our best efforts, we fear glitches and errors remain.

ACKNOWLEDGMENTS

This book would not have been possible without the help of many, many individuals and organizations. Our sponsors, Home Federal Savings Bank, kindly underwrote the cost of the volume while the Lakewood Historical Society has taken responsibility for distribution. Beyond this, the Historical Society, and especially its curator, Sandy Koozer, and its business manager, Janie Gaydos have supplied us with numerous documents, photographs, and encouragement. We also appreciate the support of the Lakewood Centennial Commission.

We selected our photographs from a pool of several thousand; many of these came from local archives. In addition to the excellent collection at the Lakewood Historical Society, the Lakewood Public Library and its invaluable staff (especially Shirley Henderson) provided us with many photographs and answered our many questions about obscure subjects. We have also benefited from John Grabowski's and Ann Sindelar's extensive knowledge of the Western Reserve Historical Society collections. The Cleveland Press Collection at Cleveland State University proved to be our most important source for photographs and we are grateful to Henry York for his assistance there. The Cleveland Public Library and the Ohio Historical Society also provided valuable visual records.

We have also received great help from a number of community organizations. It is impossible to thank everyone but we would like to express our gratitude here to Lakewood city officials, Don Hadsel and Jeff Hastings, Jan Loeder of Lakewood public schools, John Kerezy and Meg Algren of Lakewood Hospital, Anthony DiBiasio, Jr., of the Lakewood High School Alumni Association, Jim Sanders of the Rocky River Historical Society, Nick Brodella and Faith Killius at Beck Center, Dick Obermanns and Anda Cook of the Cuyahoga Plan, and Marge Ditsler of the Lakewood Chamber of Commerce.

Lakewood residents past and present also provided us with photographs and other materials. We have benefited greatly from the many individuals and families who have shared their photographs and stories with us. Some of these are recognized in the captions to their photographs throughout. Others deserve special recognition: Bill Becker, Wayne Cahoon, Jr., Dan Chabek, Larry Clark, Mike Emely, John Forristall, Charlie Geiger, Mary Jacko, Josephine Kassouf, John Kavcar, Robert and Kathy Lawther, Jerry Patno, Virginia Elias Plotz and William Plotz; Helen, Donna, and Jim Pohorence; Evie Rosenblum, Judah Rubinstein, Russ Salzbrenner, William Tiell, and Jeff Webb. For those whom we may have inadvertently left out, we extend both our sincere apologies and thanks.

Our research and especially the acquisition of photographs has been significantly aided by a number of grants. Our previous work on Lakewood benefited from grants from the Albert J. Beveridge Memorial Fund of the American Historical Association, the American Association for State and Local History, and the National Endowment for the Humanities. The Donning Publishing Company provided funding for photographs for the book as did a Research Challenge Grant from Cleveland State University.

A number of people have aided immeasurably on the drafting of the manuscript. At Donning, pictorial history coordinator Bev Hainer and editors Christina Cramer and Richard Horwege have been helpful. Nathaniel Eatman and Deborah Bell of Cleveland State University provided us with excellent copies of most of the photographs. Cheryl Brooke provided stylistic guidance and immeasurably improved our prose. Thomas Campbell, Shirley Henderson, Sandy Koozer, and Wayne Cahoon, Jr., carefully read an earlier draft and alerted us to our mistakes. The problems, errors, and inaccuracies that remain in the text are there despite the best efforts of those mentioned above, and as a result are clearly our responsibility.

We are especially indebted to Miriam Borchert whose patience we continually tested with infinite questions about Lakewood's past. We are equally thankful for the fine work of our research assistant, Dawn Likar, who braved long drives from Painesville and brought great energy and enthusiasm to her work. Finally, we must apologize to our kitten, Mao, who tolerated, not always happily, our long hours away from home.

Chapter 1
From Wilderness to Garden: Rockport's Early Years

...the most plentifull, sweete, fruitfull, and wholsome of all the worlde.
Captain Arthur Barlowe, *The First Voyage Made to the Coasts of America...*, 1584

When Collins and Rosetta French returned to Rockport in 1856 to buy a farm, Collins found his new acquisition "in a condition worse than a state of nature. There had been about 15 acres cleared off and a log house and frame barn built, but it was all run down, the fence corners and around the stumps all grown up to bushes, briars and elders, and not a rod of good fence on the premises." He wrote in his diary that "the low land between Detroit Street [near Andrews Avenue] and the Lake was covered with bushes, trees, elders, grapevines, briars, old logs, stones and water from the running spring above." With the help of his new son-in-law Edwin Andrews, Collins and Rosetta put the land in good order within a few years. The farm eventually established a considerable reputation for its excellent apples, cherries, grapes, pears, and plums.

The beautiful gardens, orchards, vineyards, stately homes, and elaborate social life that increasingly marked East Rockport during the last three decades of the nineteenth century presented a dramatic change from the landscape of this area at the beginning of the century. When settlers of European and African descent first began to push west across the Cuyahoga River and into what would later be called Rockport Township, they confronted a heavily forested wilderness cut by small streams and pockmarked by swamps. When Collins' parents and family moved to Rockport in 1828, their fifty acres near what is now Garfield School were heavily forested. Over the next eighty years, settlers and their descendents would successively carve from the wilderness a frontier outpost, a farm settlement, and finally a highly specialized and tightly-knit agricultural community. Over the years Rockport residents transformed their frontier society into a more staid, less exuberant, and more exclusionary society. In addition to constructing a series of new institutions to serve their needs—churches, schools, and social organizations—they also established patterns on the land and attitudes toward public space that would be difficult for later generations to break. By the end of the late 1880s, East Rockport residents broke away from the township government and formed a new community with a new name.

Although the Connecticut Land Company purchased from the state of Connecticut the land that comprised the Western Reserve, Native Americans still controlled the area west of the Cuyahoga River. In 1805, a treaty with the Wyandottes, Delawares, Munsees, and Senecas opened this land for settlement. In the following year the land company sent a party under Seth Pease to survey the land

"The City of Cleveland from Lakewood Bluffs" circa 1870 to 1890 (?) was painted by Henry Wood Elliott. Courtesy of Beatrice Elliott and Carl Droppers

Some years later, in 1819, Rockport formed as a township in Cuyahoga County: Township No. 7, Range 14. Rockport contained twenty-one full sections, each one mile square, and four part-sections. East Rockport and later Lakewood made up the northeastern portion of the township. Neighboring townships included Dover on the west, Middleburg to the south, and Brooklyn on the east.

To an untrained eye, the Rockport landscape must have appeared to be true wilderness. Nevertheless, Native Americans left an imprint on the land that would profoundly affect the new settlement and those to follow. Their paths, eventually named Detroit and Warren, established the major routes through the young community. Settlers adopted these paths and oriented their new settlements and community around them. The intersection of these trails became the community's center.

State government improved on these passageways. In 1809, the Ohio legislature passed a bill to construct a post road running west from the fledgling settlement at Cleveland to the mouth of the Huron River. Following the Detroit Indian trail west, workers completed construction on a corduroy (log) road to Rocky River by 1810. In April 1809 the first wagon traversed the road, bringing new settlers George Peake and his family to Rockport. Mail service through the area also began in 1809.

Although a number of settlers came to Rockport, not all remained. Despite poor roads and occasional mail, life was far from easy in the wilderness. In 1818, when the Nicholson family arrived to take up residence on their 140 acres, they had to live in their covered wagon until they could build a log cabin (near what are now Detroit and Nicholson avenues). Israel Wagar, the son of Mars and Katurah, remembered working hard to clear the forest when the family settled on their land at Detroit and Warren in 1820. Frontier life also took many settlers before their time. Within six months of his family's settlement in 1812, forty-seven-year-old Nathan Alger died, leaving his wife and son Henry, age twenty-three, as family heads. Other dangers faced settlers. When Hepsibath Wright, the spouse of tavern-keeper Rufus, went one day to visit a neighbor, she confronted a large bear. Although eighty-seven years old when he arrived in Rockport, George Peake and his son later fought a "pitched battle" with "twenty rattle snakes and four copperheads."

If the forests presented considerable challenge to new settlers, they also offered great possibilities. Henry Alger, an early settler, remembered deer and raccoon abounded in the woods while "the fish were also very abundant in Rocky River; one man could catch with a spear in one night from twenty-five to fifty or sixty large pike, and sometimes one hundred." Wild plants could also supplement the limited diets produced by frontier farming. However, not all settlers possessed the necessary skills. Since Henry "was not a hunter," the Alger family "lived five weeks without one mouthful of bread, meat,

butter or milk in their house...they lived on potatoes and beans."

Early Rockport was a frontier community made up log cabins surrounded by small clearings scattered along the post road or Indian trails. Much of the land between remained forested. Subsistence agriculture and barter governed the community's economy; survival required the contributions of all family members. With virtually n stores and few peddlers, settlers had to travel to Clevelar where they sold produce and bought necessities. While the post road proved a considerable improvement over the Indian trails, it often fell into disrepair and at best provided a long, arduous, and bumpy trip.

These conditions encouraged considerable cooper tion between settlers. Pioneers helped each other "raise" homes and barns and used the occasions for community gatherings. Despite the distance between clearings, they actively sought each other out. As Alger noted later in his reminiscences, "the settlers claimed to be neighbors if they did not live more than eight or ten miles apart, and were well acquainted for ten, fifteen, or twenty miles around."

The difficult and demanding frontier life produced a vibrant, raucous, and tolerant society; it tended to diminish differences of class, gender, and race. Settlers turned any event such as a wedding or community proje into an exuberant community celebration. Taverns often served as the center of these gatherings. Early in 1819, when Rockport formed officially as a township and settle elected their first local government, they met at Rufus Wright's tavern on the west side of the Rocky River. Henr Alger recalled the proceedings were well oiled by "Captain Wright's good old whiskey." Two years later, after a community "bridge raising" produced the first bridge over the Rocky River, the participants held a wild celebration at Wright's tavern. Neither tavern keepers or their frequenters were looked down on; one of Rockport's most respected families, the Nicholsons, kept tavern in their home in the early years.

The frontier experience encouraged a blurring of gender roles. Survival provided little room for the nicetie: of urban society. Wives worked beside their husbands in th fields; death often required widows to take on both roles When Daniel Miner died in 1813, his spouse took over the operation of his tavern. Abigail Taylor Dean used "rigid economy and good management" to keep her family of nine children together when she was widowed in 1838. Women also played an active role in the dangerous underground railroad; Lydia Foster Hawkins' home serve as a station for escaped slaves on their way to Canada.

Perhaps most striking is the large number of African Americans in Rockport. Rockport laid claim to the county first black family, the George Peakes, who arrived in 1809 By 1820, African Americans accounted for one-fifth of the township's 157 residents and over 60 percent of all blacks the county. Some African-Americans apparently worked ... Adam Wagar, who owned two hundred acres of forest ... along Warren Road. According to the Daughters of ... American Revolution's (DAR) *Early Days of Lake-wood,* Wagar employed "twenty Negroes cutting wood on ... property; they lived in temporary shacks south of the ... sent Madison Avenue at Morrison Avenue."

While information on black Rockporters is frag-... at best, they seem to have lived side by side with ... white neighbors and participated in most com-... activities. Henry Alger's numerous references to ... orge Peake and his family indicated they played an ... portant role in the frontier community. However, ... spite owning 103 acres of land, neither George or his ... took part in the first township meeting in 1819 or ... er ones; the state prohibition on black voting probably ... counted for this condition.

Over time, the frontier became settled and Rockport ... gan to take on the trappings of an established agricul-... ral community. Internal improvements helped diminish ... isolation and privation. Beginning in 1820, a stage line ... ovided the first regular means of transportation. Im-... oved conditions and a growing population attracted an ... creasing number of merchants. Initially itinerant ped-... ers served the area, walking from cabin to cabin carrying ... ir wares of quill pens, ink, needles, and scissors. Wagon ... erchants eventually replaced these peddlers, bringing a ... der range of goods, including silk and cotton cloth, ... ooms, baskets, tubs, and books.

By 1848, most farmers had replaced their log cabins ... th frame or stone homes. In 1835, the Nicholsons, who ... rlier left their log cabin for a frame house, constructed a ... ore impressive white frame colonial. (Currently being ... stored by the Lakewood Historical Society and the City ... Lakewood, it sits on the south side of Detroit at Nichol-... n Avenue.) Two years later the Wagars abandoned their ... g cabin and built a stone house at the corner of Detroit ... d Warren.

As the initial settlers added land to their holdings ... d new settlers such as the Price French family and Dr. ... red Kirtland arrived in 1828 and 1837 respectively, the ... ilderness and forest receded before the onslaught of ... rm and pasture. With improved transportation and a ... rowing city to the east, Rockport farmers began to raise ... ops more for sale than family consumption. This precipi-... ted a change in crops. As late as 1855, many farmers still ... ised wheat, corn, and potatoes; in 1852, Thomas Hird's ... heat even won first prize from the Ohio Board of Agri-... ulture. Many also kept milk cows, as Stephen Phelps did ... n the northern part of his farm at Kenilworth and Detroit. ... evertheless, Rockport's thin humus soil over a base of ... ay and shale proved difficult to farm.

The arrival of Dr. Kirtland then proved fortuitous. ... lready a well respected physician and medical school ... rofessor, Kirtland also possessed considerable knowl-

edge of horticulture. During his Rockport residence until his death in 1877, the "Sage of Rockport," as he came to be known, established himself as one of the nation's lead-ing naturalists. After evaluating Rockport soil, he con-cluded that it was more suitable to the cultivation of fruits. Kirtland both demonstrated the potential of these crops and developed several new varieties of plants; one hybrid earned him the title of "Cherry King." Local histories credit various farmers for introducing fruit culture. Reputedly Walter Phelps turned to small fruits sometime after 1840; Walter Maile first grew strawberries, although not com-mercially. Nevertheless, Kirtland is generally given credit for convincing Ezra Nicholson to convert the family's farm to grape vineyards about 1850.

By 1879, the county history acknowledged the success of these efforts: "fruit growing is one of the most important and remunerative industries in Rockport." Cris-field Johnson, the history's compiler, was careful to note that this production came largely from East Rockport. He also pointed out that "the value of fruit sent to Cleveland from Detroit street in 1867 was $10,000 while in 1872 it was no less than $50,000."

As farmers shifted from subsistence to commercial agriculture, transportation became more important. This became especially true as they specialized in fruit produc-tion. In 1848, Rockport residents met to form the private Plank Road Company to improve the passage to Cleve-land. Construction began the following year, with the road following the course of the Detroit post road. By 1850 the company built a new bridge over the Rocky River. The private road required a toll for horses and wagons.

By 1848, a stable agricultural society had replaced the frontier settlement in East Rockport. About thirty family farms lined Detroit Street from West 117th to Rocky River. The community also claimed other amenities that set it off from the frontier, including a general store at Belle Avenue, a sawmill at St. Charles, several religious groups, including two churches, and a one-room school at Nichol-son Avenue. The general store became a community cen-ter "where everyone came to hear the latest news, discuss local problems and purchase" food and other necessities.

Formal religious services were also new to the community. Baptists first organized in 1832, although by 1850 they had ceased regular meetings. Their "com-modious meeting house" at Warren and Franklin provided an important community center for some years after. Swedenborgians formed in 1841 and constructed a church seven years later. Methodists also began to meet, although their building would wait until 1876. Mars Wagar provided the first formal education in 1829 when he hired Jonathan Parshall to hold class in a room in the Wagar home. The next year, Wagar and James Nicholson constructed the first log schoolhouse on the latter's property.

Although the Baptist "Tabernacle" provided an

important community center for religious and secular meetings, taverns continued to play an important role in Rockport society. However, their clientele increasingly became teamsters and farmers traveling the Plank Road rather than local residents. Nor did the presence of whiskey and taverns go unchallenged. As early as 1827, Datus Kelley urged voters at a township meeting to take a temperance pledge. As Lakewood historian Margaret Butler noted, Rockport increasingly "gained the reputation of conducting its township meetings minus the usual bottle of liquor." Even the venerable tavern came under attack; in 1858, John Taylor, the son of an early settler, warned that the selling of liquor in the "infernal huts" along the Plank Road made it "worse than the path frequented by bears and wolves in the old days."

If the temperance movement that was sweeping the country also played a role in the life of the young agricultural community, so too did the anti-slavery movement. As with the Western Reserve generally, Rockport provided a fertile soil for abolitionists. Some Rockporters even risked arrest and punishment for aiding escaped slaves. According to historian Russell Davis, "abolitionists were known in Lakewood as early as 1820 and fleeing slaves were brought there from Medina County" to await boats to take them to Canada. Rockport African-Americans undoubtedly contributed to that effort. Although the extent of underground railroads has often been overstated, some Rockporters do seem to have served as "conductors" and "station masters." In 1848, Philander Winchester returned to his native Painesville to rescue Walter Clark from slave catchers. Margaret Butler also noted that the Winchester home on Detroit (near the street of the same name) "was the key place in Rockport for the underground movement."

In contrast to their roles in frontier society, Rockport women experienced growing limitations. While they still had to find ways to support their family when widowed, their activities in the fields became more constricted. Social custom increasingly urged married women to concentrate their efforts on keeping house and educating their children. Nevertheless, some women began to take on larger community roles through activities in the temperance, anti-slavery, peace, and women's movements.

While at least some Rockporters embraced the radical programs of the antebellum period, the production of the community's orchards and vineyards produced important changes in the years after the Civil War. The "business directory" of the *Atlas of Cuyahoga County* published in 1874, provided a sense of this transformation and even an indication of greater changes in the future. Among the entries were Henry Beach, Grower of Fruit and Vegetables; J. C. Hall, Grower of Fruit; M. C. Hall, Grower of Fruit and Vegetables; C. W. Ranney, Fruit Grower; Lewis Nicholson and Company, proprietors of Lake Erie Nursery; and F. H. Wagar, Dealer in Real Estate

and Small Fruit Grower.

As farmers who followed Kirtland's advice found increased income and wealth, the small, unpretentious, agricultural settlement of thirty families of 1848 turned into an ostentatious community of large, elegant homes and carefully landscaped yards. By 1874 nearly ninety houses lined Detroit from Highland to the river. Five years later, the county history observed that Detroit Street was lined on either side by "numerous handsome and costly suburban residences, set in the midst of tastefully kept grounds."

In the period following the Civil War, East Rockporters began a new round of house building. This time they exchanged their plain frame farmhouses for larger and more elaborate structures. Following Kirtland's model, they also carefully landscaped their grounds. In 1888, the Wagars replaced their 1837 stone house with a large frame house at the corner of Warren and Detroit. In 1879, Mathew Hall, the son of Joseph and Sarah Curtis and a superintendent of the Plank Road, replaced his simple five-room frame house at 16906 Detroit with a more elegant brick structure (later the home of the YMCA). His brother, John, built an even more ostentatious Victorian house at 16913 Detroit. The most successful of the Hall children, John surrounded his house with a "floral paradise with winding paths, a sunken garden, hundreds of unusual trees, shrubs, and flowers." Henry and Sabrina Frost Beach, who arrived late in Rockport in 1864, saw their house at Detroit and Beach grow to seventeen rooms as Henry's business as a fruit merchant improved steadily.

By the 1880s a tightly-knit community emerged. In some respects it resembled the interdependence of the frontier society; in other ways social life experienced a dramatic transformation. When Lawrence Johnson's general store burned down in 1896, his neighbors went to work to help him out. Noble Hotchkiss offered his stone house nearby for a temporary store while others installed shelves. "Within a day the stone house was buzzing with activity." With their labor no longer necessary for family survival, children's roles changed dramatically. Largely freed from toils of field and home, the children of successful Rockport farmers enjoyed the pleasures of their peers. Hope Hird Browning, the daughter of Thomas and Hope Hird, remembered "bathing parties at the foot of Cove Avenue," croquet parties on the Edward's lawn, and a yearly strawberry festival at the Church of the Ascension, where the entire community enjoyed a full course dinner. At the same time, the wives of successful Rockport farmers increasingly spent their time directing servants, entertaining neighbors and friends, and attending meetings of church groups and other organizations.

The Temperance Sunday School was one of the most important of these organizations. Organized in 1867 as an affiliate of the Good Templars, members met each Sunday in the Tabernacle; according to Crisfield Johnson, they re "very zealous in behalf of the temperance cause." elve years later, members of the Disciples and thodist churches formed a chapter of the Women's ristian Temperance Union. Members visited local erns where they lectured customers on the evils of ohol and prayed for their redemption; they usually left eral members outside to get help, if necessary.

Ironically, at the same time the temperance crusade gan to heat up again, older taverns along the Plank ad persisted while fancy new resorts appeared on the ges of the Rocky River. The new enterprises, including e elaborate Cliff House, with a first-floor bar and John oll's beer garden, often catered to church picnics. nilarly, Benno Martinetz, a Swiss emigre, produced ne from his vineyard off Madison, near Belle Avenue.

While temperance reform persisted after the Civil ar, Rockport's commitment to racial equality, as the tion as a whole, began to erode. Oral histories collected Margaret Butler reveal that after 1860, white Rock-rters tended to refer to black neighbors only by first mes, usually preceded by a racial epithet. Similarly, rs Wagar II recalled a mixed marriage between a black an and white woman that "created quite a scandal." ese changes did not affect Jared Kirtland; in 1867 he red an African-American, Andrew Farmer, to manage his m. The Farmer family lived at 1435 Winchester Avenue r many years, although its role in the community is less ar than that of George Peake. The Kirtland estate also ovided a home for at least one other African-American nily.

In other ways, East Rockport became more exclu-nary. While residents had sought to overcome the nits of the rough terrain and deep river valleys, never-eless topography exerted an influence on the emerging ciety. Not unlike the divide created by the Cuyahoga ver that led to differences between Cleveland's east and est sides, Rockport also experienced tensions between ist and west. In 1838, western Baptists briefly separated om their eastern colleagues over doctrinal disputes. nilarly, Methodists and temperance advocates formed

separate organizations on each side of the river. As East Rockport grew and matured, Detroit Street residents became linked together in multiple ways, including mar-riage, friendship, and business ventures. The first tangible evidence of this emerging consciousness came in 1871 when residents of eastern Rockport Township voted to establish a separate school district named East Rockport. By 1885, they made the break complete by petitioning the county to incorporate under the name of Lakewood.

Nevertheless, East Rockport remained profoundly influenced by the pioneers' imprint on the mental and physical landscapes of the community. Some of these imprints reflect those generally shared by other Western Reserve communities. Unlike many new settlements in this region, Rockporters did not develop a town square.

One of the trademarks of Western Reserve settle-ments, especially those established by co-religionists, was the town square. A New England tradition transplanted by settlers on their arrival in northeast Ohio, the town square represented one of the distinctive traits of the area's landscape. To New Englanders the square was more than a physical plan; it symbolized community. Moreover, the public square represented the focal point of all com-munity activities, sacred and secular.

In contrast, East Rockport settlers seem to have made little or no effort to establish either a New England-style community or even to place a public square on the land. Neither did they share a common concern for a religious community. Committed to private ownership of land, the community's form emerged organically out of daily eco-nomic activities rather than from a plan laid down by residents to guide their settlement. Moreover, save for several plots set aside for schools, East Rockport land-holders established no central public land for either civic or symbolic purposes. Even the roads that linked them to the rest of the world remained private until 1901. When their progeny subdivided farms into house lots, their harvests reaped considerable wealth but left the com-munity bereft of public space.

View of the Curtis Hall Farm from the Hall house looking north to the lake, around the 1870s to the 1890s. The artist is unknown.
Courtesy of the Lakewood Historical Society

Shown here is the second bridge built over the Rocky River. The Plank Road Company constructed it near the mouth of the river in the 1850s. The bridge was "a wooden toll bridge twenty-four feet wide with its terminals half way down the slope. Toll was seven cents for one horse, ten cents for a team and fifteen cents for a double team."
Courtesy of the Lakewood Historical Society

According to Margaret Butler, James Nicholson began construction of his white colonial home in 1835. "As the Nicholsons became more prosperous, many changes took place in the homestead" at Detroit and Nicholson Avenue. James and Betsey's youngest son, Ezra, continued to live in the house as did two more generations after him. Over the years a number of additions increased the size and comfort of the home. It is currently being restored by the Lakewood Historical Society and City of Lakewood.
Courtesy of the Lakewood Public Library

Pictured here circa 1902 is Ezra Karlon Nicholson. He was the grandson of Ezra Nicholson and grew up in the family home on Detroit at Nicholson. His grandfather, Ezra, played an important role in East Rockport; he was president of the Rocky River Railroad Company and a director of the Lakewood Savings Bank. Besides helping to introduce fruit culture into Lakewood, he also established a real estate company to subdivide and sell family property. Ezra Nicholson also invented the Nicholson Self Recording Ship Log and Speed Indicator as well as several other devices.
Courtesy of the Lakewood Public Library

Originally built around 1838, the Honam house, the oldest stone house, sat on the northwest corner of St. Charles Avenue and Detroit. It is one of the oldest remaining structures in Lakewood. Constructed by John Honam, a Scottish weaver, the building housed his family for some years. Honam's daughter, Belle, and her husband, Orville Hotchkiss, also occupied the house. In later years the house served as a doctor's office, a post office, a grocery store, a barber shop, and an upholstery company. In 1952, the house was moved to Lakewood Park. It serves as the home of the Lakewood Historical Society in its in new location at Lakewood Park. Photograph by James Thomas, October 31, 1952; courtesy of the Cleveland Press Library and Collections, Cleveland State University Libraries

This photograph was taken after Lakewood farmers adopted Dr. Jared Kirtland's advice to cultivate fruit. The Mitchells grew grapes on their forty-acre farm on Summit Avenue north of Detroit. They are pictured here taking their grapes to the Growers' Market on Woodland Avenue near Cross Street in Cleveland.
Courtesy of the Lakewood Public Library

The Wagar house was located on the
southeast corner of Warren Road and
Detroit. One of Rockport's first families,
Mars and Keturah Wagar originally
came to Rockport in 1820. They purchased land between Detroit and Madison, Warren Road and Marlowe. Mars
initially built a log cabin on the hill at
St. Charles and Detroit. In 1837 he constructed a stone house at the corner of
Detroit and Warren Road which remained until 1888. In that year Mars'
son, Francis, constructed the large
frame house pictured here. It remained
at the location until Bailey's removed it
for their department store in 1930.
Courtesy of the Lakewood Public Library

Israel Dwelle Wagar was one of Mars and Keturah Wagar's four sons. Israel became a farmer in East Rockport and raised fruit. I. D. Wagar's home was located on Hilliard near Madison. His home suggests the changes to East Rockport's landscape by the 1870s. Large formal houses and carefully landscaped yards reflected the growing wealth of community residents. From D. J. Lake, Atlas of Cuyahoga County, *page 118.*

Adam Wagar, another son of Mars and Keturah, also became a fruit farmer. Adam's residence was located near his brother Israel's, on Madison at the intersection of Hilliard. This drawing, as with others from Lake's Atlas, *(page 118),* was not drawn to scale and some were embellished by horses and buggies. Nevertheless, they were often carefully drawn and accurately depicted the built enviroment.

Shortly after Collins and Rosetta French returned to Rockport in 1856, they took Edwin Ruthven Andrews into partnership. Edwin had also married Jennie, Collins and Rosetta's adopted daughter. The French-Andrews land occupied the site that the Masonic Temple does today. The Andrews had four sons, one of whom married Lillian Spoor. Margaret Butler recorded Lillian Andrew's description of the "vine-covered verandah, the long row of white birch, the famous weeping larch, the endless variety of super-sized fruit for which the Andrews farm became famous— luscious strawberries, cherries, grapes, apples, pears, and plums."
Courtesy of the Lakewood Historical Society

William R. Maile came to the United States from St. Ives, England, at the age of fifteen. A brickmaker by trade, Maile found Rockport's clay useful for making bricks. He purchased a strip of land at Granford that stretched from Detroit to the lake. The prosperity of his brickworks appears in the brick home shown here that he constructed for his family at Detroit and Brockley avenues in Lakewood. In 1889 Maile became one of Lakewood hamlet's first trustees. His son, Christopher, continued to pursue brickmaking and established a brickworks at Hillard and Warren.
Photographed by Herman Seid on November 4, 1947; courtesy of the Cleveland Press Library and Collections, Cleveland State University Libraries

Curtis Hall was the son of Joseph and Sarah Curtis Hall. The family came to the United States from England in 1837. Joseph purchased land at Detroit and Marlowe. Curtis and his four siblings were young children when the family arrived in Rockport. Some years later Curtis married Priscilla Ranney and began farming land near the site of this house at Cranford and Detroit. Priscilla Ranney Hall died in April, 1883; Curtis later married Emma Patchen in 1886. Courtesy of the Lakewood Public Library

View looking east at the west side of the Curtis Hall house on the northwest corner of Cranford and Detroit avenues, around the 1870s to the 1890s.

The artist is unknown. Courtesy of the Lakewood Historical Society

Mathew Hall, another son of Joseph and Sarah Curtis Hall, worked as superintendent of the Plank Road. He built this house during the Civil War. According to Margaret Butler, the original structure contained "three rooms downstairs, a modified summer kitchen, and woodshed, and two low bedrooms upstairs." The house recently served as Hixson's Victorian Cottage. Donald Bryant, president of the Lakewood Historical Society and Mary McNeil, president of the Women's Junior Board of Lakewood Historical Society, place a plaque recognizing the house as a Lakewood Landmark at 16906 Detroit Avenue. Photographed by Fred Bottomer in 1970; courtesy of the Cleveland Press Library and Collections, Cleveland State University Libraries

In 1879, Mathew Hall constructed a second, more pretentious brick home at 16718 Detroit Avenue. Mathew's grandchildren, Margaret and Edward McClure, are in the foreground circa 1905. The building later served as the home of the Lakewood YMCA until the new building was completed nearby; the property is now the site of Edward's playground. Courtesy of the Lakewood YMCA

John C. Hall was Joseph and Sarah Curtis Hall's sixth child; he was born in Rockport. John constructed his Victorian home in 1875. Margaret Butler noted that the "high, spacious rooms were heated by marble fireplaces. Scrolled ceilings, parquet floors, heavy brocaded wallpaper, velvet drapes and European treasures... created a feeling of past splendor. The furniture was massive, intricately carved." Influenced by Dr. Kirtland, John "proceeded to turn his place into a floral paradise with winding paths, a sunken garden, hundreds of unusual trees, shrubs and flowers." This is now the site of the Lakewood Y at 16913 Detroit Avenue, Lakewood as photographed by Glen Zahn.
Courtesy of the Cleveland Press Library and Collections, Cleveland State University Libraries

This is the interior of the John C. Hall home many years later. The occupants of the house at the time of the photograph were the Walter H. Holtkamps. David Holtkamp is shown here in the living room of 16913 Detroit Avenue. *Photographed by Glenn Zahn; courtesy of the Cleveland Press Library and Collections, Cleveland State University Libraries*

The Farmer family was one of East Rockport's best known African-American families. Andrew Farmer, who was free-born, had managed the Eliza Jennings estate prior to coming to Rockport to manage Dr. Jared Kirtland's farm in 1867. According to Margaret Butler, Andrew's spouse, Phoebe, was a Native American who had been illegally en-slaved. Andrew and Phoebe had five children: Martha, John, Sarah, Colen, and Susan.
Courtesy of the Lakewood Public Library

The Farmer family lived on Winchester Avenue for many years. John, shown here, and his sisters apparently remained there after the death of their parents. John was a Civil War veteran.
Courtesy of the Lakewood Public Library

With her sisters and brother John, Susan Farmer lived on Winchester Avenue.
Courtesy of the Lakewood Public Library

FOCUS: George Peake

When George Peake (1722-1827) and his family arrived in Rockport in 1809, they became the first African-American family to settle permanently in the county. Their wagon was also the first to use the new post road then being constructed. At the age of eighty-seven, Peake began a new career as one of the townships first settlers. While the frontier claimed the lives of men half his age, Peake not only survived to the age of 105, he also made significant contributions to his new community.

Both George and his wife originally came from Maryland. They lived in Pennsylvania for many years while raising their family. Peake apparently arrived in Rockport with his two oldest sons; his wife and two other sons joined them later. Together they constructed a log cabin and two years later Peake pur-chased 103 acres near the Rocky River. (The property was probably just south of the site of Scenic Park on the other side of the Rocky River). Henry Alger's history of "The First Settlement of Rockport" recounts a number of Peake's exploits including his killing of a bear and battling snakes. The Peakes also introduced a new form of gristmill to the community. Earlier settlers ground the grain with a stone pestle in a mortar made from a hollow oak stump. Neighbors found the Peake mill, which used mill stones about eighteen inches in diameter, far more effective at grinding meal.

In 1816, Peak divided his farm and deeded some of it to three of his sons; Henry, Joseph, and James. As late as 1830, four Peake families still resided in Rockport.

FOCUS: Dr. Jared Potter Kirkland

Although Dr. Jared Potter Kirtland (1793-1877) did not come to Rockport until 1839, he quickly became the young community's most renowned and respected citizen. His research and experimentation with soils and plant life proved of great value to his neighbors while his reputation as a naturalist reached far beyond the boundaries of the Western Reserve and drew visitors to Rockport from all over the world.

Kirtland was born in Wallingford, Connecticut. In 1803, he remained with his maternal grandfather, Dr. Jared Potter, when his family moved to Poland, Ohio, where his father became general agent for the Connecticut Land Company. In addition to instructions on the practice of medicine, Dr. Potter also introduced young Kirtland to natural history and the practices of grafting plants. After attending an academy and studying medicine with local physicians, Kirtland entered Yale Medical Institute; he graduated in 1815. In the same year he married Caroline Atwater and settled down to practice medicine in Wallingford. Life went well for the Kirtland family until death claimed his wife and two children in the early 1820s.

Devastated, Jared and his young daughter, Mary Elizabeth, moved to Poland to join his parents. During the next few years, he married Hanna F. Toucey and gained election to the state legislature, where he served three terms. As a legislator, Kirtland distinguished himself in prison reform and became known as the "Father of the New Penitentiary." He also made several important contributions to natural history including the discovery of the snout butterfly. Kirtland again lost a spouse when Hanna died in 1837.

In the same year he began a new career as a medical college professor. He taught briefly at the Medical College of Ohio and the Willoughby Medical School. In 1844 Kirtland joined with other medical professors to found the Cleveland Medical College (now the medical school of Case Western Reserve University), where he continued to work until 1864.

In 1839, Kirtland established a country home in Rockport. His research on Rockport soil and his knowledge of fruit and other plants led to a series of hybrids that were suitable to Rockport conditions. He also experimented with exotic plant life. His campaign to convince other Rockport farmers to switch to fruit production proved successful and the community developed a strong reputation for the quality of its fruits. Kirtland's beautifully landscaped yards ad gardens also became a model for other Rockporters to emulate. As S. Newberry observed in an address to the National Academy of Sciences, Kirtland's "country home in Rockport was beautiful with flowers from every clime, and his gardens and greenhouses were the admiration of all who beheld them. His farm was stocked with all the improved varieties of fruit, many of which he was the originator."

Kirtland remained active in Cleveland and became a major contributor to the field of natural history. For years he learned about the importance of clean drinking water to avoid typhoid fever. He also assisted with Ohio's first geological survey and helped found the Cleveland Academy of Natural Sciences, which eventually became the Cleveland Museum of Natural History. Concerned about the dissemination of scientific information to the general public, Kirtland began editing the *Family Visitor* to furnish the people of northern Ohio with a kind of reading better than the light and fictitious matter that is now deluging this section of the country." The newspaper appeared weekly from 1850 to 1853.

Despite his international fame, Jared Kirtland was a most humble and unassuming man. A giant among his neighbors, the physician was one of Rockport's least pretentious residents, as numerous stories and tales about him attest. He readily shared his knowledge with his neighbors and showered them with his new discoveries. And at a time when Rockport increasingly became hostile to its African-American residents, Kirtland readily employed an experienced and highly-skilled manager, Andrew Farmer, to run his farm.

Dr. Jared Potter Kirtland, *an oil on canvas painted in the 1830s, is exhibited in the Founders' Room at the Case Western Reserve University School of Medicine.*

The "Sage of Rockport," Kirtland was equally at home with the law, medicine, and natural history. However, despite many contributions to the first two fields, his greatest attachment appears to have been to natural history. Kirtland was visited by such nineteenth-century luminaries as Louis Agassiz and Baron von Humboldt. He gave his name to the Kirtland Warbler which he discovered along with a number of other animal and plant species.
Courtesy of the Case Western Reserve University School of Medicine

This portrait, a pen and watercolor on paper, of Dr. Jared Potter Kirtland is attributed to Josephine Klippart. Courtesy of the Ohio Historical Society

Kirtland built his Rockport home in 1839. The house faced north at 14013 Detroit Avenue. Kirtland maintained extensive gardens and a farm, and he spent much of his later years tending to the grounds. Margaret Butler notes that visitors to Kirtland's home did not remember the house as much "as the beautiful grounds with ponds, winding paths, great varieties of unusual flowers, plants and trees sent from various parts of the world." From D. J. Lake, Atlas of Cuyahoga County, *page 127.*

Over the years the Kirtland house was changed considerably. According to Margaret Butler the house was remodeled in 1882 "when extra rooms were built on the second story, bay windows and an ornate veranda added." It is shown here on September 7, 1950. The house was torn down for a supermarket. Courtesy of Cleveland Press Library and Collections, Cleveland State University Libraries

Franklin Reuben and Sophia Hopkins Elliott were close friends of Dr. Jared Kirtland. Both Kirtland and Elliott shared a common interest in natural history and horticulture. In 1856, at the urging of Kirtland, the Elliott family settled on a twenty-two acre plot of land on Detroit near Cohassett where Franklin raised grapes. At a young age, Henry Wood Elliott, Franklin and Sophia Hopkins' eldest son, demonstrated an ability as an illustrator and painter of natural life. He went to work for Smithsonian Institution director Joseph Henry, and perfected his skills as an artist. He then embarked on a career as illustrator that took him to the far reaches of American territory including the Kennecott expedition to the Klondike in 1865. Seven years later at the young age of twenty-six, Henry went to the Pribilof Islands off the Alaskan coast to study the fur trade. During his work there he met and married Alexandra Melovidoff, the daughter of a Russian official. Shown here are Alexandra, Henry, and their daughter, Louise with family pets, at 1424 Grace Avenue, circa 1904. During his career, Elliott established himself as an expert on the seal industry and on the seals of Pribilof Island. For many years he fought to preserve the seals against extinction by the fur seal industry; these efforts produced the Hay-Elliott Fur Seal Treaty of 1911. Courtesy of Carl Droppers

The Henry Wood Elliotts lived in Rockport Cottage from 1869 to 1902 when they moved to 1437 Grace Avenue. Henry Wood Elliott painted this portrait of their home between 1869 and 1890. Courtesy of Pat and Marsha Julio and Carl Droppers

Henry Wood Elliott, pictured here on Grasshopper in 1871, accompanied a number of major geological surveys including the Hayden Survey (1869 to 1871). He provided illustrations for the project which surveyed the Yellowstone region. On this expedition the famous western photographer W. H. Jackson also provided visual materials. Photographed by W. H. Jackson; courtesy of the National Archives and Carl Droppers

*Although best known for his studies of
the seal populations on Pribilof Island,
Elliott gained experience on the earlier
expeditions. He is shown here sketching
on the Hayden Expedition in 1871.
Photograph by W. H. Jackson;
courtesy of the National Archives
and Carl Droppers*

Chapter 2
VIGNETTE
Henry Alger, "The First Settlement of Rockport up to 1821"

Henry Alger's reminiscences of Rockport history, fir[st] published in 1858, represent the first known history of th[e] township. In the short span of time from his arrival in 1812 to 1858 when he wrote "The First Settlement of Roc[k]port to 1821," Alger participated in the formation of a frontier society and its transformation into a farm community. By the end of the period he harbored considerable ambivalence about those changes. The dramatic sh[ift] from frontier to garden presaged even greater changes i[n] the next one hundred and thirty years.

A thinly settled frontier before 1821, Alger's early Rockport appeared to be a heterogeneous community marked by egalitarianism, interdependence, hard work, and exuberant play. By 1858, a new society emerged; bo[th] Rockport life and landscape became more formal. Large[r] houses and farmsteads replaced the log cabins and smal[l] clearings. Rockport residents of 1858, however, continue[d] to maintain close ties of friendship and business; kinshi[p] ties increasingly linked neighbors together as well. The following is excerpted from Alger's 1858 articles in the Cleveland *Morning Leader.*

The first white inhabitants in the township were Joh[n] Herbertson, an Irish refugee, with his family. He settled o[n] the east side of the river, on the top of the bank, near where the Lake Shore [Rockport] Plank Road turns dow[n] the hill. There was also another Irishman, Wm. McConke[y] who came over from the old country with Herbertson. H[e] came into the township probably in 1807 or 1808, and settled on what is known as the "Benschoter Bottom." He staid a year or two and left. . . .

Early in the year 1809, the Legislature of Ohio mad[e] an appropriation of money to open a road from Cleveland to the mouth of Huron river, and appointed Ebenezer Merry, Esq., of Mentor, Dea. Nathaniel Doan and Maj. Lorenzo Carter, of Cleveland, to superintend th[e] opening of said road. Previous to this time there was no road from Cleveland to Huron. . . .

The first wedding in the township was at Datus Kelley's, on the 9th day of January, 1814. The parties wer[e] Chester Dean and Lucy Smith, daughter of Abner Smith, of Dover. George Wallace, Esq., of Cleveland, performed the marriage ceremony. It was a splendid wedding for olden times. There were no sleighbells jingling in Rockpor[t] then. Those who were wealthy enough to own a yoke of oxen rode on ox sleds, and those who owned no team went on foot.

In olden times the settlers claimed to be neighbors if they did not live more than eight or ten miles apart, and

re well acquainted for ten, fifteen or twenty miles
ound; and could you have been present when they met
ch other, from the hearty shaking of hands and friendly
etings you would have supposed them to have been
others and sisters. But most of the old settlers are gone,
d also that unbounded hospitality and generous feeling
ich was so universal among the first settlers seems to
ve departed with them, we fear never to return. . . .

In February or March, 1819, the township was set off
d named Rockport, and a notice put up for the elec-
s to meet and elect their township officers. The first
wnship election was held at Rufus Wright's, on the first
onday in April 1819; and as they had not received the
ws of the State, so in the absence of all law to direct
em, they proceeded as in other meetings for business—
st decided how many road districts to have, took a little
Captain Wright's good old whisky, as was the custom in
ose days, and commenced business by appointing a
airman and two judges, and then proceeded to the elec-
n of officers. They first elected their Township Clerk. He
as sworn into office by the chairman, and took his seat
the table; and as they nominated their officers, one by
ne, and voted in the old way by raising the right hand,
e story was soon told. Those elected were sworn into
fice by the Clerk. It may be doubted whether the election
as conducted in every sense of the word according to
w, yet the officers performed the duties of their respec-
e offices to the entire satisfaction of the inhabitants of
e township. I think there were but nineteen voters in the
wnship all told. All were present, and eighteen officers
ere needed. Every man in the township was considered
ompetent to fill any township office; so at the close of this
ection about every man in the township either held
ffice, kept tavern, or owned a sawmill. . . .

In 1821 the first bridge across Rocky river was built,
n the lake road. It was built mostly by subscription. Capt.
ufus Wright built the bridge; and when it was raised, all
ands, far and near, turned out and spent a week in
utting it up; and when the "raising" was completed,
apt. Wright invited all hands up to his house; and the
ood and generous old Captain brought on the "oh-be-
yful" in great abundance, so much so that they had a
gular time of jollification expressive of their joy at
aving a bridge across the river. The spree went on to such
uick time that the magistrate of the township jumped on
o the table and danced a jig among the bottles and
umblers, about in keeping time with the good old tune of
Yankey Doodle,' which caused a roar of laughter, when

they parted in friendship. . . .

I will give a brief history of one family and their
sufferings. . . . When Henry Alger and his wife arrived
here, June 7, 1812, all his personal property consisted of
an old French watch, an axe, part of a "kit" of shoemaker's tools, and seven cents in cash; and no household
stuff except a bed—They had no provisions on hand, and
he owed ten dollars of borrowed money to begin with.
He built a log cabin 13 by 15 feet inside, one story high,
with a "stake and ridered" roof, as we used to call a roof
covered with wide, thin staves, and poles laid on to keep
the wind from blowing them off. He split out his floor
boards, and hewed out boards for door, a table, and a
shoemaker's bench, as he was a shoemaker by trade, and
must have a bench. . . . When they had got moved into
their hut, built their fire in one end against the logs, and
had brought in their "catamount" bedstead, table, shoe-
makers bench, and a stool or two, they found their
mansion to be quite roomy and convenient. . . .

We have now given you a part of their history for the
first two years and a half they lived in the township. They
kept house almost two years before they owned a cow,
and then he [Henry Alger] ran into debt for one. Soon
after they bought a cow, they bought a small dinner pot
that held about six quarts, and they not only boiled their
dinner in it, but made a lid and a dasher to it and
churned their butter in it. He had no team until he had
been five years, and there he ran in debt eighty dollars for
a yoke of oxen, and knew not where the first dollar was
coming from, to pay for them.

To close this chapter, I will say that they are still living
on the farm they first settled on, at the advanced age of
three score years and ten, possessed of the good old Yankee
feelings and principles that characterized them in their
youth, and invite their friends and acquaintances to give
them a call. . . .

We have now given you a brief history of the first
settlement of Rockport up to 1821, according to the best of
our recollection and what few memoranda we have on
hand; but we don't claim it to be perfect. As we have only
brought our history up to 1821, we leave the last thirty-
seven years of Rockport for those who have more time to
write and are better acquainted with the affairs of
the township.

We wish to make a few comparisons between what
the township was then, in 1821, and what it is now, in
1858. Then there was one bridge across the river in the
township, now there is four; then it was almost unbroken

wilderness and timber was of but little value, and now it is a cash article and firewood is worth from fifty to seventy-five cents per cord standing; then there was perhaps thirty families in the township, all told, now there are three or four hundreds; then they all lived in log cabins, with two or three exceptions, now they live in good houses and some have splendid mansions; then they had forest trees and mud around their cabins, now many of them have beautiful grounds, gravel walks, splendid evergreens, with shrubs, and vines, and all that taste could wish; then, I think, we had no good school house in the township, now we have good schoolhouses, built at a cost of from four to twelve hundred dollars each; then we had no regular preaching or religious society in the township, the first Methodist society being organized in 1822, the first Baptist church in 1832, the first Congregational Church in 1835, and the first Freewill Baptist Church in 1840; then there was no meeting house in the township, now there is six—two Methodist (one has a steeple and a bell), one Baptist, one Freewill Baptist, one Swedenborg and one Roman Catholic; then there was but few roads in the township, and some of them so bad that an empty wagon was a load for one team, now there are good roads running in every direction, and two plank roads and two railroads running through the township; then letters and newspapers were carried through the township on horseback at a slow pace, now the iron horse takes them along at the rate of forty miles a hour, and as several telegraph wires run through the town, if you wish to hold a conversation with your friends east or west, the lightning is at your command to carry your words, then there was not a buggy in the township, and I believe there was not even a one horse wagon, now take the buggies of all descriptions and they are to be counted by hundreds; then our wives and daughters thought it not hardship to walk two and even three or four miles on an afternoon's visit, and home again at night, now, if they have a mile to go they need a conveyance; then our young men thought it no hardship to take a knapsack on their back and start off on a journey of four or five hundred miles on foot, now if they have a few miles to go they must have a horse and buggy or go on the railroad; then our wives and daughters could spin and weave, milk cows, make butter and cheese, cook our dinners, wash the dishes, work in the garden, and raked hay if occasion required, now, they, or some of them, at least can only play on the piano or melodeon, do fine needlework, and all of them can read novels, dress fine, wear hoops, ride out for pleasure, and make calls. But perhaps I am drawing too close a comparison, if so, I beg pardon and will forebear.

From Henry Alger's "The First Settlement of Rockport up to 1821," Cleveland *Morning Leader*, November 8, 1858, page 1; and November 9, 1858, page 1.

FOCUS: Beach Family

Henry Alger's description of Rockport [prior] to 1858 contrasts with the later [ex]periences of the Beach family: Henry [18]17-1907), Sabrina Frost (1827-1894), [an]d their daughter Emma (1859-1950). [He]nry Beach brought his young family [to] Rockport in 1864. They settled on [twe]nty-eight acres near Beach and [De]troit. Arriving after Jared Kirtland and [Ja]red Nicholson had introduced fruit cul[tur]e to East Rockport, Henry set out to [cul]tivate fruit trees. While his efforts [pro]ved successful, even greater oppor[tu]nities presented themselves.

[A]s East Rockport became Lakewood, [Cl]eveland residents began to look to the [ne]w suburb for home sites. Beach dis-

covered, as did many other farmers, that he could make even more profits by dividing farm land into housing lots. Unlike many, however, Henry also constructed buildings on his property such as the ten-unit Beach Terrace on the northwest corner of Beach and Detroit. Henry's success in both endeavors could be seen in the transformation of his home into a seventeen-room Victorian house.

Emma Beach, the couple's only child, seems to have had a happy, protected childhood. In 1868, she began a diary that describes everyday life from the viewpoint of an eight-year-old. Her entry for Tuesday, January 7, 1868 read: "I fed the birds, swept the stoops, kept the smoke up under the meat, and played with my dolls awhile, and then I went over and played with Martha an hour. Then Martha came over and played with me an hour. In the evening I went over and gave Martha a new apron just like mine. Mama made them both." As other girls of the time, Emma helped her mother with sewing, cooking, and household chores.

As her father became prosperous from real estate ventures, Emma had the opportunity to attend a "finishing

school," the Cleveland Female Seminary. As a teenager Emma attended dances at the Lodge on Warren Road. At the age of twenty she married Charles Townsend. Both Henry Beach and Charles Townsend signed the petition in 1885 that led to Lakewood's incorporation. Charles became Lakewood's first chief of police, an occupation which reflected the changing rural environment. Emma and Charles had two children, Henry Burton Townsend (1880-1933) and Edith Townsend Knobloch (1889-1973).

According to Colette Sheehan Townsend, Emma's granddaughter-in-law, Emma Beach continued to be an industrious and kind person in her later years. She tended her garden, put up preserves in the fall, baked bread regularly, and produced fine needlework. Nor did she forget others. When her cousin Helen became a widow, Emma arranged several social occasions so she could meet widower Amos Kauffman, later to be Lakewood's longest serving mayor (1932-1955). The two eventually married. By the time Emma died in 1950, the quiet, garden-like atmosphere of early Lakewood had disappeared and the community had become a bustling suburb.

[Th]e Beach family at home at the corner [of] Detroit and Beach avenues, circa ['18]60s. The Beach house was named The [He]mlocks. Left to right: Sabrina Frost [Be]ach, Henry, a friend, a cousin, and [Em]ma. The horse on the right is named ["B]etty."
[Co]urtesy of the Lakewood [Hi]storical Society

[As] the Beach family prospered from [He]nry's fruit merchant business, their [ho]me grew from a modest frame struc[tu]re to an impressive seventeen-room [Vi]ctorian home. By the time of this [ph]otograph, circa 1886, Emma Beach [ha]d already married Charles Townsend. [Le]ft to right: Burt Beach, Emma Beach [To]wnsend, Sabrina Frost Beach, Henry [Be]ach, L. S. Beach, and E. A. Townsend.
[Co]urtesy of the Lakewood [Hi]storical Society

Emma wrote a diary for one year in 1868. Eight years old at the time, she chronicled what it was like to grow up in this era.
Courtesy of the Lakewood Historical Society

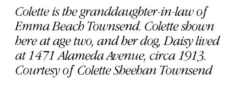

Colette is the granddaughter-in-law of Emma Beach Townsend. Colette shown here at age two, and her dog, Daisy lived at 1471 Alameda Avenue, circa 1913.
Courtesy of Colette Sheehan Townsend

This terrace on the northwest corner of Beach and Detroit avenues was one of the first row houses built in Lakewood. Construction of these dwellings, circa 1870, reflects Henry's shift from fruit merchant to real estate developer and builder.
Courtesy of Colette Sheehan Townsend

Like many large homes on Lake, the Charles Townsend home located at 12984 Lake Avenue, circa 1880, had a low stone wall; the name of the property often appeared on the wall. The name of the Townsend estate, Lake Cliff, can still be seen at the driveway entrance.
Courtesy of Collette Sheehan Townsend

Chapter 3
Machines in the Garden: Railroads, Streetcars, and Factories, 1868 to 1930

I hear the whistle of the locomotive in the woods. Wherever that music comes it has its sequel. It is the voice of civility of the Nineteenth Century saying. . . . I will plant a dozen houses on this pasture next moon, and a village anon. . . .
Ralph Waldo Emerson, *Journal,* 1842

Henry Alger's somewhat jaded description of Rockport's society documents the shift from wilderness to garden. Gone was the unbroken forest. In its place the three to four hundred settlers inserted "good houses," with "gravel walks, splendid evergreens with shrubs and vines. . . ." Writing on the eve of the Civil War, Alger could hardly have anticipated the monumental changes that lay only a few years in the future. Within ten years the first locomotive penetrated the heart of Rockport's garden. The next sixty years brought even more profound changes: a city with houses and factories arose where once forests and then orchards had dominated.

Even before Alger wrote his reminiscences, completion of the Rockport Plank Road represented a major portent of change. The same road that made it easier for farmers to take their produce to market and return with implements to ease and improve their lives also carried the seeds that would eventually destroy their garden. As Rockport farmers increasingly became linked to Cleveland, the influence of the burgeoning industrial giant to the east grew steadily. The road symbolized this growing dependence; it also reinforced the existing east-west orientation of the small farm community.

As Cleveland's industries and population grew rapidly, the quality of urban life began to change dramatically: iron, steel, and oil refining clouded the skies and dirtied the waters. If smoke meant prosperity, it also had its burdens. In comparison, bucolic Rockport on the west and Bratenahl on the east appeared pristine. Clevelanders, then, looked west and east along the lakefront for temporary escape. At the same time Cleveland industrialists and speculators laid plans to develop these areas; not coincidentally, they expected to make a handsome profit. Although leading Rockport residents joined these efforts, two interwoven Ohio City families, Rhodes and Hanna, played key roles in the transformation of East Rockport.

In April 1866 a group of Cleveland industrialists, developers, and Rockport landowners, including Daniel Rhodes, Elias Sims, and Ezra Nicholson, established the Clifton Park Association. The papers of incorporation suggest their intent: the association was to be involved in "constructing and maintaining buildings to be used for hotels, storerooms, tenement houses or water cure establishments for the treatment of invalids and for places of general public resort." The association built the resort on its large land holdings lining the east side of the Rocky

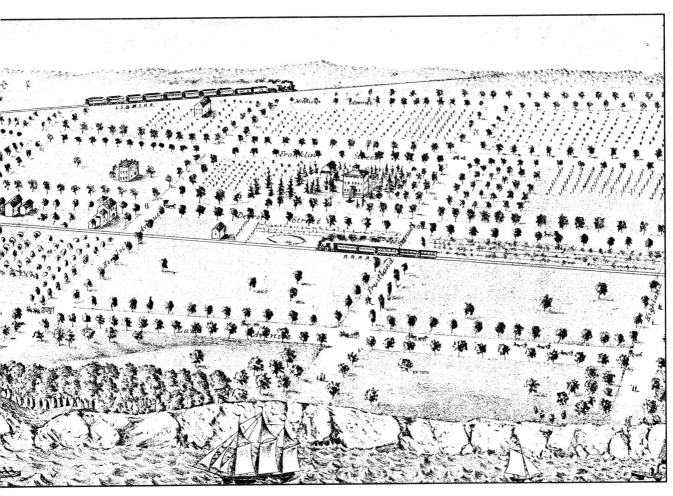

This drawing shows the area immediately east of East Rockport; Highland Avenue to the right, becomes West 117th Street. The railroad in the middle is the Rocky River Railroad while the one at the top is the Lake Shore and Michigan Southern Railroad. This orchard/garden landscape circa 1874, with most farmhouses fronting on Detroit Street, reflected that of East Rockport of the time. From D. J. Lake's Atlas of Cuyahoga County, *page 141.*

River. At the same time Marcus (Mark) Hanna joined with his father-in-law Daniel Rhodes and with Elias Sims to organize the Rocky River Railroad Company. With service beginning on September 1, 1868, the railroad provided the means to transport urban residents quickly and cheaply to and from the Park. Known as the Dummy Railroad because its smoke stack muffled the engine's sounds, the road began at the end of the city horsecar line near Bridge and West 58th and took passengers five and a half miles to the western terminus at the Cliff House where Sloane and Edanola avenues are today. Although it operated year round, the bulk of its passengers traveled during the summer. In 1872 the line carried 150,000 passengers.

As a result, the area around the mouth of the Rocky River quickly became a resort for Clevelanders. The 1874 *Atlas of Cuyahoga County* identifies John Knoll's Beech Grove as one of the area's attractions. Knoll claimed to have "the most romantic picnic ground at Rocky River, close to the Lake." It was equipped with a "dining hall, confectionery, bowling alley, shooting gallery, bathhouses, flying swings, etc." For those who wanted to fish or otherwise enjoy the lake, the Rocky River Boat House provided a "steam yacht, [and] sail and row boats to let." Other attractions included the Lake View House and the Murch House, formerly known as the Cliff House.

As the first "machine" in Rockport's garden, the Rocky River Railroad provided yeoman service in bringing city dwellers to the country. While most visitors settled for the temporary escape from work's drudgery and city pollution, they could not ignore the sharp contrasts between city and country life. No doubt many longed for the day when they could reside, if not work, in such a pastoral landscape.

The purchase of the Rocky River Railroad in 1881 by a trunk line represented the first step toward making that dream come true. The New York, Chicago and St. Louis Railroad (Nickel Plate), continued local service along the line for vacationers; it also provided direct service to downtown for East Rockport residents. Wealthy Cleveland residents could now escape from the city; from their country residences they could get comfortably to their offices downtown. By 1885, as if to underline the changes taking place, East Rockport residents and landowners, including Mark Hanna, sought to incorporate as a separate entity.

If the Plank Road represented the portent of change and the Rocky River and Nickel Plate railroads provided the initial beginnings, the machine that nurtured, formed, and shaped Lakewood the suburb was the electric streetcar. In the decades before the automobile became the major means of commuting, the streetcar provided the only cheap, reliable, and frequent transportation system. To a great extent it made possible the development of middle-class suburbs some distance from the central city.

The streetcar, however, imposed a new pattern on the rural landscape. Although Thomas Knight noted in h 1902 promotional pamphlet "Beautiful Lakewood" that "between Highland Avenue [West 117th] and Belle Avenue there are no store buildings of any kind as is the case between Warren Road and the River," the impact of the streetcar increasingly undermined Detroit Avenue society. Even on the north-south side streets they imposed a density that eventually rivaled that in central cities. Dependence on streetcars encouraged small lots, vertical houses, and multiple family homes. The single-story, rambling ranch home, shaped by the constraints of the automobile, had to wait for more than a generation and appeared in significant numbers only in more distant suburbs.

In 1893, Cleveland streetcar lines consolidated into two major companies; the Cleveland City Railway provided service to the west side. On Detroit, the line reached to West 117th. In the same year, the hamlet of Lakewood granted a franchise to extend service to Rocky River. Service began on September 23; the Nickel Plate then discontinued local service. In October 1897 the new suburb gained a light-rail connection to Lorain by way of the Lorain and Cleveland Electric (interurban) Railway. Within five years, the Clifton streetcar line began service; the Lake Shore Electric then shifted to these tracks and continued service west to Toledo until the line closed in 1938.

The completion of these streetcar lines profoundly affected Lakewood's growth. The hamlet's population leapt from about four hundred and fifty in 1890 to more than fifteen thousand in 1910. Most of the newcomers purchased new homes close to one of these two streetcar lines. As a result much of the subdividing and home-building activities took place immediately north and south of Detroit Avenue and then north and south of Clifton. Although the Madison line reached West 117th by 1898, service into Lakewood did not begin until 1917. As result, south Lakewood, save for the southeast section, developed last.

In retrospect it is difficult to fully appreciate how important streetcars were to the new suburb. Not only did they shape the landscape, but they also provided Lakewood with a vital connection to the economic, cultural, and social life of the central city. In contrast to the Rocky River Railroad's 150,000 customers in 1872, the Detroit line from Sloan Avenue to Cleveland's Public Square carried nineteen million in its peak year in 1920; the Madison line carried fourteen million two years earlier.

Transportation also played a key role in suburban factory location. The number of Cleveland's industrial sites declined as land costs climbed. Industrialists began to turn to suburban sites along the major trunk lines. Serviced by two such railroads, the Nickel Plate and the Lake ore and Southern Michigan (LS&SM), and situated close Cleveland, the hamlet of Lakewood became a potential e for factories. The industrial corridors that developed ong these rail lines needed workers; the long hours manded of industrial employees required housing arby. As a result, industrial workers became an impor-t part of the Lakewood story.

In 1892, Washington Lawrence, president of the ional Carbon Company, purchased a large tract of land tween Madison Avenue and the LS&SM tracks for a new fice building and factory. The preceding year Lawrence ught the carbon department from his former associate, e inventor Charles Brush, and added it to his growing siness. On part of the new site the company built a ctory complex in 1894 and an office building in 1896. cause the location lacked a streetcar line to bring orkers out to the factory, a subsidiary, the Pleasant Hill nd Company, planned housing lots for workers. Even-ally, other industries located their factories in the same ea. Alexander Winton built his automobile plant to the st in Cleveland along Berea Road, as did Glidden Paints, idland Steel, and Empire Brass. In 1917, Templar Motors rporation built its new factory immediately west of the sidential neighborhood. Although Templar's efforts ere short-lived, other industries, Standard Dry Battery d Lake Erie Screw came to occupy the site.

Fires, residential construction, and zoning laws cir-umscribed industrial development along the Nickel Plate acks. In 1919, fire consumed the Edgewater Lumber and pply Company on West 117th. One year later Theodor undtz's lumber yard (between Clifton and the tracks, anor Park, and Giel Avenues), erupted in a massive fire. undtz sold the property to the C. O. Frick Company hich developed the land for housing lots. Eventually, e only industrial sites along the Nickel Plate tracks con-

centrated on Hird and West 117th Street; these factories were small compared to those along the LS&SM tracks.

By 1900, the successive introduction of railroad, streetcar, and factory had transformed the East Rockport garden landscape into a new environment. Increasingly orchards and vineyards gave way to a suburb of "beautiful homes." Yet even as the streetcar and railroad dominated and transformed the landscape, technological develop-ments began to challenge the iron horse's position. A new machine, the horseless carriage began to appear on Cleve-land streets. Initially, many dismissed the newfangled creation as a toy at best and a nuisance at worst. Alexander Winton, a bicycle manufacturer and Lakewood resident, disagreed. As early as 1896, he began building and testing self-powered vehicles. On March 24, 1898, with four horseless carriages in stock, Winton sold the first Ameri-can-made, standard model, self-propelled road vehicle in the United States, a sale that Cleveland auto historian Richard Wager marks as "the beginning of the American automobile industry."

The automobile's relatively late arrival meant that it had much less influence on Lakewood's emerging spatial and physical forms. The automobile had a more profound impact on the younger suburbs of Rocky River, Bay Village, and Westlake. Nevertheless, Lakewood's history is inextricably intertwined with the automobile. City resi-dents and businesses have made major contributions to the industry while the community has grown increasingly dependent on the automobile for transportation. Many Lakewood residents found work in the numerous auto-mobile factories located on the west side of Cleveland. For residents of southeast Lakewood, and especially the Village, these plants offered important sources for employment.

Shown here is a Rocky River Railway Company Stock Certificate, circa 1869. Mark Hanna, Daniel P. Rhodes, Elias Sims, and Ezra Nicholson organized and promoted the railroad. According to Margaret Butler, the railroad cost $160,000 to construct. Half of these funds came from the sale of bonds to William Barrett and the rest from stock sales. Apparently the stockholders never earned dividends, but as Rockport's "first machine" the railroad brought major changes to the rural community. Courtesy of James Sanders

Organized in 1867, the Rocky River Railroad began service in September, 1868. According to John Rehor, three Baldwin seven-ton coal-burning tank engines worked the five-and-a-half-mile line "from the end of the city horse car line near Bridge Street and Waverly Avenue (now West 58th Street) in Cleveland to the east bank of the Rocky River in Rockport township. The Rocky River Railroad terminated at the Cliff House [Murch House]." Initially the railroad's three engines were named the "Rockport," the "Brooklyn," and the "Elias Sims," shown here with a closed coach car circa 1880. The first two were renamed the "Hanna," and the "Rhodes." With major business in the summer, the railroad offered ten trains in each direction on weekdays and seventeen on Sundays. In 1881, the Nickel Plate Railroad acquired the road.
Courtesy of the Lakewood Historical Society

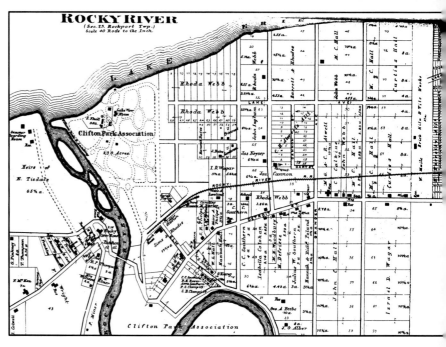

This map provides the location of the Rocky River Railroad and its western terminus at the Murch House, earlier known as the Cliff House. It also shows the location of the area's other recreational attractions. The east side of the river featured J. Knoll's beer garden, the Lake View House, and Williams' Boats and Landing. On the west side of the Rocky River, visitors could find the Rocky River House and a summer Boarding House near the lake. The Plank Road's toll house is also visible on the west side of the river. By 1874, some land owner had already subdivided their property although few of these lots as yet had houses upon them. Most residences still line Detroit. From D. J. Lake, Atlas of Cuyahoga County, page 135.

The Cliff House, later named Murch House, opened in 1869. According to Margaret Butler, it was "especially favored by Clevelanders for picnics, balls, parties, and even plays. It had an elaborate three story building with an observation tower on the roof, and a verandah along the second story. The first floor contained the bar, the second floor the dining room and the third floor a large ballroom." Daniel P. Rhodes and Elias Sims owned the Cliff House. By 1873, J. H. Murch was proprietor of the Cliff House and changed its name. From D. J. Lake's Atlas of Cuyahoga County, page 132.

The Lake View House was located in the Clifton Park area near the lake. It appears on the 1874 county atlas and was located near John Knoll's Beech Grove beer garden. The atlas notes that Beech Grove was "the most romantic Picnic ground, at Rocky River, close to the Lake. Dining Hall, Confectionery, Bowling Alley, Shooting Gallery, Bath-houses, Flying Swings, etc. in connection." Nearby the Williams Brothers, proprietors of the Rocky River Boat House, provided a "Steam Yacht, Sail and Row Boats to let. Picnics, Fishing Parties, etc. supplied at all times." Courtesy of the Lakewood Public Library

Located in Rocky River valley near the Detroit Avenue bridge, Scenic Park was an amusement park and sold liquor. According to the Early Days of Lakewood, the park featured a "car, suspended on a cable" that carried passengers to a boathouse on the other side of the river; the trip cost twenty-five cents for a round-trip. It also contained a two-fifth-mile bicycle track. Passage of the Beal Law in 1905, which prohibited the sale of liquor in Lakewood, greatly affected Scenic Park's attendance. In 1906 it became Lincoln Park and was later sold to the city in 1917. Courtesy of the Lakewood Public Library

An even more important "machine" in Lakewood's garden, the streetcar came to be the major means of transportation in the period before the Great Depression. The tracks shown here circa 1919 on West 117th and Detroit connected the Madison and Detroit lines and provided transfer of equipment. On the right is the recently opened Cleveland Trust branch and in the center, the Lakewood Tire Shop. The latter suggests the growing importance of the automobile.
Courtesy of Jim Pohorence and Peter McGrew

Service on the Detroit Avenue line in Lakewood began in 1893 and continued until 1951. Bus service then replaced the streetcar.
Courtesy of George Snyder

Pictured here are the Rocky River Streetcar Barns, circa 1942. The Detroit car barns were located near the "L" turn on Detroit at the west end of Lakewood. An apartment complex now occupies the site.
Courtesy of George Snyder

The Madison Avenue Car Barns at the corner of Madison Avenue and West 117th, circa 1949 are pictured here. Service in Lakewood along Madison was the last to begin. Starting in 1917, the Madison streetcar line operated until 1954 when bus service replaced it.
Courtesy of George Snyder

The Clifton line began service in Lakewood in about 1902. From that time until 1938, the Clifton line also carried the Lake Shore Electric (interurban) railroad that provided service west to Toledo. Clifton streetcar service ended in 1947. The tracks occupied the tree lawns on both sides of Clifton.
Photograph by Walter Kneal; courtesy of the Cleveland Press Library and Collections, Cleveland State University Libraries

Westbound Clifton streetcars can be seen on the left of the photograph. Eastbound tracks are on the right. The westbound car on the left appears to be a Lake Shore Electric interurban car circa 1930.
Photograph by the Lakewood Police Department; courtesy of Home Federal Savings Bank

In addition to streetcar lines, roads and automobiles became an important part of the Lakewood landscape. Here E. H. Schupp and Sons, General Contrac- tors from Lakewood are building a road. Courtesy of the Lakewood Historical Society

The opening of the Hilliard bridge in 1926 helped alleviate traffic across the Detroit Avenue bridge. Courtesy of the Cleveland Press Library and Collections, Cleveland State University Libraries

By 1913, another "machine" entered the Lakewood landscape. Early residents were aware of natural gas on their property. A natural gas boom began in Lakewood after 1910 and reached a peak in 1914 and 1915. According to Margaret Butler, wells at National Carbon Company and Winton Motor Company produced a million cubic feet of gas daily. The Beach property contained three wells "which supplied gas for several years to the tenants in the numerous apartments of Clifton Prado." George Lindstrom notes that some residents, fearful of the impact of these wells on their property, put pressure on city government to regulate their locations and operations. However, the gas deposits were apparently fairly shallow and many wells failed to produce. Nevertheless, at least one operating well continues at Lakewood Park. In 1949, Lakewood Nursery was located at 17920 Detroit Avenue; it is unclear if the well is at this site or elsewhere.
Courtesy of the Cleveland Press Library and Collections, Cleveland State University Libraries

FOCUS: Lakewood's Automobile and Automakers

If Detroit rightly claimed the title of "motor city," Cleveland ran a close second. As Cleveland's largest suburb for many years, Lakewood also played a key role in automobile development. Two long-time Lakewood residents, Alexander Winton and Walter C. Baker, made pioneering contributions to automaking, while many others worked for one of the area's numerous auto-related enterprises. Lakewood also produced its own distinctive automobile, the Templar. Largely forgotten, the story of Templar Motors (1917-1924) is a chronicle of innovation and of the difficulties faced by the auto industry during the 1920s.

The Templar: "Superfine Small Car"

Organized in 1916 by Cleveland industrialists, including M. F. Bramley, Templar Motors selected a twenty-acre tract of land between the LS&MS Railroad tracks, and Athens, Halstead and Clarence avenues as the site for its office and factory. Company literature boasted of a factory worth $2.5 million that had three hundred thousand square feet of production space under its roof. Fronting on Halstead, the company referred to the area as Templar Park.

Although automobile production started in 1917, the onset of World War I quickly altered company plans. With two large government contracts Templar produced artillery shells during the war. Full automobile production resumed in late 1918. In 1920 the factory turned out 1,850 cars; Templar production ranked sixth that year among Cleveland automakers. Despite a production capacity of over 5,000 cars per year, Templar seldom turned out more than one-third of this number. The automobile's relatively high price, a glutted auto market, Henry Ford's mass-produced, inexpensive Model T and worsening economic conditions at the end of 1920 all played key roles. Templar suffered further from a disastrous fire on December 13, 1921, that left only one building remaining. Nevertheless, Templar continued production and quickly rebuilt. Before its financial collapse in 1924, Templar turned out 6,000 automobiles. Unfortunately, the company's bankruptcy left its twenty thousand investors with a combined loss of more than six billio dollars.

Drawing on the imagery of the medieval crusades and using a Maltes cross as its emblem, Templar Motors advertised its product as "The Superfi Small Car." Clearly ahead of its time, Templar offered economy, quality and reliability in a small car when most car makers produced either large, expens automobiles like the Peerless or small cheap cars like the Ford. The sleek roadster and speedster models qualifi as some of the first sports cars produc in the United States. Templar's performance matched its car's racy lines. 1919 the car broke the New York to Chicago record, averaging nearly thirty seven miles per hour for the thousand mile trip. The following year a Templa established several new transcontinen records. In 1921, despite combination of dirt and poorly paved roads, a Templar raced from Akron to Cleveland in less than twenty-six minutes at an aver age speed of over sixty miles per hour

Templar offered five basic models: a five-passenger touring car or sedan, a four passenger sportette, a three passenger coup, and a two-passenger tou ing roadster. Although prices varied depending on demand, in 1920 Temp charged (f.o.b. Cleveland) $3,585 for t five passenger sedan and $2,685 for th other three models. The company also offered custom construction and produced a small number of taxicabs for Checker in Chicago and Waite Taxicab and Livery Company of Cleveland.

Clearly the touring roadster was Templar's most interesting and unique model. It carried the Maltese cross on the side panels; lacking doors, it provided a step panel just below the insignia. The roadster came equipped with two spare tires mounted in the rear de well. It also featured a clock, a clinometer (grade indicator), a spot light, a power tire pump, and, perhaps most unusual, a side panel housing a folding Kodak camera and a compass. It came with a full hammered aluminum body and was available in gray, cream, wine or bronze. In 1921, the roadster sold fo $2,885; its more expensive competitors included the Pierce Arrow three-seater, which cost $8,000. In contrast, a 1924 Model T Ford Coupe sold for $520.

Shown here is the "No. 39 Templar Motors Corporation Factory Plan," circa 1917 to 1924. Templar Motors used sterograph cards like this to help boost stock sales. The site contained a factory, company offices, and a hospital. Suggestive of gender roles at the time, it also featured a two-story restaurant, the first floor for men and the second for women. In this drawing the neighboring area to the east (the Village) appears to be undeveloped; in fact, the area was densely settled.
Courtesy of the Western Reserve Historical Society

his view, circa 1917 to 1924, suggests
 leisurely and spacious environment.
he large, open office, with railings sepa-
uting departments, stands in sharp con-
ast to many modern workplaces. Tem-

plar Motors president M. F. Bramley was also president of the Cleveland Trinidad Paving Company. Bramley did not live in Lakewood but resided nearby on Harbor-View Drive. Company advertise-

ments frequently used his attractive home as a backdrop to exhibit their new models.
Courtesy of the Western Reserve Historical Society

Templar Motors constructed its own engines based on company design. Contractors produced most of the other parts according to Templar specification. Workers at the Templar factory, shown here, circa 1917 to 1924, then assembled the automobile. Under the direction of a foreman, on the right, workers on this primitive assembly line put together Templar's four-cyclinder, 197 cubic-inch, 43 horse-power engines. Courtesy of the Western Reserve Historical Society

Templar's pride and joy, the roadster attracted the most attention. The Western Reserve Historical Society's Crawford Automobile Museum has a 1922 Templar roadster on exhibit.

TEMPLAR

The Superfine Small Car

The Pioneer Builder of Quality Small Cars

TO build a fine small car in a finer way has always been the Templar purpose.

Templar began where other motor car makers stopped. Templar is a light car so distinct in appearance, so exceptional in performance, so luxurious in riding qualities that only weight marks its variance with high-priced heavy cars.

Motorists accustomed to every refinement in an automobile find in Templar qualities heretofore associated only with cars of large size and superlative cost.

Five-Passenger Touring, $2885
Four-Passenger Sportette, $2885
Five-Passenger Sedan, $3785
Two-Passenger Touring Roadster, $2885
Three-Passenger Coupe, $3775
Price f. o. b. Cleveland

The Templar Motors *Co.*

2200 Halstead St., Lakewood, Cleveland, O.
Export Dept. 116 Broad St., N. Y. City.

FOCUS: Alexander Winton

Alexander Winton (1860-1932) was one of the most important pioneers in the fledgling U.S. automobile industry. Born in Scotland, Winton migrated to the United States at the age of nineteen. After working in several machine shops, he founded the Winton Bicycle Company in 1891 to manufacture his own improved bicycle design. In 1896, he built his first automobile and the following year founded the Winton Motor Carriage Company. Two years later he sold the first manufactured automobile in the United States.

A major innovator in automobiles and engines, Winton eventually held more than a hundred patents. He pioneered in the design and manufacture of diesel engines; in 1912 he founded the Winton Gas Engine and Manufacturing Company and produced America's first diesel engine the following year. General Motors purchased the company in 1930 to form the Cleveland Diesel Engine Division.

In 1902, Winton moved his automobile factory to the new industrial corridor along the New York Central tracks near West 117th at 10601 Berea Road; the plant was close to the new hamlet of Lakewood. About the same time Winton built his estate, Roseneat at 12590 Lake Avenue in Lakewood.

To meet the increased demand for war material in 1917, Winton, like Templar, drastically cut its auto production. Early in 1915, the company reorganized under the new name of Winton Motor Car Company and began production of a lighter car model with a thirty-four horse-power, six-cylinder engine. Winton also continued production of heavier forty-nine horse-power model both models came in eleven different body styles. At prices ranging from twenty-five hundred to thirty-five hundred dollars, only the well-to-do could afford a new Winton. However, as he increasingly focused attention on manufacturing diesel marine engines, Winton's automobiles began to lose their hard-earned reputation for innovation. By the 1920s the saturated market for expensive automobiles and the growing attraction of the inexpensive Ford helped push Winton out of the automobile business in the same year that Templar folded.

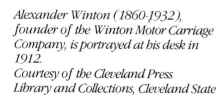

Alexander Winton (1860-1932), founder of the Winton Motor Carriage Company, is portrayed at his desk in 1912.
Courtesy of the Cleveland Press Library and Collections, Cleveland State University Libraries

Alexander Winton, Jr., also lived in Lakewood on Erie Cliff Drive for many years. He is shown here with his 1917 Winton automobile on December 17, 1951. The Western Reserve Historical Society's Crawford Automobile Museum has on exhibit a 1921 Winton Model 25, a four passenger touring car. Photograph by James Thomas; courtesy of the Cleveland Press Library and Collections, Cleveland State University Libraries

FOCUS: Walter C. Baker

Alexander Winton was not the only Lakewood resident to make major contributions to automotive technology. Walter Baker (1868-1955), who moved to Clifton Park sometime after the turn of the century, lived in Lakewood for many years. Born in Hinsdale, New Hampshire, Baker studied engineering at Case School of Applied Science. He helped found both the American Ball Bearing Company in 1895 and the Baker Motor Vehicle Company in 1899. In 1905 Baker Motors located its new factory on West Eighty-third along the same industrial/rail corridor that Winton had three years earlier. In 1915 the company merged with Rauch and Lang Carriage Company, producing its last car the following year. Baker helped pioneer the electric automobile, introduced left-handed drive, and sold more electric cars than any other manufacturer.

By 1910 electrics could travel seventy-five miles on a set of fully-charged batteries. Because it was clean, quiet, and required only forward and reverse gear shifting, the Baker Electric came to be known as an "urban ladies car." In contrast to the genteel electric automobiles the company produced, Baker's experimental race cars virtually flew. Powered by twenty battery cells wired to a 110-volt, direct-current motor, the "Torpedo," a larger version of the "Torpedo Kid" reached speeds of 120 miles per hour.

Walter C. Baker, undated.
Courtesy of the Cleveland Press
Library and Collections, Cleveland State
University Libraries

*Walter C. Baker in his "Torpedo Kid"
car 999, second from right lined up for
a race at the Glenville mile race track,
September 1903. The Western Reserve
Historical Society's Crawford Automobile
Museum has Baker's racing trophies on
exhibit.
Courtesy of the Cleveland Press
Library and Collections, Cleveland
State University Libraries*

*Pictured here is a Baker Electric, circa
1900. The Western Reserve Historical
Society's Crawford Automobile Museum
has a Baker electric on exhibit.
Courtesy of the Cleveland Press
Library and Collections, Cleveland
State University Libraries*

Chapter 4
VIGNETTE
Jan Pankuch, "Slovaks in Lakewood"

In 1889, farms and forests dominated the Lakewood landscape. Over the next forty years the community underwent the dramatic transformation from orchard to suburb. However, for new settlers in the last decade of the nineteenth and the first years of the twentieth century, Lakewood's rural landscape still held sway.

For workers at National Carbon's new factory in Lakewood, this meant limited transportation facilities and services. It also required these pioneers to confront the difficulties of climate and terrain when they purchased building lots from the company and began to build homes, churches, stores, and businesses. Despite long work hours, low wages, and limited resources, residents of the Pleasant Hill Land Company's development and other parts of southeast Lakewood slowly replaced trees with homes.

In this process, Slovaks and other immigrants from Eastern Europe played a major role. On the eight streets of the company's allotment, five of which were named for birds, these newcomers constructed a village modeled, in part, on those they had left behind. As Margaret Butler correctly noted, "although most of Lakewood refers to this section as Carbon District or the Bird's Nest, [or more recently Birdtown] the people who live there call it the 'Village,' and it is really just that."

By 1930, when Jan Pankuch compiled his *History of Slovaks of Cleveland and Lakewood*, southeast Lakewood was densely settled. The following excerpts from Pankuch's book provide a good sense of the process of settlement and institution building that marked the neighborhood. Since Pankuch did not move to Lakewood until 1917, he drew on the memory of Andrew Babej, one of the first Slovaks to move to Lakewood:

The National Carbon Company started to build a factory in 1892. People were seeking work in all directions around Cleveland because it was so tough getting a job. I got a construction job on the factory. After I had worked there for a couple days, the boss told me to bring in a couple more men. I asked him how many I should bring; he answered as many as I could, even a dozen would do, he said. So I called up my brothers: George and John, and John and George Nemec, A. Chovana, and many others; Michael Urban and A. Goda also came; all got hired. All the Scerbas, John Scerba, John Scerba, Jr., Adam Scerba, Andrew Rybarik and many others came later.

When the construction was finished, the men were hired to work in the factory, but the Nemecs didn't work there long.

Since there were no houses, except a couple of farms on Highland Avenue [West 117th Street] up to Madison, we came to work from Cleveland in a horse driven wagon. But the wagon only followed Highland Avenue on to Detroit Street and on to Madison after they had constructed a railroad starting at Gordon Avenue which is now called West 65th Street. I found an empty house leased by the farmer Warner, his farm was situated around today's Wagar Avenue. So I moved there, it was evidently closer to walk to work from there than it was from town. Living in town one had to get up around five AM in order to get to the factory on time, around seven o'clock. Several times the horses slid on the icy road, mainly on the shore leading from the old Superior bridge

Pearl Road. [West 25th]. The passengers had to get out help push the wagon. When we finally reached a flatter etch we got back up and sat down continuing our urney on to Pearl Road where a new team of horses s added.

That part of Lakewood, south of Detroit Street, nsisted mainly of farms and it was only after National rbon Company was built and after the factory started operate that things changed. The company acquired a ge piece of property which spread from Highland enue to today's Madison Park. The Company kept what needed for its expansion and had the rest divided into ilding lots which were handed over to the workers for all down-payments. The cheapest lots were the ones xt to the railroad on Plover Street—that is why the orkers bought these lots and right away houses were con- ucted and in a very short time a fairly large Slovak ony appeared. After that, Slovaks kept coming to Lake- od gradually, almost every month. Shortly after these rivals, the lots which the Company sold to its workers re taken over by a private real estate company and omptly sold. Several years later houses were built. The other neighborhoods around Madison Avenue, ere the streets used to spread out beautifully on to the cky River, were all empty, and it wasn't until many ars had passed that they started building on that land.

Once the Slovaks had settled in Lakewood in larger umbers, they yearned for their own organized life. At the ginning there were more Protestants in the group. They nted to have their own church there, but they were not le to come to an agreement on how to achieve such a oject. One group wanted an independent parish, while e other was proposing to create an annexation of the rish of Holy Trinity [in Cleveland]. And that is how they rted into two groups from the beginning. One group nstructed a little church on Quail Street, not far from over Street (the annexation of the Parish of Holy Trin-), and the other group constructed the church of Sts. ter and Paul on the same street nearer to Madison, on e corner of Thrush. The Parish of Sts. Peter and Paul as founded on March 21, 1901.

They called the church near Plover Street "Scerba's urch" since it was the Scerba family who invested and crificed the most for it; as for the church on the corner Quail and Thrush Street—that one was called "Babej's urch" because the Babej family put into it the greatest nount of effort and sacrificed just as much for its reali- tion. This separation continued for many years, up to

the year 1910, I think.

Catholic Slovaks came to Lakewood along with other Slovaks, and very quickly there were so many of them that they founded their own parish; they named it "The Parish of SS. Cyril and Methodius." They built the church on the corner of Madison and Lakewood Avenue in 1903. By then associations, businesses and even a savings bank 'Orol' [Eagle] were founded in Lakewood.

With the construction of houses in the neighborhood of Madison Avenue, an interesting field opened up oppor- tunities for the streetcar business, and since horse driven carriages were replaced by electric streetcars, a railroad was constructed on Madison, but for some time people took the so-called "Dinky" to commute from Highland Avenue. At present Madison Avenue and its surroundings represent the most beautiful part of Lakewood. Who would have imagined that in a quarter of a century such a change would occur, that those farms, forests, and swamps would become such beautiful streets. No one would have thought that Slovaks would be living in such homes which they are now lining the new streets south of Madison, since most of all the Slovaks that established themselves here during the first years worked for the "Carbon Shop" [National Carbon Company] and their wages barely met their needs. By saving dollar by dollar they took care of their wives and children, contributed to their church, their associations. Needless to say all the old settlers knew how to save and raise large families who bore faith and national pride.

The great progress made by the Slovaks in Lakewood, really occurred after 1900 when they started to settle down in larger numbers. And one must take Mr. Andrej Babej's word for granted, since the most beautiful part of Lakewood was actually built by Slovaks in the last years.

Translated from Slovak by Allice Nemcova and Dr. Michael J. Kopanic, Jr. Mrs. Cyril (Jean) Pankuch and Jewell Pankuch Muffler gave permission to use these passages from Jan Pankuch, editor and compiler, *Dejiny Clevelandskych a Lakewoodskych Slovakov* (The History of Slovaks of Cleveland and Lakewood), 1930.

This December 28, 1940 scene shows the
Village's central business district looking
east from Lakewood Avenue along the
north side of Madison Avenue. Begin-
ning on the left the stores include:
Sunnyside Soda Grill with George E.
Fedor's law offices above, Andrews 25¢
to $1.00 store, Stoyanoff's Market,
Lakewood Sweet Shop, Gamary's Barber
Shop, D. Dreueny Grocery, Cort's
Shoes, Mansky's Shoes, and Fisher
Brothers' Grocery Store on the corner
of Ridgewood and Madison.
Photograph by John Goski; courtesy
of the Cleveland Press Library and
Collections, Cleveland State
University Libraries

Saint Gregory the Theologian Byzantine Rite Catholic Church and Calvin
Presbyterian Church, Quail Avenue, are
shown here on November 14, 1931. This
street scene on Quail Avenue looking
south from Madison suggests the importance of religion to the Village. Note the
small group of residents congregated a
the corner of Quail and Thrush. Neigh
borhood interaction was an importan.
part of the Village social life.
Courtesy of the Cleveland Press
Library and Collections, Cleveland Stat
University Libraries

FOCUS:
Jan
Pankuch

Born in Saris County, Hungary (Slovakia), Jan Pankuch (1869-1952) came to the United States with his family in 1886. When his father died in a coal mine accident in Pennsylvania the following year, Jan became head of a family of four. In search of a spouse he returned to Europe, where he met Rozalia Gasber; they married in Cleveland in 1889. Jan and Rozalia had eleven children and were married for sixty years; Rozalia died in 1950.

Jan worked variously as a blacksmith, streetcar driver, and factory hand; he also operated a grocery store and a bookstore while he attended school at night. His real vocation, however, was as a printer, editor, writer, and publisher; he began his first newspaper in 1892. In 1907, he took over the weekly *Hlas (Voice)*, which he published until 1947. From 1915 to 1925 he also published a daily, *Denny Hlas.* Pankuch directed these papers to the Cleveland Slovak community. His interest in Cleveland area Slovaks led him to collect a vast amount of information about the community, and ultimately to the publication of his history, excerpted here in part. His collections, book, and other writings continue to be important sources for Slovak history.

In 1917, the Pankuchs moved to Lakewood; they purchased a house at 1581 Alameda Avenue. In 1936, they moved to 2159 Elbur Avenue. Eventually Jan also relocated his printing company to Lakewood as well. While a number of their children worked for the printing company, only Cyril continued until its demise in 1949.

The Pankuchs belonged to Sts. Peter and Paul Lutheran Church located at Grace and Madison avenues, where Jan served as president of the congregation. He also played a prominent role in Slovak-American activities. He helped organize the Slovak League, served as treasurer, presided over the National Slovak Society, and held membership in the Czecho-Slovak National Council.

Pictured here are Mr. and Mrs. Jan Pankuch, on their fiftieth anniversary in 1939. Jan and Rose were married for over sixty years.
Courtesy of Jewel Muffler

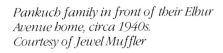

Pankuch family in front of their Elbur Avenue home, circa 1940s.
Courtesy of Jewel Muffler

Chapter 5
From Orchard to Suburb: The Making of Lakewood's Five Landscapes, 1889 to 1930

The farms which no longer than ten years ago flanked Detroit street on either side, have given place to artistically laid-out streets. . . . Lined with shade trees that are characteristic of Lakewood; garnished with well arranged lawns and gardens. . . these streets present model locations for the erection of the home, the ultimate end towards which every man strives.
Thomas Knight, *Beautiful Lakewood*, 1902

For the many Clevelanders who experienced the quiet pastoral beauty of East Rockport, the prospect of owning a home in such a setting must have seemed like an impossible dream. To make it possible someone had to translate the dream into reality. In the process these visionaries made decisions that profoundly shaped the emerging physical landscape and set parameters regarding who could participate in this suburban dream. Ultimately the answers arose piecemeal from the thousands of individual decisions by landowners, developers, builders, home buyers, and renters as well as from realtors, bankers, and local government officials. Nevertheless, transportation profoundly affected the shape and form of the new community. Thus, Lakewood emerged as a densely-settled streetcar suburb; by 1930, the community reigned as the county's "second city" with a density even greater than Cleveland's.

With so many different influences shaping the city, it is hardly surprising that the end result appears both confused and confusing. Nevertheless, there are discernable patterns: at least five major landscapes, physical and social occupy much of the city's turf. Four of these are residential and one commercial. The residential landscapes include a densely-settled, working-class urban village in southeast Lakewood; elite residential areas along the lake and riverfronts; a "middle Lakewood" comprised of a broad swath of modest single- and double-family houses and an apartment house landscape on Madison and Detroit and parts of Clifton and Lake. The commercial landscapes, with centers at West 117th and Warren Road, came to dominate the once residential Detroit Avenue as well as Madison.

Relations between Lakewood's five landscapes have not always been cordial. Native-born residents of more affluent sections have often looked down on immigrants with fewer resources. Village residents regularly experienced nativist condescension from other parts of the city while homeowners throughout Lakewood viewed apartments and apartment dwellers as threats both to their property values and lifestyles.

Urban Village

"To understand the neighborhood," a former village said recently, "you have to think of it as if someone took village from Slovakia and set it down between National Carbon and Madison Park." It is the mix of Old World an

w, and village ambiance and urban texture, that makes
e area so distinct and interesting.

Its origins were far more domestic and utilitarian,
wever. In 1894, National Carbon Company's subsidiary,
e Pleasant Hill Land Company, platted eight narrow cul-
-sacs and 424 small lots. Surrounded by forests and
lds and lacking streetcar connections that could bring
ban workers to the factory, the company apparently
cided to build housing adjacent to the factory.

Seeking work, Slovak, Polish, Carpatho-Rusyn, and
her Eastern European immigrants soon moved into the
ighborhood and began to construct homes. Long hours
d low pay meant few resources on which to draw; vil-
gers countered with sweat equity and innovations in
ancing and architecture. Low-rise, multi-family housing
oduced income for homebuilders and provided small,
w-cost apartments for workers. To lower construction
sts, villagers did their own work or called on neighbors
d relatives. Families took in boarders to supplement
comes while boarders shared in family life. Nor were
ese efforts restricted to residential development; despite
ry limited resources, villagers produced some of Lake-
ood's most distinctive and beautiful churches.

Unlike much of suburban Lakewood, the Village
eceded the arrival of the streetcar and its population
alked to work at the neighboring factories. Low incomes
d demand for housing produced a neighborhood as
ense as many inner-city areas; at its population peak in
20, the Village counted more than four thousand resi-
ents, over one-tenth of Lakewood's population in
at year.

These factors and others produced a unique land-
ape that combines elements of Old World villages with
ose of New World cities. Single- and multiple-family
ouses nestled close to each other while nearby churches
gged the sidewalk. Small shops and stores, pushed out
om house fronts, furthered the urban ambiance, as did
llagers' active street life. On the other hand, carefully-
nded lawns garnished with bright flowers, the presence
several dairies, and the widespread use of domestic
imals to supplement family incomes, provided a rural
mbiance. Villagers, then, produced a neighborhood that
flected and met their needs.

lifton Park and Lakefront Estates

Having increasingly experienced difficulties as a
sort, the Clifton Park Association in 1894 commissioned
the office of landscape architect Ernest W. Bowditch to
develop plans for an exclusive residential community.
Unlike the rest of Lakewood, which closely follows a grid
pattern, the plan introduced curvilinear streets and divided
the land into 96 lots of about an acre each. A later plan
increased the number of lots to 232. In 1899, the Clifton
Park Land Improvement Company bought the Park and
began to press land sales. It promoted the area as "the
finest suburban residence property accessible to Cleveland combining all the conveniences of city homes—
water, gas and sewage—with exceptional advantages of
pure air, forest grounds, private parks, bathing beaches,
boating and fishing privileges with every lot." A later
brochure pointed out convenient streetcar service "only
32 minutes from Public Square," and a private club
"around which social life in the Park centers." The company assured potential homeowners that "the property is
restricted in such a manner as to secure to all purchasers
alike, immunity from the depreciation of value which
would follow the location of business places of any kind,
apartment houses, or terraces within the limits of the
Park."

Within a few years some of Cleveland's most successful industrialists and professionals built homes in the
Park. Initially some built summer homes. In 1899, John J.
Jennings, an officer and director of Lamson and Sessions
Company, constructed a summer home "Restcliff." As with
many Clifton Park residents, Jennings belonged to a
number of elite metropolitan social organizations including the Union Club. Within a few years, however, old
and new residents alike increasingly established permanent residences in the Park. Frederick Glidden constructed "Franklyn Villa" (17840 Lake Road) in 1905,
while five years later, eighty-year-old Francis Glidden constructed "Inglewood" (17869 Lake Road). Francis founded
the Glidden Paint and Varnish Company. The Park also
served as home to automobile pioneers Walter Baker
(18131 West Clifton Road) and in about 1925, Alexander
Winton (18102 Clifton Road). Architect W. Dominick
Benes (1857-1935) also resided in Clifton Park. As a
partner in the architectural firm of Hubbell and Benes, he
helped design such Cleveland landmarks as the West Side
Market and the Masonic Auditorium.

As the advertisements promised, Clifton Park's emerging landscape contained only large, expensive homes; no
apartment houses, businesses, schools, or churches in-
truded on the park-like atmosphere. While park planners
avoided the large gates and walls found in private street

developments throughout the United States, they did privatize access both to river and western lakefront.

Unlike the planned Clifton Park, the lakefront estates represented a continuation of a pattern already established in West Cleveland. Beginning with the house and farm of millionaire real estate promoter Jacob Perkins, Cleveland's Lake Avenue soon acquired the large summer homes of other important leaders, including Mark and Leonard Hanna. Other well-to-do Clevelanders soon built estates in Lakewood. Eventually about fifty large residences occupied the land north of Lake Avenue from Edgewater Park to just west of where Lakewood Park is today. in Lakewood, industrialists and businessmen Alexander Winton built Roseneath, C. L. F. Wieber built Elmhurst, and Charles T. Reed built Waterside. Others also constructed large homes: Theodor Kundtz, Robert R.

Rhodes, Roland T. Meacham, J. A. Paisley, A. E. R. Schneide William Prescott, and John McMyler.

Considerably larger than the Clifton Park lots, the lakefront estates ran from Lake Avenue back to the lake. Owners located their homes close to the water and constructed long teardrop shaped driveways to provide access from the street. To maintain privacy, they installed stone walls and gates; the latter frequently carried the estate's name.

Ironically, the development of Clifton Park and lake front estates gave Lakewood its largest and most expensive homes; it also removed from the vast majority of residents one of the amenities that had attracted them to the city in the first place. Only the purchase of the Rhodes' estate for Lakewood Park in 1918 would partly remedy th loss of the city's most important natural feature.

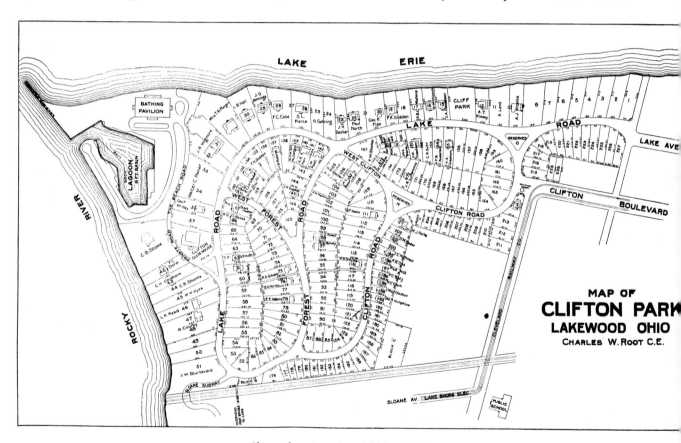

Shown here is a circa 1905 to 1915 map of Clifton Park, Lakewood, Ohio, by Charles W. Root, C. E., for the Clifton Park Land Improvement Company. Source: The Clifton Park Land Improvement Company. Courtesy of Jack E. Rupert

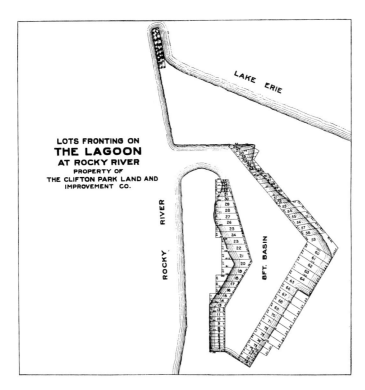

Lots fronting on the Lagoon at Rocky River, circa 1905 to 1915 from The Clifton Park Land Improvement Company.
Courtesy of Jack E. Rupert

Harry and Mabel Hanna Parsons' home at 17890 Beach Road was built in 1911. Harry Parsons served as a confidential secretary to Sen. Mark Hanna and belonged to a variety of automobile clubs and the Cleveland Yacht Club. Mabel Hanna was the senator's daughter. The house contained thirty-six rooms. In 1965 the house was razed and the property was converted into Clifton Park Lane with four houses. Some artifacts from the Parsons' home were incorporated into these new dwellings.
Photograph by James Thomas; courtesy of the Lakewood Historical Society

Margaret Butler is pictured here in the Mabel Hanna Parsons' home in Clifton Park on October 1, 1965. Also shown is the free-standing statue in the dining room. Other rooms were equally elegant. Photograph by James Thomas; courtesy of the Lakewood Historical Society

The dining room of the Mabel Hanna Parsons' home in Clifton Park, was photographed on October 1, 1965. According to Blythe Gehring, "the interior of this house was far more grand than the exterior." There was a free-standing fountain on the right in the dining room and each bedroom contained a fireplace. According to the Cleveland Plain Dealer, the living room walls were "hung with free-hanging draperies of silk linen and fourteen-karat gold threads." The same room featured a two-ton Carrar[a] marble fireplace brought from Italy in 1912; it was covered with symbols fro[m] Greek mythology.
Photograph by James Thomas; courtes[y] of the Lakewood Historical Society

Developers of middle Lakewood sought to reach a
broad range of urban families whose breadwinners held
skilled laboring or white-collar positions. With more
income they could command larger houses than could
most Village residents, but they had much less income
than did dwellers along the lakefront or in Clifton Park. It
was largely for this group that Thomas Knight wrote
Beautiful Lakewood. Noting the "fruit trees and vineyards" were "relics of the fast-disappearing garden farm,"
Knight highlighted some of the community's features:
"well-kept lawns and beautiful homes," "perfectly
equipped schools," and "the fact that there is absolutely
no smoke in the hamlet . . . the soot and grime that makes
life a burden in Cleveland."

In contrast to the Village and Clifton Park, middle
Lakewood's layout reflected the decisions of many
different landowners and developers. In most cases a
developer subdivided only several streets. This process
produced a patchwork pattern, with built-up streets
surrounded by farmland or woods. Usually, developers
merely sold improved building lots with hookups for
water, gas, electricity, and sewers; sidewalks also accompanied the property.

Often builders purchased several adjacent lots and
constructed speculative housing; in other cases individuals purchased a lot and contracted with a builder for
their home. The former accounts for the presence of iden-
tical "twin" and "triplet" houses next door to each other;
the latter explains the relative diversity of house forms
across middle Lakewood. Some new suburbanites selected their home from the pages of a Sears & Roebuck
catalog.

The middle landscape that emerged from this
process was closely tied to the speculators' concern for
profit and to the home-buyers' modest incomes. Since the
grid was easiest to impose and rendered the greatest
profit, middle Lakewood is set on a veritable right angle.
But if most streets are a straight line, few adjacent streets
have the same width or setback; the texture is an undulat-

ing one that ebbs and flows every two or three blocks.

Oriented to the streetcar, the middle Lakewood landscape reflected the constraints of the transportation
system. Densely settled to provide residents easy access to
the streetcar; middle Lakewood, like the Village, could
support a plethora of shops and stores. By 1930, virtually
every resident was within walking distance of the numerous grocery stores, bakeries, fruit and vegetable dealers,
meat markets, confectioners, and druggists who lined
Madison and Detroit avenues at regular intervals. The
presence of only seven gas stations in 1930 underlines the
continuing import of the streetcar even at that late date.

Nor is this sufficient to describe the complexity of
commercial activities of the streetcar suburb. Before the
introduction of modern refrigeration and heating technology, residents relied on innumerable home delivery
services: ice for iceboxes, coal for furnaces, and milk.
They also benefited from the many peddlers who daily
paraded along Lakewood streets, shouting their wares of
fresh fish, poultry, and vegetables, as well as such services
as knife and scissors sharpening and "paper-rags" buying.
Only a block or two away, on Detroit or Madison, a house-
wife could find a small grocery store, meat store and pos-
sibly a fruit and vegetable dealer; not far away she could
find a home bakery and a druggist. Walking to and from
shopping brought neighbors into frequent contact; stores
became informal community centers where neighbors
regularly met and chatted.

By incorporating front porches in the designs of
most houses, builders furthered the potential for neighborhood interaction. Although most single and double
homes of the streetcar suburb lacked the elaborate, broad,
wrap-around porches of the mid- to late-nineteenth
century, its front porches proved adequate for families to
share sheltered space on warm summer days. They also
permitted space for neighbors to visit. In contrast, builders
of automobile suburbs of the post-World War II period
exchanged front porches for backyard patios.

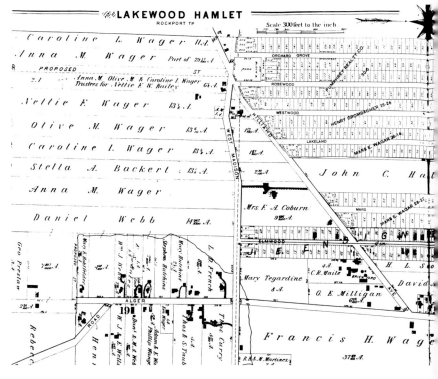

Shown here is a part of Lakewood Hamlet in 1898. From Mars Avenue west to Orchard Grove, between Detroit and Madison nearly every street was sub-divided and sold by a different real estate company: Mars E. Wagar, Henry Grombacher, and Pumphey Realty Company. Neighboring areas have yet to be subdivided as in the case of the John C. Hall property between Mars and Lakeland and Mrs. F. A. Coburn's property south of Mars between Hilliard and West Madison. Much of the land north of Madison remained undeveloped. From Thomas Flynn, Otto Parthel, R. H. Bunning, and Thomas Hassan's Atlas of the Suburbs of Cleveland, Ohio, plate 25.

Mars E. Wagar, (1858-1944) was the grandson of Mars Wagar and the son of Francis and Serena Wagar. As president and treasurer of the Wagar Land Company, Mars played a major role in the transformation of Lakewood from orchard to suburb. He subdivided and sold much of his family's extensive land holdings. According to Margaret Butler, Mars and Wagar avenues were named for Mars Wagar I, and the Wagar family respectively. Wagar graduated from Harvard University in 1881 and did further study at the Sorbonne and the University of Leipzig. He helped found a Cleveland literary club, the Rowfant Club, and served as a board member of the Cleveland Public Library. He is pictured here with his grandchild about 1944.
Courtesy of the Lakewood Public Library

Keep Your Eye on Cherry Grove Farm

Seventy-five acres of the best fruit land in the County : : : : : : : : : : :

To be Converted Into the Choicest Residence Property

FRONTAGE ON DETROIT ST., LAKE AVE. AND THE BOULEVARD

The well known fruit farm of Andrews Bros. has a frontage of 850 feet on Detroit Street and extends back to Lake Erie. It is covered with the best of fruit trees so situated that they would not have to be disturbed through building operations : : : : : :

TWENTY ACRES OF VALUABLE LAKE FRONT PROPERTY NOW ON ══════ THE MARKET ══════

This portion of the farm is heavily timbered with second growth trees and is very desirable for the more pretentious residences. 1700 feet of Boulevard property and 800 feet of Lake Avenue property will also be disposed of at an early date. Write or telephone for full particulars and you will be repaid for your trouble : : : : : : : : : : : :

Andrews Brothers
Residence 2974 Detroit Street
──── Opposite Elmwood ────
Cuyahoga Phone Cliff 199

ne land owners offered their property
developers to subdivide. The Andrews
others appeared to do this when they
k out this advertisement in Knight's
mphlet offering "seventy-five acres of
best fruit land in the County. . . to be
nverted into the choicest residence
operty." From Thomas A Knight's
autiful Lakewood: Cleveland's West
d, page 16.

OLIVEWOOD AVENUE
THE CHEAPEST GOOD PROPERTY in LAKEWOOD

A nice modern home, with all improvements, at a moderate price.

Lots have sewer, water, flagging and trees, and range in price from $225 to $400.

MONEY FURNISHED TO BUILD.

THE HAMBY REALTY CO.
345 Superior St.
Phones: Main 2386, A 905

Some developers divided land into house lots for sale as the Hamby Realty Company did with this property on Olivewood Avenue circa 1902. Lots generally had sewer and water connections and sidewalks; buyers had to construct their own homes or find a builder. From Thomas A. Knight's Beautiful Lakewood: Cleveland's West End, *page 20.*

THE LAKEWOOD REALTY COMPANY

MAKES A SPECIALTY OF GILT EDGED RESIDENCE PROPERTY IN LAKEWOOD

We can locate you either on Lake Avenue, Clifton Boulevard, Detroit Street, Belle Avenue, Cook Avenue, Warren Road or St. Charles Avenue. Choice Lake Front lots.

Six elegant houses with every modern improvement are now being completed on BEAUTIFUL BELLE AVENUE, the banner street in Lakewood.

Come and look at them before purchasing elsewhere. "Seeing is believing." Easy payments.

Take Detroit Street car to Belle Avenue or call at
CITY OFFICE, No. 246 THE ARCADE
Phone M. 2347

Some developers also constructed speculative housing as did the Lakewood Realty Company on Belle Avenue. From Thomas A. Knight's Beautiful Lakewood: Cleveland's West End, *page 42.*

Genck Realty Company allotments included this house, originally the Joseph and Sarah Curtis Hall stone house on the southwest corner of Detroit and Marlowe. The building was razed in about 1916.
Courtesy of the Lakewood Historical Society

Detroit Avenue looking east from Summit, circa 1900s is shown in this postcard by B. E. Williams, Photo Views. The gates in the foreground are at the entrance to Arthur Avenue near the site of the library and Saint Paul Lutheran Church. The church spire on the left is the Church of the Redeemer, now the Latvian Evangelical Lutheran Church. The large building in the middle is the "new" high school, later to be Wilson School on Warren Road. The water tower near the fire station and to the left of Wilson School is also visible.
Courtesy of the Lakewood Historical Society

"Mars Avenue didn't even exist when Mr. Rudenauer pointed his camera west out of an upper window of his home at 1646 Elmwood Avenue just north of Madison Avenue. . . . Mars Avenue in 1910 was a cornfield and grape vineyard." From the Cleveland Plain Dealer Pictorial Magazine, *March 4, 1956. Photograph by Frederick E. Rudenauer; courtesy of the Lakewood Historical Society*

"Summer of 1919. Oldtime horse-powered scoops are digging the basement for another house at 1645 Mars Avenue. (Note dump wagons at curb)." From the Cleveland Plain Dealer Magazine, *March 4, 1956. Photograph by Frederick E. Rudenauer; courtesy of the Lakewood Historical Society*

The Rudenhauer house at 1646 Elmwood Avenue is pictured here about 1906. The tower on the left is probably a gas well.
Courtesy of the Lakewood Historical Society

Elsie Rudenauer picking cherries circa 1920. Some developers subdivided orchards and vineyards and put them up for sale with the added attraction that the buyer would collect the proceeds of the harvest of his lot in the fall. Presumably the land would then be cleared and a house constructed.
Courtesy of the Lakewood Historical Society

Arthur Rudenauer is shown at the wheel of his Studebaker touring car, circa 1920. Adelaide Rudenauer and Elsie are in the rear seat of the car in the driveway of their home at 1646 Elmwood Avenue. Lakewood was clearly a streetcar suburb but automobiles represented a proud possession and provided residents with an opportunity to travel more freely than streetcar schedules and routes permitted.
Courtesy of the Lakewood Historical Society

The Whitehall was a Sears, Roebuck and Company house model circa 1912 to 1926. Not all new Lakewood residents turned to local builders to construct homes for their lots. Some selected their house from a catalog. Between 1908 and 1940, Sears, Roebuck and Company offered about 450 different ready-to-assemble houses ranging from summer cottages to bungalows to mansions. Sears sold nearly 100,000 houses during the time period. Each customer received an instruction manual with blueprints, some as long as seventy-five pages; the manual was designed for both the owner and the contractor who would assemble the house. According to Houses by Mail, all materials for the house were sent by rail; the lumber "was precut to size and numbered at the factory for assembly on the site." From Katherine Cole Stevenson and H. Ward Jandl's Houses by Mail: A Guide to Houses from Sears, Roebuck and Company, page 278.

A neat and roomy house at a very low price. Was designed with two objects in view: economy of floor space and low cost. The dining room is connected with the living room by a large cased opening which practically makes one large room of the two rooms. Has a kitchen and good-sized pantry.

Details and features: Six rooms and one bath. Full-width front porch with wood column; projecting two-story bay in front; front door with beveled plate glass. Cased opening between living and dining rooms.

Years and catalog numbers: 1912 (181); 1913 (181); 1916 (264P181); 1917 (C181); 19 (3035); 1921 (3035); 1922 (3035); 1925 (3035); 1926 (P3035A)

Price: $687 to $1,863

Locations: Plainville, Conn.; Aurora, Ill.; Gary, Hammond and LaPorte, Ind.; Cresco and Davenport, Iowa; Morristown, N.J.; Eastwood, Hempstead and Richmond Hill, N.Y.; Allentown, Galeton, Hadley, Hellertown, McKeesport and New Castle, Pa.; West Point, Va.

Sometime in the 1920s the owners of t lot at 2208 Glenbury, perhaps Econom Management Company, purchased th Whitehall model from Sears, Roebuck. The packaging label discovered in the house's attic many years later indicate the materials were shipped via the Baltimore and Ohio and the New York Central railroads from Norwood, Ohio As the advertisement for the house shows, the price for the Whitehall mod ranged from $687 to $1,863. It "was designed with two objects in view, economy of floor space and low cost," and contained six rooms and a full porch across the front.
Photograph by Jim Borchert; 1988, information courtesy of Russ Salzbrenner

Lakewood residents could rely on a wide range of street vendors and delivery services. Mike Foltin with his No. 1 Milkwagon, circa 1910, regularly provided milk deliveries to his customers in the Village and elsewhere. Such service was the hallmark of the streetcar suburb prior to the 1950s. His horse is wearing a cord netting with a long fringe to help keep the flies away.
Courtesy of Mary Dvoroznak

ithout electric refrigerators, Lakewood sidents needed ice for iceboxes; they so had to shop regularly for perishable oods. They relied on regular deliveries of such necessities as ice and milk as well as coal for heat. Street vendors offered vegetables, fruits, fish, and a variety of other goods. Paul W. Combs is pictured here with his City Ice and Fuel Wagon circa 1924; his route included the area from Bonnieview to West Clifton.
Courtesy of Mary Emma Walker

John, Katherine, Ralph, and Louis Ulrich at 99 Coutant Street, circa 1902. Most homes in middle Lakewood featured front porches. As many photographs indicate, new suburbanites took advantage of this feature especially in warm summer months.
Courtesy of Virginia Elias Plotz and William A. Plotz

Middle Lakewood neighborhoods are filled with many nice surprises. The H. E. Hackenberg house on Grace Avenue, shown here circa 1902 is one of the most spectacular of these. Hackenberg was vice president, secretary, and treasurer of National Carbon Company. He also served on the board of a Lakewood bank. From Thomas A. Knight's Beautiful Lakewood: Cleveland's West End, *page 21.*

Apartment Houses and Cliff Dwellers

Lakewood's apartment landscape was the last and lowest to develop. In part it reflected the rising land costs along streetcar lines and the strong demand for rental housing in the new suburb. Homebuyers were not the only ones who had earlier enjoyed outings and picnics at Clifton or Scenic Park. White collar singles and young married couples also sought the benefits of suburban living. Realizing the potential profits, developers began construction of multi-family apartment houses and buildings.

By 1930 Lakewood had about two hundred apartment structures; most fell into one of two general patterns with each closely tied to the streetcar. The majority of apartments occupied sites along Detroit, Madison, or around the corner on side streets. Most of these were small brick buildings of two or three stories; developers also placed apartments above stores. In some cases merchants lived above their stores as did the Lodzieski family who, for several years, lived over their Lakewood Bakery store on Detroit at West 117th. These small apartments blended into the emerging commercial landscape of Detroit and Madison. While residential streets also have terraces, they are not as common as other housing forms and are often close to major streets as in the case of the Lakeland Avenue terraces.

In contrast, "cliff dwellers" moved into much larger three- and four-story buildings with brick and stone facades that increasingly claimed lots on Clifton, Lake, and Edgewater. Unlike the dispersed patterns on Detroit and Madison, the cliff dwellings clustered near the two prime shopping areas. The largest concentration formed at the east end along Clifton, Lake, and Edgewater, while a smaller one emerged along Clifton near Warren Road and in Lake west of Cook.

With great bulk and little setback, this new landscape stood in sharp contrast to the single- and double-family homes and estates that lined Clifton and Lake. The buildings also introduced into this family-oriented, home-owning population new elements: singles, childless couples, and small families who rented. While many cliff dwellers hoped eventually to own homes of their own, property owners nearby felt threatened on several accounts.

Driven by concerns over declining property values and a deluge of city "riff-raff," they formed the Lakewood Home Owners' Protective Association to fight further real estate development on Clifton and Lake. In response city council "rather hurriedly" passed a zoning ordinance in 1918. According to the *Suburban News*, council acted "to prevent the ruin of certain beautiful residence sections of the city by the erection of unsightly, cheaply built, congestion-breeding apartment houses." Two years later council enacted a more comprehensive zoning ordinance "to protect Lake avenue, Clifton boulevard and adjacent territory against business and apartments and to restrict business and apartments to Madison and Detroit avenues." As the *Suburban News* reported, the law restricted all heavy manufacturing to the "vicinity of Berea road and Madison avenue at Highland avenue." These ordinances did not stop the debate, however. In 1924, the Lakewood *Post* reported a council meeting that "broke into a storm of repartee" between homeowners and developers. Speaking for Lakewood homeowners, William David warned that "we cannot allow massive structures to destroy our home sections without losing our claim to having a beautiful city."

Unlike the buildings they occupied, many cliff dwellers appeared more anonymous than their counterparts in other sections of Lakewood. With lifestyles less tied to the community and few institutions to hold them, apartment dwellers appear to have been largely ignored and forgotten by much of the rest of Lakewood. Nevertheless, some apartment dwellers became central figures in community life, for example, community activist and businesswoman Bernice Pyke lived for many years in the Edgecliff Apartments on Lake Avenue with her husband Arthur and son John.

Because the Madison streetcar line did not begin operation until September 1917, much of south Lakewood was not constructed until after that date. Clearly by 1929, most lots were already built upon as this view of Elmwood at Madison suggests. This apartment-store combination became important parts of the commercial landscape that developed on Detroit and Madison. As in this case, the apartment buildings frequently wrapped around the corner onto side streets. In some cases these buildings reached considerable volume and size; nearby are shop-apartment buildings of three stories or more.
Courtesy of Lakewood Historical Society

This attractive English Tudor building, the Edgewater Cove Apartments at 12065 Edgewater Drive, is one of the more interesting buildings that made up the apartment landscape along Edgewater, Lake, and Clifton. Shown here circa 1954, it was built prior to the Great Depression and contained twenty-five suites. It faced the Lake Shore Hotel. Courtesy of the Cleveland Press Library and Collections, Cleveland State University Libraries

The Erie Cliff Apartment Building, shown here circa 1964, also reflects the pre-Depression architecture that appeared in the cluster near Warren Road. Located at 14901 Lake Avenue on the corner of Cook and Lake avenues, the four-story brick apartment building is an imposing structure. Lakewood businesswoman, suffragist, community activist, and politician Bernice Pyke and her family lived in the Erie Cliff for a number of years.

Photograph by C. O. Frick; courtesy of the Cleveland Press Library and Collections, Cleveland State University Libraries

Commercial Landscapes

As the first road through East Rockport, Detroit Avenue became the preeminent commercial street. While residents of the fine homes along Detroit resisted the intrusion of commercial activities, they fought a losing battle. Stores and shops gradually replaced these residences. On Madison, the late arrival of the streetcar meant that commerce could claim much of this land directly from landowners and developers.

Neither street developed unbroken rows of stores and shops. Rather, the building patterns reflected the streetcar's influence. For example, most stores located at or near trolley stops. Here developers placed two- and three-story brick buildings; groundfloor shops sought to catch customers as they waited for or alighted from the streetcar. Some second floors contained professional offices; others, apartments. Close by, on either main thoroughfare or just around the corner on side streets, small two- and three-story apartment buildings blended into the commercial architecture; together they represented urban outcroppings on the suburban landscape.

This commercial landscape may well have influenced the placement of churches and other buildings on the major thoroughfares as well. While both Madison and Detroit contain a number of large, impressive, and monumental church structures, with a few important exceptions, these buildings sit close to the street and lack the perspective of churches in newer communities. In fact, Saint James, Saints Cyril and Methodius, and Lakewood Presbyterian churches front immediately on the sidewalk, many others are set back only slightly from the street. Even Lakewood's Greco-Roman temples, the First Federal Bank, the Masonic building, and the Christian Science Church, hug the sidewalk. Thus the religious landscape both mirrors and provides continuity with existing commercial patterns.

In addition to this highly dispersed commercial pattern, Lakewood also developed two commercial centers. When East Rockport was still a struggling farm community, the Rockport Plank Road Company, influenced by Native American patterns, selected the site that would become Lakewood's central business district. Other merchants located their businesses near the company's toll house at Warren Road. As late as 1902, Thomas Knight explained that the only store buildings on Detroit lay between Belle and Warren. From 1912 to 1919, the city located its city hall at the intersection while a number of government activities clustered nearby. In 1923, the five-story Detroit-Warren Medical Building on the southwest corner became the city's first high rise building with the city's first elevator. Seven years later Bailey Department Store further confirmed the intersection's importance when they erected a major suburban store on the southeast corner.

Another business center emerged around the intersection of Detroit and West 117th. This business center spilled across both Lakewood and Cleveland and lined both sides of Detroit and West 117th; it even extended east along Clifton. Young's Department Store in Cleveland helped cement this location, as did Reidy's Furniture Store in Lakewood. With two large theaters, the Homestead and the Granada and a dance hall above the Homestead, the area offered recreational attractions. Gold's Market, Lakewood Bakery, Cleveland Trust, and Fanny Farmer's candy store also drew customers to the area.

By the time the Great Depression arrived Lakewood was largely built. The result reflected the interaction between the constraints of the streetcar and the efforts of landowners, developers, builders, and residents. The streetcar suburb that sprouted from East Rockport's garden mocked its former origins. While much of Detroit Avenue still contained the outcroppings of the prosperous farm community, the new landscape reflected much of the metropolis to the east. In the process, the city lost much of its two most important amenities: lake access and woods.

For their part, the landowners, developers, builders, homeowners, and renters had shaped the community into a series of different and sometimes discrete and conflicting landscapes. Businesses and apartments undermined the once thriving social life of Detroit Avenue; apartment and commercial developers battled homeowners along Clifton and Lake. While residents of Clifton Park and the lakefront estates retreated into private clubs or behind stone walls, Village residents endured the slights of much of the rest of the community. These conflicts presented leaders with one of their greatest and continuing challenges: to make the community's diverse constituencies cohere and at the same time demonstrate respect for the needs and concerns of each.

This scene shows Detroit Street west near Marlowe, circa 1914. By 1914, the farms that had once lined Detroit were largely in retreat and stores with apartments above began to fill in where farm houses once stood. This scene shows two streetcars in the distance, one east-bound and the other west-bound passing each other at about Warren Road. Horse-drawn wagons still plied Lakewood's streets making deliveries to stores and shops. Peddlers also hawked their wares from such wagons. *Photograph by Perry Corell; courtesy of the Lakewood Historical Society*

Detroit Avenue West near Marlowe in downtown Lakewood as it appeared sometime after 1916. The sign of Guardian Bank is barely visible in the distance. On the left, new construction is taking place on the southeast corner of Marlowe. Across the street, Lakewood Presbyterian Church's new building hugs the sidewalk as does the Marlowe Exchange of the telephone company on the northeast corner. By this date trucks have begun to replace horse-drawn wagons, thus reducing the amount of physical waste on Lakewood streets. Note the air pump in front of the tire shop on the right. *Photograph by Perry Corell; courtesy of the Lakewood Historical Society*

is photograph of Detroit Avenue east
m Victoria Avenue, demonstrates the
ent to which downtown Lakewood
s already built up by 1920. As with
er photographs of the time, only a
v automobiles grace the scene, but
re is also the ubiquitous presence of
Detroit streetcar. The small house on
far left (site of Ameritrust building)
iy well be that described by Marie
ers in her "Memories of Early Lake-
od" (Chapter 6), where she describes
i the east corner was a small real
ate house where Mr. Allen sat out
nt talking to passers-by." Guardian
ist Bank occupies the site of today's
st Federal Bank. In about 1917,
ewood National Bank constructed
building that Guardian Trust took
er. Guardian Trust collapsed during
Depression leaving many Lakewood
titutions and residents without access

to their deposits. Colonial Savings Bank,
on the right, advertising 5 percent inter-
est on savings is on the south side of

Detroit in today's "Colonial Building."
Photograph by Perry Corell; courtesy of
the Lakewood Historical Society

owntown Lakewood from just west of
mwood Avenue as it appeared on a
arm summer day, looking east from
ars Avenue down Detroit Avenue.
urrows Brothers store here is located

near Elmwood and provided lending
library services as did Bernice Pyke's
Bookstore at Cook and Detroit. The
woman in front of Burrows is using her
umbrella to ward off the warmth of the

sun.
Courtesy of the Lakewood
Historical Society

This is the Curtis Block at 14501-15 Detroit Avenue at Marlowe, circa 1920s to 1930s. Grocery stores were an important part of the streetcar suburb's commercial landscape. These small stores dotted Madison and Detroit every few blocks. In 1923 the Fisher Brothers alone had six stores, including this one, on Detroit; they also had four stores on Madison. On Detroit the stores were located at West 117th, Marlowe, Westwood, Bonnie View, Wayne, and Riverside. The stores on Madison were at Ridgewood, Wyandotte, Warren, and Winton. In addition to the Fisher Brothers, there were other grocery chain stores and many independents, like the Gold Brothers and Frank Sinagra's Lakewood Fruit Market.
Courtesy of Mary Hall

This cartoon-advertisement for Arthur Kellogg and his original Shanty auto parts store on July 22, 1933 was drawn by Lee W. Stanley. The Shanty became a Lakewood institution featuring a wide range of auto parts. The cartoon shows the store at its original site. It later moved to larger quarters in the block that now houses Lakewood Center North. For some time it shared the block with the State Liquor Store and Rozi's Wine Store.
Courtesy of Pauline Groth

Detroit and West 117th streets also became a major shopping area. The Cleveland Trust Bank (now Ameritrust) branch is about to open on the left in this picture on the southwest corner of 117th and Detroit Avenue circa 1919. Dentists' offices occupy the second floor of the Brown Building, while furnishers and hatters have a store in the same building. The next store sells cigars and candy while a book store appears to occupy the same or neighboring space. The shop on the extreme right also sold cigars and candy while the Coffinberry Insurance Company had offices above. On the left several people are waiting for the east-bound streetcar while two young newsboys are looking for customers. Courtesy of Jim Pohorence and Pete McGrew

Shown here is the northwest corner of Detroit Avenue at West 117th Street on August 22, 1951. The large building that housed the Fanny Farmer candy store dominated the Lakewood side of West 117th. The building was later destroyed by fire. On the left, two passengers wait to board the east-bound Detroit streetcar. Courtesy of George Snyder

FOCUS: The Village

The Village landscape represents an amalgam of rural and urban, and of residential, commercial, industrial, and religious uses. It is the mixture of these elements along with the creativity of Village home builders and residents that make this neighborhood most interesting and distinctive.

While many houses in the neighborhood look like standard Cleveland doubles, some are, in fact, small apartments of six or eight units. What appears to be the front door in fact provides access only to one unit. The real entrance to the apartments is on the side of each building. Two stairways each provide access to two units per floor. This layout gives residents more privacy than the standard apartment layout. The small units offered young immigrant families inexpensive rents. For the more affluent, traditional double- and single-family homes dot the neighborhood. Others constructed front and back houses on the same lot, a pattern common in older parts of Cleveland and other industrial cities.

The importance of religion to the Village is underlined by the presence of eight churches in the immediate neighborhood. They reflect the diverse ethnic and religious origins of the neighborhood. Initially Saints Peter and Paul Evangelical Lutheran Church organized in 1901, Saints Cyril and Methodius Roman Catholic Church founded in 1903, and the Calvin Presbyterian Church begun in 1921, served largely Slovak-American congregations. In 1905 Polish-Americans founded Saint Hedwig's Roman Catholic Church, while Ukranian-Americans, Carpatho-Rusyns, and Galician-Americans organized Saint Nicholas Ukranian Orthodox Church in 1916, Saint Gregory the Theologian Byzantine Catholic Church in 1905, and Saints Peter and Paul Orthodox Church in 1917. If Village houses are utilitarian and modest, the neighborood churches provide unusual visual splendor. Their gold domes, and brick and stone bell towers dominate the neighborhood skyscape, while church sanctuaries are some of the most elaborate and beautiful in the city.

Finally, the Village has its own commercial center. Initially it was located on Plover; most businesses eventually moved to Madison. Lakewood's first and only locally-owned department store, Schermer Brothers, started on Madison in 1906 and remained to the 1960s. A savings and loan, Orol (Eagle) Federal (now Home Federal), began here, while several funeral homes also served the neighborhood. Some dance halls and a gym located on residential streets, although Madison became the principal recreational area housing several bowling alleys, dance halls (including Mahalls), and a movie theater: first the U-NO and then the Royal.

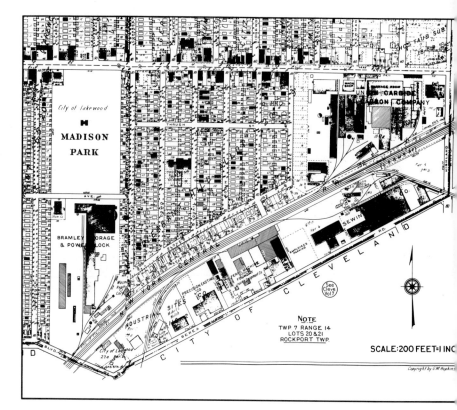

By 1927 the Village was largely constructed. Only a few lots remained undeveloped; many of the churches and schools were already built. By 1927 Templar Motors had folded and Bramley Storage replaced the automobile factory. Union Carbide and Carbon Company, the White Sewing Machine Company, the Crucible Equipment Company, Precision Casting Company, Castle Auto Parts, and Howell Automatic Machine Company are also shown. From G. M. Hopkins Co., Plat Books of Cuyahoga County, Ohio, *1927, plate 4.*

The Vavrek family and friends are shown in front of their home at 2090 Quail Avenue, in the 1920s. Born in 1875, John Vavrek left Slovakia for the United States at the age of twenty-four. About 1910 he built this house at 2090 Quail Street, next to Harrison School. The Vavreks probably lived on the first floor while two tenant families occupied separate apartments on the second. Some years later this house was moved to 2135 Dowd Street. John and Elizabeth Pohlod Vavrek are on the left with their family and friends. Their baby daughter, Julia, is in the baby carriage on the front porch. A neighbor child is looking out from the second floor window. Courtesy of Monica Adipietro

Although National Carbon Company laid out the Village, not all residents worked at the company's factory. John Vavrek, pictured here on the far right in the 1930s worked at Empire Brass Manufacturing Company at 10301 Berea Road; other Villagers worked at Winton or Templar Motors or at other factories located along the industrial corridor that lines the New York Central Railroad tracks. After living on Quail for a number of years, the Vavrek family moved to 1604 Winchester; John died in 1936 at the age of fifty-nine. Courtesy of Monica Adipietro

The Mescon family and home at 2104 Dowd Street, circa 1921. Left to right: Mary Miholik Mescon, Joseph, John Jr., and John Mescon, Sr. Villagers carefully tended their yards; the abundant foliage here adds to the village ambience. Courtesy of Lisa Hoy

In addition to building their own homes, many Villagers established businesses, often as an appendage to their house. Frank and Mary Janusz migrated to the United States from Rzeszow, Poland, in about 1906. Nine years later, Frank built an eight-unit house at 2023 Halstead; the family combined two units on the first floor and rented out the other six two-room units. In 1920, Frank built

a store and house next door at 2025 Halstead. The interior of Janusz Meats and Groceries with the Janusz family is pictured here, left to right: Mary, Frank, Adele, Barbara, and Frank, circa 1920. Until business began to flourish, Mary worked at National Carbon. In 1928, Frank sold the house and store, which was then taken over by George Gluvna. The Januszs moved to Waterbury Avenue. Courtesy of Barbara Janusz Jedlinka

The Village business district included both locally owned and chain stores. In 1930, over thirty grocers competed for neighborhood customers. The five chain stores included the Fisher Brothers store, pictured here at the northwest corner of Madison and Ridgewood avenues, circa 1937, as well as two Kroger and two A and P stores. The Fisher Brothers store is next door to Mansky's Shoe store; Cort's Shoe store is on the far left. This block is the present site of Fedor Manor Apartments.
Courtesy of John J. Loksa

Orol Federal Savings and Loan Association, at 12223 Madison Avenue, circa 1930. Orol (eagle in Slovak) Federal was one of the Village's key institutions. Initially located on Plover, the bank soon moved to Madison Avenue. Chartered by the state of Ohio in 1911, Orol Federal Savings and Loan Association (now Home Federal Savings Bank) is Lakewood's oldest locally owned bank. Despite the Depression, Orol Federal reported over one million dollars in deposits and assets in excess of $1.5 million in 1933.
Courtesy of Home Federal Savings Bank

FOCUS: Lakefront Estates

Residents of lakefront estates included some of Ohio's most prominent and wealthy citizens. While some initially used their property as a summer retreat, many constructed large, permanent homes that demonstrated the extent of their wealth. Although the lakefront elite chose to live in Lakewood, their business and social circles often took them well beyond the boundaries of the new suburb. Only a few focused their efforts on their new hometown. Robert R. Rhodes, Alexander Winton, and Theodore Kundtz provide different examples of the lifestyles of Lakewood's rich and famous.

In about 1874, Rhodes, the son of prominent Cleveland industrialist Daniel Rhodes, constructed a large frame summer home in what would become Lakewood Park. Eventually his family would occupy the home year-round. Although important figures in Cleveland social and philanthropic life, the Rhodeses also took an active interest in Lakewood. Kate Castle Rhodes served on the board of the Visiting Nurse Association; Lakewood Hospital's dispensary in the Village was named for her.

Shortly after the turn of the century, Alexander Winton, the automaker, constructed a large, rambling frame house near the present site of the Winton Place. Named Roseneath, the house and grounds reflected a more imposing and impressive structure than the Rhodes' "summer home." Despite his wealth

The lakefront estates stretched in 1912 from Edgewater Park to beyond Lakewood Park. Beginning at Alexander Winton's estate, Roseneath, (12924 Lake Avenue) and moving west, the following estates lined the lakefront: Alexander Winton, Elva L. Reed (Waterside), Frederick W. Stecher, Brougham E. Harris (Lake Cliff), Byron Harris (Rock Bluff), Alexander C. Mackenzie, The F. Zimmerman Realty Company, Jean C. Hutchins (North Anchorage), and Theodor Kundtz. Estates west of the Kundtz property included: Alfred Arthur, Gertrude W. Crider, William and E. Prescott (Rosecliff), Robert R. Rhodes, H. F. Hopkinson (Beechwood), and the Sisters of Charity of Saint Augustine. From C. M. Hopkins Co., Platbook of the City of Cleveland, and Suburbs, *vol. 2, plate 28.*

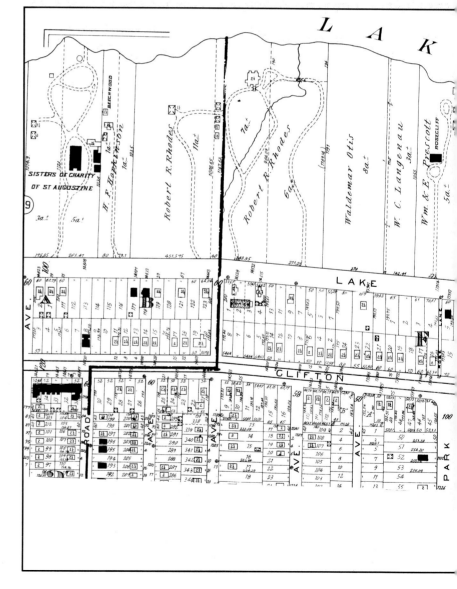

d the grandeur of his estate, Winton's personal life was not always easy. Shortly er completion of the house his first e drowned in the lake; his second ouse died in 1924. A third marriage, to rion Campbell, a Native American hts advocate and theater devotee, ded three years later. Winton remar- d for a fourth time two weeks after his orce. Although he was a noted yacht- enthusiast and a member of the kewood Yacht Club (now the Cleve- d Yacht Club), Winton's social and ofessional contacts often took him far yond the bounds of the small suburb. Born the son of a cabinetmaker in ter-Metzenziefen, Hungary, Theodor ndtz (1852-1937) came to Cleveland he age of nineteen. Beginning work

as a cabinetmaker, he soon established his own business producing sewing machine cabinets for White Sewing Machine Company. By 1900, the Theodor Kundtz Company employed over twenty-five hundred workers, many of whom were Hungarian immigrants. By 1915 Kundtz owned five plants in Cleveland and a lumber yard in Lake- wood. In contrast to Rhodes and Winton, Kundtz's social life revolved around the Cleveland Hungarian community, of which he rapidly became a prominent member. He helped underwrite the construction of the Hungarian Hall and participated in Hungarian community activities. As with Winton, Kundtz's other ties linked him to Cleveland; he belonged to the Cleveland Chamber of

Commerce and attended Saint Rose Church.

Kundtz's "castle" was clearly Lake- wood's largest and most elegant man- sion. Built on land that originally extended from Lake Avenue to the lake, the house took four years to construct. Kundtz used skilled workers from his factory to hand-carve interior decora- tions; they also made all the mansion's furniture. Each room was finished in a different wood and handpainted murals graced many walls. The mansion also contained a ballroom, bowling alley, and music room. In 1937 William Morrow purchased the estate and in 1961 it was torn down.

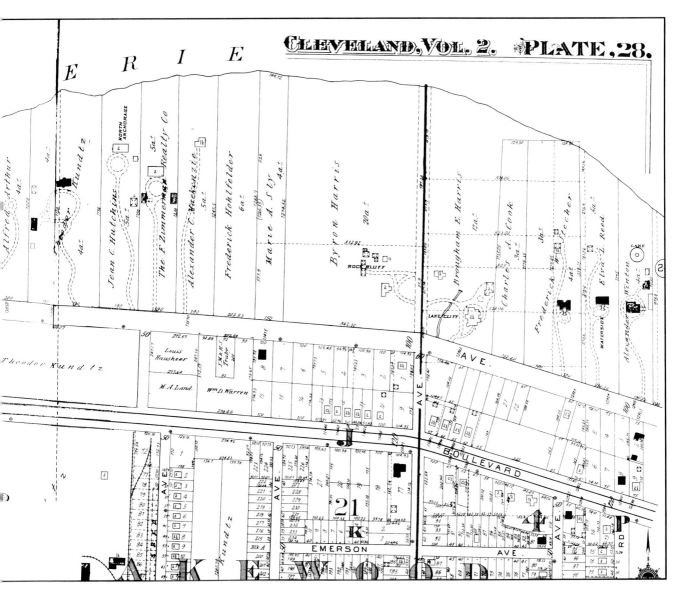

The former estate of Robert R. Rhodes is pictured here circa 1950. Built sometime around 1874, the Rhodes home was one of the earliest lakefront estates. The family remained in the house until shortly after Robert's death. In 1918, his widow then sold the estate to the city for $215,000. The house served as a convalescent hospital for wounded soldiers during World War I and handled overflow patients from Lakewood Hospital during the deadly influenza epidemic of November 1918. In 1920 the house became City Hall; the building was torn down following completion of a new city hall in late 1959. The glassed-in area on the first floor was a veranda where the Rhodes family spent quiet afternoons reading and entertaining at tea. After the city took over the building the veranda became the offices of the Telephone Exchange and the Building Department.
Courtesy of the City of Lakewood

This living room and master bedroom circa 1910, were on the second floor of the Rhodes home. These rooms became the site of Lakewood's Engineering Department when the building became the city hall.
Photograph by P. J. Corell; courtesy of the Lakewood Historical Society

Shown here is a bedroom of the Rhodes estate circa 1910, now Lakewood Park.
Photograph by P. J. Corell; courtesy of the Lakewood Historical Society

The rear of Alexander Winton's estate, Roseneath, on Lake Avenue around the 1900s to the 1920s.
Courtesy of Elsa Watters and the Lakewood Historical Society

The north view of the grounds of the Winton estate, from the house, around the 1900s to the 1920s.
Courtesy of Elsa Watters and the Lakewood Historical Society

Marion Campbell, of Clifton Park, pictured here in Native American dress on December 10, 1929, was the third Mrs. Alexander Winton. During her marriage she presented an opera, "The Seminole," in the yard of their home; guests included Cleveland high society and the governor of Ohio. The marriage apparently was a steamy one; the third Mrs. Winton reported that she received an out-of-court settlement of two hundred thousand dollars. Both parties remarried shortly after the divorce.
Photograph by Trout Ware Studios; courtesy of the Cleveland Press and Library Collections, Cleveland State University Libraries

Theodor Kundtz is portrayed here at his desk at the Theodor Kundtz Company in 1915.
Courtesy of the Cleveland Press Library and Collections, Cleveland State University Libraries

Shown here is the former estate of Theodor Kundtz at 13826 Edgewater Drive in 1961. When the Kundtz-Morrow house was destroyed for the

Kirtland Lane Homes, the developers promised "each new home will contain some item taken from 'The Castle' which once occupied the site."

Photograph by Byron Filkins; courtesy of the Cleveland Press Library and Collections, Cleveland State University Libraries

Mike Tischler, a cabinetmaker who worked in the Theodore Kundtz factory worked on the home as well. He helped construct the dining room table, around the 1920s to the 1930s.
Courtesy of Duncan Gardiner

According to the Cleveland Press, the coach house, shown here in 1978, was "larger than most mansion-size houses. The Kundtz family moved in here . . . five years before the main house was completed. . . . The main house was a copy of a real castle in Hungary which Kundtz recalled from his boyhood there."
Courtesy of the Cleveland Press Library and Collections, Cleveland State University Libraries

Hall of Theodor Kundtz Home.
Courtesy of the Lakewood Historical
Society

A bedroom in the Theodor Kundtz
Home. Note the mural near the edge of
the ceiling.
Courtesy of the Lakewood Historical
Society

Hall of Theodor Kundtz Home.
Courtesy of the Lakewood Historical
Society

A bedroom in the Theodor Kundtz
Home.
Courtesy of the Lakewood Historical
Society

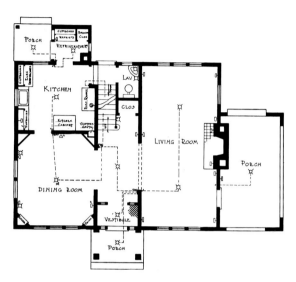

Unlike many homes in Lakewood, this model home offered an electric refrigerator, dishwasher, and electric range. The brochure noted that "the air of the electrical kitchen is so pure that plant life will thrive." The house also featured a half bath on the first floor. Courtesy of William and Virginia Elias Plotz

hile far from the grandeur of Kundtz' 'astle," this large home called "The 'odern Electric Home," is located at 126 Lake Avenue. Constructed by the el-Bilt Homes Company, it offered ur bedrooms and many modern conniences, circa 1922. urtesy of William and Virginia as Plotz

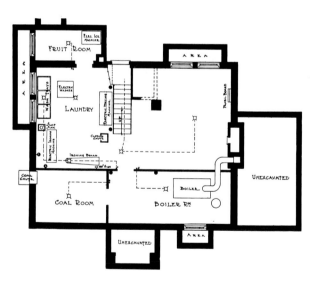

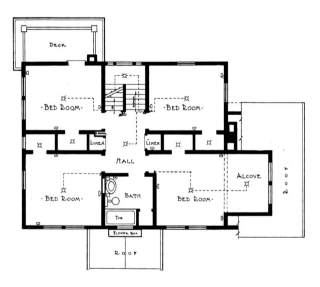

ke most Lakewood basements, "The 'odern Electric Home" contained a al room and a fruit room. It also fered an electric washer, dryer, and n ironing machine. The fruit room ntained an electric ice machine. ourtesy of William and Virginia ias Plotz

With four large bedrooms and an alcove off the master bedroom, this house offered considerable space for its residents. Among the other appliances available for the bedroom of this electric home, the brochure recommended "wired furniture," a warming pad, an immersion heater (for the quick heating of children's food or water), a curling iron ("to properly curl milady's hair"), and a vibrator. "The Electric Vibrator has two important functions, viz.; stimulating blood circulation in the case of local ailments or, in the lady's boudoir, as a beautifier." Courtesy of William and Virginia Elias Plotz

Chapter 6
VIGNETTE
Sister Stanislaus, Annals of the Congregation of the Sisters of Charity of Saint Augustine's

If Lakewood presented diverse physical landscapes, it also produced considerable religious diversity. Founding a new institution or transplanting an older one, however, presented considerable difficulties. In the new suburb, young families confronted mortgage payments or rent as well as expenses for food, clothing, and transportation. Financial support for religious and other institutions had to come out of the money left over from these expenses. Institution building also demanded considerable time and expense in other ways as well.

For the Sisters of Charity of Saint Augustine, as for other groups, institution building was not an easy task. One year before Lakewood adopted its name and became a hamlet, the Sisters of Charity took over a summer home recently vacated by Mark Hanna. From their isolated Lake Avenue site just west of the Robert Rhodes estate, the Sisters struggled to bring some semblance of order to their new environment. Death was never far away; it seemed to lurk about the new community, often snatching away the youngest of the order. Sister Stanislaus chronicled those sad passings and traced the Sisters' successes in establishing the convent. The following passages are excerpted from her *Annals*.

In April, 1888, the Sisters took possession of their new home on Lake Avenue, Lakewood Hamlet. The Hon. M. A. Hanna had a lease on the place until June 1st of this year, but through kindness he vacated in April, he only using it as a summer residence; paying, however, his full rent. The Sisters at once took possession of the cottage; several coming to live in it until the erection of the present building. All new foundations are accompanied with more or less hardships and toil; the Lake Avenue foundation being no exception to this rule. Situated as it is, five miles from the business section of the City, it entailed either fatigue to get the necessaries, or else much deprivation. The street railway came no nearer at the time than at the intersection of Lake Avenue and Detroit St. Sister Mary Gertrude was the first Sister placed in charge. At first they had not the blessing of having the Holy Sacrifice offered at the home, and often did the Sisters walk to St. Colman's or another church to hear Mass. The large room in the upper story of the cottage was fitted up as a Chapel, and in November of this first year the Rt. Rev. Bishop permitted the Blessed Sacrament to be reserved here; and through the kindness of Reverend G. F. Houck the Sisters had the consolation of assisting in their own little Chapel at the Holy Sacrifice on Sundays and Holy-Days; and occa-

nally the Jesuit Fathers gave them this great blessing. Ah!
o can describe the delight of the Sisters when the God,
 Lord of Heaven and earth, found here on this beauti-
 spot, a home!

April 20th Sister Margaret Mary (Carrollton) was
led to her reward; scarcely four years since her en-
nce, when she gave herself to God with a fervent and
erous heart. God was pleased with her sacrifice. She
k pneumonia and lasted but a few days. All hoped she
ght battle with the disease and recover; but it was
erwise ordained for her and she was willing.

One day while the greater number of the Sisters were
ing the weekly washing, fire broke out in the laundry,
d but for the able work of the Fire Company, all would
e been ashes. A day or two after, another fire; this time,
 barn. . . . How these originated, could not be told; yet
looked as if an evil one had perpetrated the deed, and
 a purpose.

During the summer the Right Reverend Bishop made
visitation. The new convent was now nearing comple-
n and would be ready for dedication at the will of the
hop. It was decided, as the building was in debt, to
rge a fee of entrance on the day; for some attraction
st be used as a draw. The Knights of St. John kindly
eed to give a dress drill on the grounds. A train on the
kel Plate Railroad was chartered from the City; the fare
be fifty cents, and with this, a coupon admitting them to
 house and grounds.

On Sunday, August 28, 1892, the feast of the great
hop and Doctor, St. Augustine, patron of the Com-
nity, the Right Rev. Bishop Horstmann blessed the
apel and convent. . . . The Bishop went from one apart-
nt to another, sprinkling holy water and reciting the
yers prescribed, followed by a great number of priests
m the various City parishes, as well as many from out-
town. The convent was thrown open for the day that all
o came might have the opportunity to visit every part.
lly two thousand people, friends of the Sisters, came to
tness the impressive ceremonies. . . . The day was warm,
d the cooling breezes from the lake made it enjoyable.
e Knights acquitted themselves most creditably on their
rt, making a fine appearance in their uniforms. Two
ass bands discoursed good music. Ice cream, cake, and
ft drinks were served at booths on the grounds; every-
ing being done to give satisfaction and enjoyment to
ose who came.

[The event raised $1,084.] To finish the building it
as necessary to borrow from the bank at 6 percent,
$10,000.

In the Summer of this year [1896] the cottage on the
grounds was opened, with the sanction of the Rt. Rev.
Bishop, to summer boarders. This was a source of income
and materially helped to lessen the debt, which at the time
was $14,000.

On the 8th of June Sister Mary Hilda, who on May
30th the year previous had been clothed with the holy
habit, soon after began to decline in health. It was evident,
after the physician had pronounced her disease Tuber-
culosis, that she would go to an early grave. . . .

The year of 1898 entered severely cold, and
continued so the balance of the winter. Owing to the
weather, there was much sickness throughout the City. The
Sisters had a goodly portion of the grippe and kindred
troubles. The hand of Death entered the Community,
taking from it several members.

A very successful orchard festival, which indeed had
become annual, was held this summer [1900]. The
proceeds helped materially toward the erection of a long
felt needed addition—a laundry. This is a substantial
brick and stone structure, 75' x 45', and three stories high.
In it is a large dormitory, a well arranged hospital apartment for the sick children, to be used especially when an
epidemic breaks out; bath-rooms, etc.; a complete
laundry, bake rooms, ovens, etc., boiler rooms. From this
the entire building is heated.

Many improvements were made on Lake Avenue
during the past year [1900]. During the past year the
avenue was widened; the street paved, a fence of iron in
front of the property, and the City water turned into the
convent, the pipes having been laid the year previous.

These excerpts are from Sister M. Stanislaus Clifford,
CSA Annals of the Congregation of Sisters of Charity of
Saint Augustine. Sister Cheryl Keehner, CSA, archivist for
the Sisters of Charity of Saint Augustine, in Richfield,
Ohio, kindly granted permission to reprint excerpts from
the Annals; she also provided information on Sister
Stanislaus and the Sisters of Charity.

FOCUS: Sister Stanislaus of Saint Augustine's Convent

With its fresh lake breezes the new Lakewood site offered an excellent location for the sick to recouperate from illness. The Sisters treated patients suffering from pneumonia and diptheria and nursed victims of industrial accidents, such as John Stevering who had his hand crushed in a machine at Excelsior Iron Works. The Sisters also took in the sick who had no family to care for them.

In 1921, a novitiate high school opened, affiliated with the Catholic University of America; it later became Saint Augustine Academy. In 1975, the Sisters of Charity handed over the operation of the academy to the order of the Holy Family of Nazareth which took over responsibility for the academy. The academy recently added a day care center.

Born in Ohio's Richland County, Elizabeth Clifford (1842-1911) joined the Sisters of Charity in Cleveland in 1859. One of the founding group of sisters who established Saint Augustine Convent in Lakewood, Sister Stanislaus chronicled the important events of the order in Cleveland and Lakewood. Her *Annals* cover over fifty years and document the order's activities. Her attention to detail and knowledge of convent life provide an interesting view of life in the new suburb.

The Sisters of Charity began in Cleveland when four Sisters arrived from France in 1851 to serve the diocese's sick. In 1865, the Sisters staffed and ran the new Saint Vincent Charity Hospital and its adjacent orphanage for boys. By the 1880s the order needed a new mother house; in 1888, the Sisters moved to the Lakewood site.

Sister Stanislaus Clifford shown here circa 1900, was one of the founding sisters of the convent in Lakewood. She was a skilled nurse who, along with her colleagues, cared for many religious and lay people at their Lakewood convent at 14808 Lake Avenue. Courtesy of Sister Cheryl Keehner and the Sisters of Charity of Saint Augustine Archives

Mark Hanna and his family leased this cottage, shown here with the addition circa 1925, for three summers prior to 1888. In that year it became the first convent building when the Sisters of Charity moved to the property in Lakewood west of the Robert Rhodes estate (Lakewood Park). The Sisters of Charity lived here until the brick convent building opened in 1892.
Courtesy of Sister Cheryl Keehner and the Sisters of Charity of Saint Augustine Archives

[The] Sisters of Charity purchased the [pro]perty for the mother house and novi[tiat]e in 1886. The three-story convent [buil]ding was dedicated in 1892. It took [ma]ny more years to pay for the property [and] the new buildings under construc[tion]. In 1921, the Sisters opened their [aca]demy for high school instruction for [girl]s. Four years later they added kinder[gar]ten through sixth grade for both boys [an]d girls. The initial enrollment was [sixt]y-four pupils. In 1925 the Sisters of [Cha]rity dedicated the building shown [her]e; a year later the school added [gra]des seven through nine.
[Cou]rtesy of Sister Cheryl Keehner [an]d the Sisters of Charity of Saint [Au]gustine Archives

By 1952, the Sisters had added a number of new buildings to their academy, as shown here. The rapid growth in enrollment brought about construction of a new elementary school in 1928. As demand grew for the high school, Saint Augustine's discontinued elementary education. In 1963, the academy added a new building with ten new classrooms and other facilities. Ten years later the Sisters of Charity turned over control of the academy to the Sisters of the Holy Family of Nazareth.
Photograph by Kucera and Associates; courtesy of Sister Cheryl Keehner and the Sisters of Charity of Saint Augustine Archives

FOCUS: Lakewood Churches

While religion and religious institutions came to play a major role in East Rockport and Lakewood, churches took some time to develop. Henry Alger's account of the "First Settlement to 1821" provides a limited discussion of religious activities. It is unclear if clergy performed the first two weddings of Rockport settlers while Deacon Daniel Miner "kept a tavern." Alger's limited household inventory did not even include a Bible. Certainly the small population, the difficulties of establishing farmsteads, and the rugged conditions contributed greatly to these conditions.

Nevertheless, as pioneer outposts became settled farm landscape, Rockport's pioneer families organized several churches. With suburbanization, however, came a wave of church founding and building. By 1930 Lakewood became home to a wide range of denominations and some very impressive church structures. After 1930 the founding of new churches slowed considerably, although the city continues to add to its complement of churches and faiths.

Baptists organized first in 1832 but dissension between those east and west of the Rocky River split the meeting in two. Several years later the two factions joined and in 1846 constructed a "commodious meeting house" at Warren Road and Hilliard. Apparently this church fell into decline shortly after. In 1841 the Nicholsons and the Wagars helped established the New Jerusalem (Swedenborgian) Church, and seven years later erected a building. Shortly after, Wesleyan Methodists formed a class but they did not construct a church building until the 1870s. These early churches often had difficulty attracting

ministers and frequently had to rely on circuit preachers who served a number of other congregations.

To a considerable extent church formation and construction awaited Rockport's ascendence into affluence. In the 1870s as Rockporters began to construct new homes and lay out elaborate gardens, they also turned to church founding and building. With financial help from the Webb family, Methodists put up a frame structure at the corner of Summit and Detroit. Two years earlier, the Disciples (Christian Church) organized a Sunday school and held classes at West School. In 1878, aided by the Franklin Circle Disciples Church in Cleveland, the fledgling congregation constructed a chapel. Similarly, Cleveland's Episcopal Trinity Chapel established a mission in East Rockport. By 1875, mission members had founded the Church of the Ascension and erected a small church. After the turn of the century parishioners of these churches would build larger, more substantial buildings.

In general, these first churches tended to reflect the views and concerns of Rockport pioneer families. While many new suburbanites joined these churches, many more chose to found churches of their own, especially when their faith was not represented. Between 1897, when the Detroit Avenue Methodist Church began, and 1930, Lakewood residents founded some twenty-five churches.

These new institutions greatly expanded the city's religious offerings. Roman Catholic churches joined Lakewood's Protestant landscape: Saints Cyril and Methodius (1903), followed by Saint Hedwig's and Saint Gregory's Byzantine Rite (1905) and Saint James's (1908). In 1922, Lakewood Catholics added Saint Clement's and Saint Luke's. Eastern Orthodox worshipers also founded two churches: Saint Nicholas Ukrainian (1916), Saints Peter and Paul (1917). New Protestant churches also sprouted up on the new suburban landscape. Presbyterians founded four churches: Lakewood and Faith United in 1905, Calvin in 1917 and Grace (1924), while Lutherans established Saint Peter and Paul Evangelical (1901), Saint Paul's Evangelical (1903), Pilgrim (1914), and Pentacostal Lutheran

(1918). Congregationalists started Lakewood (1904) and Parkwood (1916).

Other denominations also founded churches, including The First Church Christ Scientist in 1909, and Evangelic United Brethren in 1912, while Bapti reappeared in 1904. Nor were these efforts limited to Christian denominations. In 1918, Jewish residents organized a Sunday school when they discovered "about two hundred Jewish children" living in the area. Despite much effort and prominent articles in both the Lakewood *Press* and the *Jewr Review and Observer*, their attempts to establish "a Temple of our own in Lakewood" were futile. In recent year the West Temple in nearby Cleveland has filled this need.

As James McDowell noted in his history of Lakewood churches, founders "were actually few in number: Faith Presbyterian—20, Lakewood Baptist—28, Lakewood Congregational—27, Lakewood Presbyterian—15, Saint Gregory—about 17, Saint Paul Lutheran—13." Many churches began as prayer meetings in members' homes, did the Methodist Episcopals. Faith Presbyterian emerged from such meetings, but the church became a "mission of First United Presbyterian Church of Cleveland.

During the second stage of organization members held services in rented halls or schools; in some cases other churches offered their facilities until a group could construct its own building In 1910 Rev. Michael Leahy, the pastor Saint James, leased "the entire second floor over store-room numbered 1480 on the north side of Detroit. . .for church purposes." Lakewood Presbyterian Church held Sunday school classes in a tent at Robinwood and Detroit while regular services took pla at the Church of the Redeemer. Eventually, most groups constructed small chapels on church land.

As Lakewood and its church membe ships grew, so did their resources. Mos congregations constructed larger and more permanent structures before 193 This third stage often involved considerable dedication and sacrifice on the part of parishioners to raise the necessary funds. Church groups held bake sales, bazaars, and plays to raise mone ile building committees handed out dge cards to help cover costs. These orts produced impressive results. All oss the city, and especially along troit and Madison, large and imposing irches began to appear in about as ny architectural styles as there were ldings. Even some of the smaller irches produced magnificently decorated interiors that might seem improbable from their exterior. In 1915, members of Lakewood Congregational urch laid the cornerstone for a Geor-

gian colonial building on Detroit at West Clifton. Members of the Baptist Church worshiped in the basement of their new church for five years until construction was completed in 1923. Dedication of Saint James' striking church building took place in 1935.

Church formation did not end with the Depression. Since that time a number of new groups have established themselves while some older denominations have constructed new buildings. Detroit Avenue Methodists built a new

church at Cove and Lake. Gethsemane Evangelical Lutheran formed in 1948, and members constructed their church at Saint Charles and Madison. In contrast, Jehovah's Witnesses converted a former night club into their church on Madison, while the West Shore Assembly of God rented the Masonic Temple. Others took over vacated churches as the United Latvian Evangelical Lutheran congregation did with the Church of the Redeemer. By 1980, Lakewood claimed nearly forty churches.

This is the "People's Window," at Lakewood United Methodist Church, circa 1963. The window was designed by John W. Winterich and Associates. Courtesy of the Lakewood United Methodist Church and the Lakewood Historical Society

*The Nicholson and Wagar families
helped found the New Jerusalem
"Swedenborgian" Church in 1841. By
1848, congregants constructed a church
at the corner of Detroit and Andrews
avenues. Ten years later they improved
and formally dedicated the building. In
1906 they built a new structure nearby;
the new church was called the Church of
the Redeemer. In 1964 the facility
became home to the United Latvian
Evangelical Lutheran Church.
Courtesy of the Lakewood Public Library*

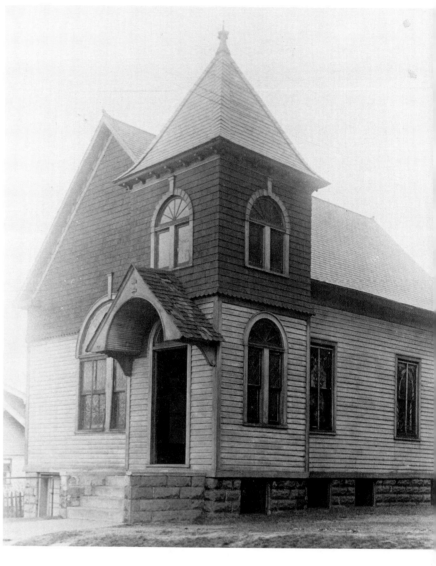

*Methodists formed a class in the 1870s.
In 1876 they constructed the first Lake
wood Methodist Church on the corner o
Summit and Detroit. In 1911, they brok
ground for the current building, a
Sunday school wing was added in 191
By 1927, the church had the second
largest Methodist congregation in the
country.
Courtesy of the Cleveland Press
Library and Collections, Cleveland Stat
University Libraries*

Baptists were one of the first groups to organize in East Rockport. Their founding dates to 1832 and in 1846 they constructed a meeting house at Warren Road and Hilliard. Apparently this church was abandoned. In 1904, twenty-eight Baptists founded a new church. They constructed this building, Lakewood Baptist Church, in 1906 on Detroit near Grace Avenue; the church served the congregation until 1918 when it was sold to Garfield School to use as an annex. Members of Lakewood Baptist Church constructed a new church on the corner of Detroit and Lincoln. Begun in 1918, the building was not completed until 1925; in the interim they met in the church's basement.
Courtesy of the Cleveland Press Library and Collections, Cleveland State University Libraries

Cyrus Eaton is shown here at graduation from McMaster University in 1905. Shortly after graduation Eaton, later to become a leading industrialist, served as a lay minister for the newly founded Lakewood Baptist Church. He held the pastorate from 1905 to 1906. Confronted by family responsibilities that required financial support beyond what the small congregation could afford, Eaton took a job with John D. Rockefeller as a trouble-shooter for the Standard Oil owned East Ohio Gas Company.
Courtesy of the Cleveland Press Library and Collections, Cleveland State University Libraries

The first building of the Church of the
Ascension on Detroit near Grace
Avenue, is pictured here circa 1875 to
1915. The Church of the Ascension
began as a mission founded by Trinity
Chapel in Cleveland. According to Albert
Fowerbaugh's history of the church, the
first families to pledge for a new build-
ing included: the Frys, Hirds, Beachs,
Halls, Nicholsons, Mailes, Newmans, the
Westlakes, and Dr. Jared Kirtland. In
1875, members of the Episcopal Church
of the Ascension erected this church. They
dedicated the present building in 1918.
Courtesy of Albert Fowerbaugh and the
Church of the Ascension

Pictured here is the Church of the
Ascension rug sewing bee at the home of
Ethel and Connie Hanna on Fry Avenue
on October 27, 1911. Women played
critical roles in the formation of Lakewood churches. Through a variety of
organizations they raised money for
church buildings and directed many of
the social and other activities that
churches sponsored.
Courtesy of Albert Fowerbaugh and the
Church of the Ascension

Aided by Cleveland's Franklin Circle Disciples of Christ Church, Lakewood Disciples organized a Sunday school and held classes at West School beginning in 1875. By 1878 they erected the Rocky River (Lakewood) Christian Chapel on Detroit just west of Park Row. Fire destroyed the chapel in 1895. Courtesy of Mary Emma Walker and the Lakewood Christian Church

Founded by former members of Cleveland's Old Stone Church, Lakewood Presbyterian Church began in 1905. One of the original sites of the Lakewood Presbyterian Church was in the hall above Lakewood market on the northwest corner of Detroit and Warren. The billboard on the right announces services under the direction of the church's pastor, Rev. A. J. Wright. The church also held services in the Church of the Redeemer at Detroit and Andrews avenues. In 1907, the congregation purchased their current site at Marlowe and Detroit; they dedicated their first structure in 1908. A larger sanctuary followed in 1916. Photograph by G. B. Young; courtesy of the Lakewood Historical Society

Lakewood Christian Church members constructed their second building on the site of the chapel. Under the name of Lakewood Church of Christ, congregants began construction of a new building in 1897; it served the congregation from 1897 to 1906. The current home of the church is at the corner of Roycroft and Detroit avenues; it was dedicated in 1912. Courtesy of Mary Emma Walker and the Lakewood Christian Church

The original building of Saints Cyril and Methodius Church was photographed in 1971. Saints Cyril and Methodius Church grew out of a meeting held in November 1902. By 1905, the congregation completed its first church and school building. Saints Cyril and Methodius was Lakewood's first Roman Catholic church. Founded by Slovak Catholics the church still provides Slovak language services. This was also Lakewood's first parochial school.
Photograph by Bill Nehez; courtesy of the Cleveland Press Library and Collections, Cleveland State University Libraries

The blessing of Saints Cyril and Methodius Church on September 7, 1931, was photographed by Bachna Studio. This cropped photograph shows only a portion of the participants in the dedication. Cleveland Bishop Joseph Shrembs and Msgr. Francis Dubosh dedicated the new church. Monsignor Dubosh served the parish from 1927 to 1967.
Courtesy of Joseph Kavcar

Members of Saint James Catholic
Church celebrated their first mass in July
1908 with their pastor, Rev. Michael F.
Leahy. In 1910, the church rented the
second floor of a store at Warren Road
and Detroit. Two years later the congregation established a school and in 1926
they laid the cornerstone for the church
at Detroit and Granger avenues. It was
dedicated in 1935 in the heart of the
Depression. One of Lakewood's most
impressive churches, the building came
at considerable expense to its parishioners and to Father Leahy who donated
personal and family funds to the project.
When Father Leahy died in 1941, he left
a congregation of twelve hundred
families.
Photograph by Superior Studios circa
1935; courtesy of the Cleveland Press
Library and Collections, Cleveland State
University Libraries

Saint James Church, circa 1935, is one
of the best examples of Sicilian
Romanesque style architecture. The
great narthex screen took a year to
carve; it was done by the Liturgical Arts
Guild of Cleveland. The ceiling was
painted in gold, red, and blue.
Photograph by Superior Studios;
courtesy of the Cleveland Press Library
and Collections, Cleveland State
University Libraries

Pictured here is the First Church of
Christ Scientist, Lakewood, at 15422
Detroit Avenue, in the 1920s. The
congregation laid the cornerstone for
their "Greco-Roman Temple" at Detroit
and Arthur avenues in 1914. As many
Lakewood churches, they held services in
the basement for eight years before the
church was completed.
Courtesy of Marilyn Brace and the
Christian Science Church

As with many Lakewood churches, Saint
Nicholas' Ukrainian Orthodox Church
emerged from meetings held in private
homes. The congregation formed in
1914; from 1922 to 1948 they held
services in the basement of the present
church. In 1980 the church acquired the
current gold, onion-shaped dome and
cross. Father Lewis Opeka is standing by
the altar.
Photograph by Paul Toppelstein, 1960;
courtesy of the Cleveland Press Library
and Collections, Cleveland State
University Libraries

This photograph shows the new gold dome being placed on Saint Gregory, The Theologian Byzantine Catholic Church in August 1980.
Photograph by Fred Noe; Courtesy of the Lakewood Historical Society

Saints Peter and Paul was the Village's first church. Slovak Lutherans founded the church in 1901; they constructed their first church at the corner of Quail and Thrush in 1902. In 1927, they moved to the current church on the corner of Madison and Grace. Members of Saints Peter and Paul included journalist and publisher Jan Pankuch and his family.
Photograph by Bill Nehez, 1971; courtesy of the Cleveland Press Library and Collections, Cleveland State University Libraries

Chapter 7
From Township to City: 1889 to 1930

What the final municipal programme of the new city will be, one can only conjecture, but that it will be a programme making for a better civilization, a larger life, and increased comfort and opportunity, the gradual progression of society gives assurance.
Frederick Howe, *The City: The Hope of Democracy,* 1905

As the railroads and then streetcars increasingly introduced more residents to the community, both the nature and form of government began to change dramatically. In the short space of twenty-two years, East Rockport abruptly changed names and moved rapidly from rural township to hamlet, village, and city.

Behind these changes stood Cleveland's ascension to an industrial giant. The decision to convert garden plots into housing lots, however, came from East Rockport land owners and developers. To faciliate these effo[rt] land developers needed a more expansive government provide the infrastructure necessary to attract potential home buyers. The government they formed reflected th[e] founders' desire for a utilitarian and privatized landscap[e] a concern that left a lasting imprint on the young community. In contrast, urban dwellers attracted by the promise of lake, woods, and inexpensive home lots sup[-] plied with urban services, arrived with different conceptions of government, electorate, and civic landscape. Th[e] newcomers, then, painted over the founders' canvas where they found shortcomings and enlarged it in impo[r-] tant ways.

Residents of the new suburb of Lakewood who voted their community "dry" probably would have been offended to learn that Rockport held its first election in 1819 in a tavern. In a sparsely-settled, rural area, township government reflected the limited conceptions and resources as well as the personal nature of civic life.

However, East Rockport did change in perceptible ways as Henry Alger noted in his 1858 reminiscences. By the 1880s, railroads, resorts, and summer homes encroached on the garden while most permanent resident[s] clustered along Detroit Avenue in large formal homes. Already East Rockporters had established a separate school district from the rest of the township. Sensing the possibilities for profit by converting farms into suburban home lots, a group of 103 prominent residents and land holders petitioned the county commissioners for incorporation of East Rockport as the hamlet of Lakewood.

The name change here is perhaps the most telling indication of their concerns. East Rockport was unlikely [to] inspire potential homebuyers, but their first choice, Arling[-] ton, already had a place in Ohio. With a profound grasp [of] the obvious, they settled on the area's greatest natural attractions, those that clearly set it apart from the city. Wi[th] Cleveland incorporated in the names of their new suburbs, residents of East Cleveland and Cleveland Heights could never forget from whence they came. In contrast, ewood conjured up both sylvan beauty and indepen- nce. It is little wonder that the new community to the st became Cleveland's largest suburb. Ironically, as we ve seen, Lakewood gave up lake access and cleared ests to make way for houses.

If land owners and developers could see the benefits incorporation for their account books, owners of the vate Plank Road saw only debits. Fearing a new govern- nt would end their control of the road, the company ught suit. Although the county commissioners quickly roved incorporation, the lawsuit delayed formal adop- n of the plan. Finally, on July 11, 1889, the community ected its three trustees and on August 31, I. E. Canfield, ble Hotchkiss, and William Maile met at the Hotchkiss me at Detroit and Saint Charles for their first official nlet meeting.

The trustees and their successors confronted a series problems and concerns much different from those nfronting their counterparts in 1819. If the first town- p government concerned itself with carving civilization t of the wilderness, hamlet officials wanted to protect inst civilization's excesses. In effect they sought a nmunity for themselves that would also be attractive to tential homebuyers from Cleveland. Their first ordi- nces, designed to prevent speeding, cruelty to animals, orderly conduct, gambling, prostitution, Sunday games, d Sunday alcohol consumption, clearly reflected both ncerns. They also approved a tax ordinance to finance e new government.

As the pace of suburban development quickened, e hamlet's officials struggled to create the infrastructure cessary to support the new population that began to kle into the community. In the 1890s, when the Illumi- ting Company proved unwilling to extend electric vice, the hamlet built and operated its own light plant. ewood also granted the Cuyahoga Telephone Com- ny permission to establish service and gained free mail livery. Successive administrations established ordi- nces for allotments, building regulations, street paving, ter mains, fire hydrants, sewer lines, and a streetcar nchise.

In 1902, Thomas Knight praised the results: "one y stand at Detroit Street and look up towards West dison Avenue or down towards the lake on any of the oss streets and not see one building out of line.....on a jority of the streets the regulations provide that struc- es shall not be built closer to the sidewalk than 35 t." Knight further noted that the municipally-owned

light plant provided residents with "cheap rates."

Prospective homebuyers had more concerns. To at- tract them, a new community needed an educational sys- tem and health care facilities. A key part of the former required the institution of a high school. While Lake- wood's first high school class had graduated in 1889, a separate high school building did not open until 1900. This building, now the Board of Education Building, served as the high school for only four years before a newer, larger structure replaced it. Even this structure could not contain Lakewood's rapid growth; by 1918, a new high school opened at Bunts and Franklin avenues.

Health care in the new community drew on both the public and private sectors. As early as 1900, hamlet officials established the position of health officer and physician "to care for the sick, poor, and other needy persons." Seven years later, Dr. C. L. Graber mortgaged his home to start a hospital in a frame house at the corner of Belle and Detroit avenues. Supported by the Women's Board of Lakewood Hospital Charitable Association, the hospital soon became a voluntary, non-profit institution. The fledgling hospital rapidly expanded its activities. In 1910 it began nurses' training and the following year opened the Kate Castle Rhodes Dispensary in the Village. The dispensary sought to reduce the neighborhood's high infant mortality by providing medical care, information, and formula. Student nurses received public health training there. In 1921, the dispensary became the hospital's out-patient treatment center.

These improvements encouraged more Clevelanders to move west. The community grew from about 450 residents in 1890 to 3,355 ten years later. By 1910, the city topped 15,000. Responding to this growth, Lakewood reincorporated as a village in 1903. The 1910 census confirmed that the community was large enough to become a city. On February 17, 1911, Lakewood officially became a city just twenty-two years after its initial incorporation.

The ease with which Lakewood could successively incorporate as hamlet, village, and city reflected both a desire for local control and Ohio's permissive incorpora- tion laws. Nevertheless, Lakewood's continued inde- pendence was far from assured; Cleveland's growth had always been premised in part on annexation of neighbor- ing land. Cleveland absorbed its rival Ohio City in 1854. In 1890, Brooklyn joined the growing metropolis as did West Cleveland in 1894. In 1922, even West Park succumbed.

Cleveland residents who moved to Lakewood must have felt some ambivalence. By 1910 Cleveland had grown rapidly to become the nation's sixth largest city. Unlike many American cities of the time, Cleveland had a well deserved reputation for model urban government. Lincoln Steffens, the noted muckraker and author of *The Shame of the Cities* (1904), remembered Cleveland under Mayor Tom Johnson as one of the nation's few well-run cities.

In contrast, young Lakewood, with its new name, remained largely unknown. Nevertheless, new residents quickly developed roots and an attachment that length of residence alone could not explain. In the first two decades of the twentieth century Lakewood residents established a profusion of new civic, religious, social, educational, fraternal, recreational, and cultural organizations. Although many of these organizations were branches of national groups, they were Lakewood organizations in membership and often by name as well. Newcomers quickly developed loyalties to the new community that must have both surprised and amused natives.

Residents of Cleveland's new suburbs came to these communities accustomed to a wide range of urban services. Suburbs such as Lakewood, East Cleveland, and Cleveland Heights which could supply those services, were likely to maintain their independence. Lakewood voters rejected annexation efforts in 1910 and 1922. In the latter years the *Plain Dealer* attributed the rejection to the fact that "Lakewood now provides ample school facilities, police, fire, city planning, zoning, and sanitary protection to its inhabitants and uniformly good street paving and improvements." Moreover, the city appeared "ready, able and willing to enlarge these facilities as the population increases, according to a standard of excellence which Cleveland cannot afford."

There were, of course, other reasons for the defeat of annexation. Suburbanites wanted to avoid urban problems they had left behind in the city. While Cleveland remained "wet," Lakewood temperance supporters finally succeeded with the passage of the Beal law. In 1905 voters endorsed a referendum to prohibit "the sale of intoxicating liquors as a beverage." In 1918 Lakewood residents and the Lakewood *Press* opposed a county consolidation measure that would have brought all communities under one government. The *Press* argued that unlike Cleveland, "Lakewood has no tenement houses, no slums, no saloons, no centers of disorder. It is a clean community. By preserving jealously its own identity it has for years been a 'dry' city, while Cleveland continues the center of the liquor interests of the state."

Moreover, as separate political entities, Lakewood and her sister suburbs of East Cleveland and Cleveland Heights could more effectively restrict access to their communities. Immigrants and racial minorities would find it harder to gain entree. Most of these efforts took place outside the official jurisdiction of city government, but municipal administrations did little to discourage them.

Over the years, the private sector developed a series of devices to restrict access. The minorities who managed to evade restrictive covenants, real estate steering, and denied loans, had to confront a range of hostile responses legal and illegal. While the position of African-Americans in East Rockport society deteriorated over the nineteenth century, it became more marked as the new suburb emerged. As early as 1892, B. K. Smith, an African-American, encountered community resistance when he "purchased two lots on Winchester avenue opposite the carbon works." The extent of the change is suggested by the fact that Winchester Avenue gained its name from an slavery leader Philander Winchester, while the Farmer family had previously lived on the same street for many years.

Ironically, the suburbs that sought to limit access proved more receptive to expanding democracy within their borders. For some years Ohio law permitted women to vote in school board elections, but gaining the right to vote or to run for other offices proved much more difficult. While suburban men generally supported these efforts, in Lakewood the Woman's Suffrage Party, organized in 1912, helped bring this to fruition.

For some years the national woman's suffrage movement had focused on a strategy designed to gain the vote in each state. In Ohio, suffrage workers successfully placed constitutional amendments on the ballot in 1912 and 1914 only to see them go down to defeat at the polls. The Ohio Suffrage Association then sought a dual strategy to gain the vote in municipal and presidential elections. Following East Cleveland's successful campaign for local suffrage in 1916, Lakewood suffragists, led by C. E. Kendel, Bernice Pyke, and Maude C. Waitt, pressed for an amendment to Lakewood's city charter. With the strong support of Councilman George Palda, the measure passed council and appeared on the November 1917 ballot. A statewide referendum on a presidential franchise for women shared that ballot.

Members of the Woman's Suffrage Party left few stones unturned in their dual campaign for these issues. Suffrage workers raised money with bake sales and campaigned in every section of Lakewood. The Lakewood *Press* reported some women canvassed at night "accompanied by their husbands, who are now showing their loyalty to suffrage and their belief in our cause of municipal suffrage." Their hard work paid off. Although presidential suffrage went down to defeat state-wide, Lakewood men voted to extend the municipal vote to women.

The measure's success also reflects the ethos of the new suburb. Lakewood's suburban families began to replace the paternalistic orientation of late nineteenth-century East Rockport with a more egalitarian one. If one of the keys to Lakewood's strong sense of identity was its large number of community organizations, then Lakewood women could claim a large share of the respon-

lity both for the founding and the day-to-day opera-
ns. World War I drove home the important role women
yed in the community. Not only did they join the work
ce to replace men gone to the front, they organized
l ran the war's domestic support structure. As the
ogressive" Lakewood *Press* editorialized, "the men of
ewood by their votes have shown that they believe
t woman is a man's equal partner. They have invited
to participate equally with them in the performance of
nicipal work....they have declared that the age long
istice done to woman should be rectified."

The suffrage movement also left a lasting legacy for
community. Immediately after their electoral victory,
Lakewood Woman's Suffrage Party sponsored a lec-
e series on citizenship by Florence Allen a suffragist
yer. The series challenged voters, old and new, to re-
nk their views of government. Out of these public
ication efforts, locally and nationally, emerged the
gue of Women Voters; Lakewood's league grew out of
local Women's Club and gained a League charter in
2. Equally as important, the suffrage movement pro-
ced a number of women, including Democrat Bernice
ke and Republican Maude Waitt, who went on to have
portant careers in politics.

Clearly, founders and newcomers differed in their
ws on prohibition, racial exclusion, and the women's
e. They also held different opinions on the importance
civic landscapes. East Rockport landowners had set
de only a minimal amount of land for schools; they
l established neither a traditional Western Reserve
wn square or a community center. In contrast, new
urbanites benefited from a vision of civic landscapes
sented by the 1893 World's Columbian Exposition in
icago. The exposition's brilliant design provided a
del for "City Beautiful" movement planners to intro-
ce order and beauty to civic centers across the land.
eveland quickly drew on it for its Group Plan, which
t public buildings on opposite sides of a broad mall. In
kewood the influence most clearly appeared in the
velopment of Clifton as a broad boulevard, in Alameda
enue's green island, and in Clifton Park's curvilinear
eet pattern.

Nevertheless, the community landscape remained
gely utilitarian and privatized. Although something of a
ic center did emerge reluctantly along Warren Road
ar Detroit Avenue. Construction of East Rockport Cen-
l School in 1879, the adjacent first high school building

in 1899, and the second high school (later Wilson School)
in 1904, directly across Warren Road, established an educational center. Not until 1911, however, did the community gain a city hall when it purchased the Tegardine
house at the corner of Detroit and Warren Road for this
purpose. Three years later the city constructed the police
and fire department building on Warren Road north of
Rockport Central School. When the Tegardine house soon
proved inadequate, the community chose to move its city
hall to the Robert R. Rhodes home in the newly-acquired
Lakewood park rather than build a new structure in the
existing municipal center on Warren Road. Despite construction of new police and court buildings, commercial
interests eventually absorbed large parts of the public
center on Warren Road and the public presence here
atrophied.

Similarly, while Lakewood as a hamlet, a village, and
a city developed a wide range of services and a fine educational system, the community was slow to purchase
park land. Because private owners held much of the lake
and riverfront land, most city residents had to go to
Edgewater Park to swim.

At the instigation of the Chamber of Commerce, the
city corrected part of this problem with the purchase of
the Rhodes estate. Lakewood Park provided lake views as
well as well landscaped grounds for a variety of uses.
Unfortunately the use of the park's lakefront as a dump
site for many years undermined its value here. Although
other major park acquisitions at Rosewood (Wagar-1904)
and Madison (1917) provided important neighborhood
centers, Lakewood Park alone became Lakewood's symbolic and recreational center. The home for municipal
July 4 celebrations and other community-wide events as
well as for City Hall, the park represented the belated
efforts of suburbanites to correct the excessive privatiza-
tion introduced by earlier settlers.

From the perspective of 1930, Lakewood presented a
sharp contrast with an earlier Rockport. The frontier
community had welcomed all races, aided escaped slaves,
conducted government in a tavern, privatized its land, and
limited the franchise to men. Suburbanites banished
alcohol, extended the vote to women, attempted to limit
access to the community, and sought to establish a
stronger civic presence. At the same time, suburbanites
revolutionized Rockport's social and cultural life and
brought the benefits of urban life to the garden.

The Tegardine house was on the south-west corner of Warren Road and Detroit. J. E. Tegardine served as Lakewood mayor from 1900 to 1901. During Nelson Cotabish's term as mayor (1911), the city purchased the house for Lakewood's first city hall. They purchased the home for $15,500. By 1917 the house had become inadequate to house city business; in 1920 city hall moved to the recently purchased Rhoa estate in Lakewood Park. From Thomas A. Knight's Beautiful Lakewood: Cleveland's West End, *page 25.*

Lakewood's City Hall is shown here in the 1940s. Besides official city business, city hall also provided a snack bar for visitors to Lakewood Park. The children and adults standing under the awning by the building are waiting to be served. The house sat adjacent and to the east of the enclosed pavilion.
Courtesy of the Lakewood Public Schools

Lakewood residents generally opposed annexation to Cleveland and voted against such action on several occasions. This button from the 1920s was used by the anti-annexation forces to publicize their efforts.
Courtesy of the Lakewood Public Library

For many years Lakewood has had one of the best records of fire prevention and protection in the nation. The fire department can claim credit for much of these efforts. The Chamber of Commerce has also played a major role in alerting the public to the need for fire prevention. Lakewood's first motorized apparatus shown here circa 1912 was an American La France Type 75. Bill Curry and Addis Hallock are on the back step; E. Buhl is the driver and J. Dooley is seated next to him.
Courtesy of Jim Anderson

By 1915 the Lakewood Fire Department's motorized equipment had grown to three fire engines and an automobile. Two of the engines are pictured here on the south side of the building on Warren Road. Left to right are: Lieut. F. H. Hoffstetter, J.N. Hennie, W.J. Curry, E.T. Bendernagel, L.M. Slavick, and J. M. Rafferty. The Fire Department tended to have a strong presence of German-Americans among its staff.
Courtesy of Jim Anderson

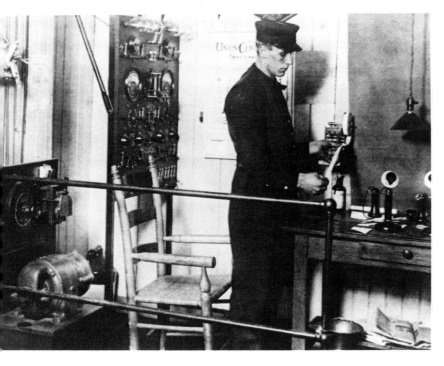

Shown here is the Fire Alarm Office with Jake Hennie, circa 1913.
Courtesy of Jim Anderson

Engine No. 3, a Sutphen 1250/500, arrived new in December 1983. It is shown here at the Clifton Boulevard fire station.
Photograph by J. McCown; courtesy of Jim Anderson

The Lakewood Police Department's bicycle brigade is shown here in 1916. Left to right: H.J. Swickard, Henry Calvert, Peter Christensen, Clayton Tyler (mayor), Herman Lang, Henry O'Dell (police chief), Howard Amstus, and Andrew Kennelley. The brigade was photographed in front of the high school, later Wilson School on Warren Road across from Police Headquarters. Irish Americans tended to have a strong presence on the Police Department.
Courtesy of the Lakewood Public Library

Clearly a step up from the bicycle days, by 1925 the force shown here had four Indian motorcycles on which to patrol. American-made, the Indian was one of the the best motorcycles made in its day.
Courtesy of Captain Matt Biscotti, Lakewood Police Department

The Lakewood Police Department headquarters are shown here in 1930. In 1923 the Police Department moved from its quarters at the fire station to the newly remodeled Cuyahoga Telephone Building at 1484 Warren Road. That site is currently occupied by the Kirtland Apartment Building.
Courtesy of Capt. Matt Biscotti, Lakewood Police Department

is is a cell in the men's section of the Lakewood jail on Warren Road, ca 1950. Lakewood's low crime rate s largely the product of a well-trained d organized police force. Jail condi- is like these might also have discour- ed crime. They led to the construction a new city hall and jail facility only a years after this photograph was en.
urtesy of the Cleveland Press rary and Collections, Cleveland State iversity Libraries

Lakewood Municipal Court made up
another part of the public center on t
west side of Warren Road. The buildi
was dedicated in March 1929. The K
land Apartment Building currently oc
pies the site.
Courtesy of the Lakewood Public Sch

The swearing-in of Judge Matt J.
Walther in Lakewood Municipal Court
on December 21, 1933.
Courtesy of the Western Reserve
Historical Society

The original Lakewood Hospital Build
ing at Belle and Detroit avenues is pic
tured here. Almost from Lakewood's
beginning as a suburb, some residents
realized the need for health care. With
the nearest hospital four miles away, I
Lee C. Graber and several other physicians began planning for Lakewood
Hospital. In 1907, Graber mortgaged h
own home to raise funds to build a
hospital on Detroit at Belle. Just in cas
the venture failed, the building was
designed so that it could be converted
into a two-family house. The hospital
opened in 1907 with Alice Brooks, a
registered nurse, as superintendent ar
three doctors.
Courtesy of Mary Hall

1914, the fifteen bed hospital had
*ved inadequate to the growing
*munity's needs. Community leaders
*an a fund-raising campaign for a
* building. In 1917 the new building
*ned; it faced on Detroit Avenue with
* original hospital house in the rear.
*munity groups then participated in
*ther fund-raising drive to furnish
*eighty-five bed hospital. Pictured here
*e first wing at Lakewood Hospital
*a 1934.
*rtesy of the Cleveland Press
*ary and Collections, Cleveland State
iversity Libraries

*Previously a private, non-profit hospital,
the city purchased the building in 1931.
It continued to grow to meet community
needs. In 1939-1940, a second wing
along Belle Avenue was added to the
original brick structure.
Photograph by John Nash, 1939;
courtesy of the Cleveland Press Library
and Collections, Cleveland State
University Libraries*

*the 1950s Lakewood Hospital had
*panded once again. This addition
*shed further up Belle Avenue and
*ovided a new entrance. The hospital
*so began a school of practical nursing
*ring the 1950s.
*otograph by Robert C. Hoffner,
*ril 26, 1956; courtesy of the
*eveland Press Library and Collections,
eveland State University Libraries

In 1910, Lakewood hospital opened a school of nursing that continued until 1937. After construction of the new hospital wing, the original hospital building was used to house the student nurses.
Courtesy of the Lakewood Hospital

In addition to support from the Woman's Board, the Children's Board, the Junior Board of Lakewood Hospital, the Hospital Helpers, and the Volunteer Association, many other community groups aided the hospital. Representatives of Lakewood Hospital and the Business and Professional Women's Club are, from left to right: Florence Joles, Olga Schleuter, Leona Fretter, Mildred Morian, Dr. Crawford, and Ruby Wilder. The Club donated the baby incubator to Lakewood Hospital in 1951.
Photograph by Edna Sauber; courtesy of Rose Schroeder and the Lakewood Business and Professional Women's Club

Lakewood Hospital appears in miniature with Mayor Robert Lawther and Arthur Lepinot, hospital superintendent, February 1, 1966. By the mid-1960s, Lakewood Hospital again projected an expansion. The model here shows the proposed $3,800,000 L-shaped addition on the right. By 1986, Lakewood Hospital contained 410 beds and a wide range of specialized services.
Photograph by James Thomas; courtesy of the Cleveland Press Library and Collections, Cleveland State University Libraries

...kewood Park East End, just after the ...y acquired it from the Rhodes Estate ...1918. In the center is a small bridge ...r a creek that ran through the park. ...e Chamber of Commerce played an ...portant role in the acquisition of the ...rk.

...otograph by Perry Corell; courtesy of ...e Lakewood Historical Society

...e of Lakewood's most active civic ...ganizations, the Chamber of Com-...rce played a major role in Lakewood. ...unded in 1911, the Chamber pro-...ted the development of many of the ...y's most important institutions and ...nenities. It attracted many of the ...mmunity's leading citizens; at one ...int the chamber claimed eight hun-...ed members. Organizational drives ...e that pictured here helped swell ...mbership. This July 1931 promo-...nal photograph of a membership ...ve included one current mayor, ...ward Wiegand and a future one, ...os Kauffman. Between them they led ...kewood for thirty-two years (1924 to ...56). From left to right: Anne Zagaros,

R. C. Hyre, Brian Bowman, Dr. C. B. Crawford, Amos Kauffman (then city finance director), Edward Wiegand (mayor), Edythe Perlman, Alice Evans, and unidentified. The photograph was taken on Detroit at Warren Road in front of Bailey's Department Store.

Within a year of this photograph Mayor Wiegand would be dead and Amos Kauffman would succeed him. Courtesy of the Cleveland Press Library and Collections, Cleveland State University Libraries

A leading citizen, Judge Willis Vickery was an important member of the Chamber of Commerce and was instrumental in the acquisition of Lakewood Park from the Rhodes estate.
Photograph by Frank Moore Studio, circa 1929; courtesy of the Cleveland Press Library and Collections, Cleveland State University Libraries

John C. Bethel was one of the founders of the Chamber of Commerce and served as its secretary during its first years. Bethel helped found the Lakewood Republican Club, and along with George Hansen and George Lindstrom, he also founded the Lakewood Pioneer Historical Society.
Photograph by Jack Clifford, February 27, 1924; courtesy of the Lakewood Public Library

State Senator Maude C. Waitt (1875-1935) moved to Lakewood with her husband in 1914. A former school teacher, she became a key leader in the Lakewood and Ohio suffrage movements. After Lakewood passed municipal suffrage in 1917, she helped organize citizenship classes for new voters. As did Bernice Pyke, Waitt found a new career in politics. A Republican, she was first elected to the state senate in 1924 and went on to serve three terms. She was chair of the senate legislative committee and worked on state prison reform.
Photograph by Harris and Ewing; courtesy of the Cleveland Press Library and Collections, Cleveland State University Libraries

FOCUS:
Nelson
Cotabish

Madison, and on Cohassett, he subdivided these areas and named Cohassett after the Boston suburb. Cotabish played an important role in the formation of several key institutions. With other Lakewood business leaders he helped found two banks: People's Bank and later First Federal. An active member of the Lakewood Chamber of Commerce and the Westside Chamber of Industry, Cotabish served on Lakewood Hospital's

board of directors, promoted construction of the Masonic Temple, and served as an active lodge member. He was also a member of the Lakewood Yacht Club.

Vida Cotabish, Ellen's and Nelson's daughter, established the Cotabish Charitable Fund which greatly benefited Lakewood Hospital's capital improvement drives. The fund also sought to provide housing for Lakewood's senior citizens.

Although not a founder of suburban Lakewood, Nelson Cotabish (1867-1942) played a critical role in the community's formation. Clearly one of Lakewood's most active "live wires," Cotabish participated in a wide variety of community building activities. He was a corporate leader, politician, promoter, developer, and philanthropist. His vision for the needs of the community left an important imprint on the young suburb.

Born in Cleveland, Cotabish became responsible for the support of his family when his father died. He went to work as a laborer at Otis Steel Company; eventually he gained a white-collar position at Variety Iron Works. His opportunity for advancement came when he went to work for the National Carbon Company as chief clerk. In 1890, Cotabish became sales manager for the company, a position he would hold for forty-five years. Several years later when National Carbon's new factory opened, the recently married Cotabishes (Ellen "Nellie" McBride) moved to a house at Grove and Detroit. Cotabish frequently commuted to work by bicycle. They later moved to Cohassett and Detroit, where they built one of Lakewood's more distinctive houses.

As a Republican in a Republican town, Cotabish had an active political career. After serving one term as council member, Cotabish gained election as mayor in 1910; Lakewood became a city during his administration. He authorized the purchase of the Tegardine home at Detroit and Warren for Lakewood's first city hall. He later held the position of director of public service for three years.

Cotabish also placed his imprint on the young community in other ways. As a developer of land on Bunts, north of

Nelson Cotabish with his mother, his daughter Vida, and his grandson are portrayed here circa 1920. Nelson Cotabish was Lakewood's mayor from

1910 to 1912. He also served as Public Works Director and helped found the Masonic Temple.
Courtesy of Alice Cotabish

In addition to his busy life as a corporate leader, politician, civic father, and real estate developer, Cotabish, pictured here on September 26, 1936, also maintained a half-acre garden at Grace Avenue adjacent to his Dutch colonial home at Detroit and Cohassett. He took great pride in his tomatoes, corn, and other vegetables.
Courtesy of the Cleveland Press Library and Collections, Cleveland State University Libraries

FOCUS: Bernice Pyke

Working for women's suffrage gave many Lakewood women political experience and skills that could be applied to a career in politics. Among these women, Bernice Pyke (1880-1964) stands out. She was the first woman delegate to a national political convention, the first woman to run for Lakewood mayor, and the first woman to hold a cabinet position in Cleveland city government. Pyke helped found several Lakewood institutions, ran her own business, and had a long career in political office.

Born in Frankfort, Ohio, Bernice Secrest graduated from high school in Chillicothe and earned an A.B. degree from Smith College in 1902. After a brief career teaching mathematics in Illinois, Bernice married Arthur Pyke in 1905, and the couple moved to Lakewood.

Prior to her work on Lakewood's suffrage campaign Bernice Pyke helped found the local parents-teachers association and served on the school board. With Belle Graber, she was also instrumental in the founding of Lakewood Public Library. Following the successful campaign for municipal suffrage in 1917, the Lakewood *Press* editorialized that "it was her [Pyke's] direct, eloquent appeal to the city council that won for her and her sisters the instant support of the members of the council."

In 1920, Pyke gained election as delegate to the Democratic National Convention; during her career she attended four more. In the same year, Pyke organized women voters for Gov. James Cox's unsuccessful presidential campaign; she also became Ohio's first National Committeewoman. Only one year later, Pyke, a Democrat, challenged traditional Republican and male dominance in Lakewood city government. Initially, the five seasoned Republican mayoral candidates, all men, refused to take Pyke's campaign seriously. However, when Pyke supporters staged an impressive parade just before the election, four of the Republican candidates immediately withdrew from the race and threw their support behind incumbent Louis Hill. Hill won re-election but only by a narrow margin, and Bernice Pyke established both a Democrat's and a woman's presence on the Lakewood political landscape.

In addition to these impressive political achievements, Pyke established a career in business. Her interest in books led her not only to found the public library but also start her own

okstore on Detroit Avenue at Cook.
gun in 1923 with a capitalization of
thousand dollars, the Bernice Pyke
ok Shop sold a range of books and
ionery supplies and provided circu-
ng library services. The store re-
ined in business for about seven
rs.

In 1931, Pyke became supervisor of
Cuyahoga County Board of Elec-
ns; a year later she gained appoint-
nt as Cleveland's director of Public
alth and Welfare. In 1934, Pres.
nklin D. Roosevelt appointed her
lector of Customs for the Cleveland
trict; she held the position until 1953.
ear later, at seventy-four, Bernice
e ran unsuccessfully for congress.

Bernice Pyke's Book Store, pictured here
on April 28, 1928, was at 14824 Detroit
Avenue. At the time the Pykes lived in the
Edgecliff Apartments at 14901 Lake
Avenue; during the 1930s they resided
at the Lake Shore Hotel.
Courtesy of the Cleveland Press
Library and Collections, Cleveland State
University Libraries

ortly after the passage of Lakewood's
arter amendment regarding woman's
ffrage in 1917, the Lakewood Press
nored Bernice Pyke with a front page
rtoon. The caption provided glowing
aise: "To Mrs. A. B. Pyke, the women
Lakewood are chiefly indebted for
eir enfranchisement. . . . Her work is
t yet done, but . . . if a just cause,
ergy, ability, devotion, and enthusiasm
esage victory, then woman's suffrage
ill be victorious under the leadership of
rs. A.B. Pyke."
otograph by Frank R. Bill, circa 1916;
urtesy of the Cleveland Press
brary and Collections, Cleveland
ate University Libraries

Bernice Pyke, U.S. collector of customs
for the Cleveland District, is shown on
the left, with customs agent Jeanne
Cambran in 1949.
Photograph by Rebman Photographic
Service; courtesy of the Cleveland Press
Library and Collections, Cleveland State
University Libraries

Chapter 8
VIGNETTE
Marie Albers, "Memories of Early Lakewood"

By 1906, when the Albers family moved from Cleveland to a house at 1356 Cook Avenue, the village of Lakewood was experiencing rapid growth; within five years it would be a city. Marie Albers' "Memories" of this period describe a farm community in the process of becoming a residential suburb. The two landscapes exist side by side in apparent harmony; greenhouses, vineyards, forests, and brickyards share space with schools, churches, hospitals, businesses, and houses. If the days were numbered for the garden, its continued presence, nevertheless, provided children with infinite opportunities for play and pleasure.

Albers provides a good sense of the changes taking place in the new community. The following is excerpted from Marie Albers' "Memories."

I moved to Cook Avenue in 1906. It was June, and Mother and I rode on an open-sided Detroit Avenue streetcar. The seats were like two long benches, the length of the car. When we got off at Cook Avenue, and walked north to 1356, the huge poplar trees arched the street and we remarked how beautiful they were. On the east corner [Cook and Detroit] was a small real estate house where Mr. Allen sat out front talking to passers-by.

Detroit Avenue had many lovely old homes. Lakewood Hospital started in a home on its present site. The Wagar home was on the southeast corner of Warren Road. Two Wagar sisters lived there. One was a teacher, the other a principal. After Gladys Avenue was laid out, they lived there. Andrews Avenue was an old street with Reformed Church [Swedenborgian] on the northeast corner, and a huge pond on the NW [corner]. Kids would swim and ice skate on this pond. Later, the Masonic Temple was built there. Lakewood Market was on the north side of Detroit, east of Cook Avenue; it was a butcher shop with saw dust floors. You were given half a wiener when you bought two pounds of round steak ground in a huge wall grinder. There was Bailey's Grocery with rooms upstairs where St. James Church first met [Warren Road and Detroit]. My neighbor, Miss Leahy, would take me along as her nephew, Father Leahy, was the priest there. On the NE corner of Warren Road was a sunken empty lot with grass, an iron fence and center circle of red cannas plants and "elephant ears." Next was Stalls Drug Store with its urns of colored water in the window and an enticing candy counter and soda fountain inside. Then there was the Boston Dry Goods store where I spent much time gazing in the window at Christmas time. It was packed with dolls, tea sets, etc., filling every corner. On the NE corner of St. Charles was a house set back with the sign "Mastick-Daniels Funeral Home." In back of the house was the Fire Department with its horse and water tank. On the NW corner set back was the old sandstone house with the sign "Furniture and Upholstering." This house is now in Lakewood Park as a museum. Between St. Charles and Belle, on the north side, was a group of small buildings set back. One was Bakers Bakery. The Bakers lived on Cook Avenue and had a barn and horse in the back to deliver bread, etc. One hot summer day, spontaneous combustion caused a fire which destroyed the barn. they went out of business and Mr. Baker became janitor at Grant School. Before Gladys Avenue was cut through there was an old orchard in back of our house. Looking out from our back porch we could see Clifton Boulevard streetcars

ss. On the south side of Detroit from St. Charles east the ad was about fifteen feet higher. ther were board ewalks. . . . There was also a creek that ran across troit from east of Belle. An old wooden bridge crossed it.

I attended the old school at Grant. There was no ctoria Avenue. South of Grant School was a "brick rd" [Christopher Maile's] that was still in operation. ross from Grant School on Warren Road was the old ewood High, from which Harold Albers graduated. en Grant School became overcrowded, some of its 7th d 8th graders had some classes across the street in the gh School [later named Wilson School]. We had to walk ross mud and ice for these classes. Manual training for s and cooking for girls was one afternoon a week at Kinley School. Walking to and from in groups there s much teasing and fun.

Kids had fun on Cook Avenue. When we heard the in whistle, we would run down to the tracks to watch cars go by. The man on the caboose would wave to us. ring World War I, when troop trains passed they some- es threw out papers with names or messages. In winter ok Avenue was roped off for coasting down the hill. e slope near the railroad track would halt the ride. The er boys had a wooden toboggan and would give the e kids rides and pull them back up the hill. I loved to be eadlight."

The empty lot in back of the real estate office on the rtheast corner of Cook was filled with weeds and cockle- rrs. We gathered the burrs to make baskets and some- es threw them at each other. One time some burrs got ught in my hair and Mother had to cut them out. After pper the kids would play "hide and seek," until the rbon street lights came on. It was fun to watch the city en come to put in new carbon sticks for the lights. They uld lower the globes, replace the carbons, and give us e old ones to use for writing on sidewalks. There were er street venders—the "paper rag" man would call out d buy papers or rags. The fish wagon was always smelly. e ice man would let us climb on the back step of the rse-drawn wagon to retrieve ice chips to eat. The milk an came early to leave milk bottles at the door. In winter would freeze and the cardboard top would pop up out two inches. In summer the fruit and vegetable man uld call out "straawberries-vegetables." Sometimes there uld be a "knife and scissors" sharpener who carried his etstone on his back. Then there was the organ grinder ith his pet monkey who would tip his little red cap if you ve him a penny. Once there was a photographer with his

donkey. He raised his black box to take our picture after he sat us on the donkey. I still have the picture. One winter when the snow was very deep, the city plowed the side- walks with a horse-drawn wooden wedge plow. I stood at the front window to watch. I also loved to watch the horses and wooden plows dig out the basements for four new houses across the street on Cook Avenue. Horses and wagons also delivered coal to our house and a man shoveled it down a chute into the coal bin. He had to borrow planks to cover a grass path for the horse and wagon to cross.

When Victoria was made a street, Huffman's Greenhouse was on the east side north of Grant School. It was an experience to go inside the glass roofed sheds and smell the dank earth mingled with the fragrance of flowers.

Arthur Avenue had a stone wall entrance on Detroit. I remember when the library was built. Our Grant School class walked over to see it and learn how to use the library. Clifton Boulevard streetcar rails were laid in the tree lawns on the south side of the street. There was no car line on Madison Avenue until later. Lake Avenue still had fields of grapes as this was an area for raising grapes. Between Lake Avenue and Lake Erie all was woods. In spring we would walk down to pick "Spring beauties" and violets. St. Augustine Convent was there. One time Dad was given a box of candy to deliver to one of the nuns. Dad, Mother and I took a walk down to deliver it in the evening. I remember how scared I was, walking into the dark grounds and almost bumping into a statue. When we approached the convent we heard loud voices and laughter. As soon as Dad rang the bell—dead silence!

Mother, Dad and I often took evening walks to in- spect the new streets with their new houses such as French and Virginia Avenues. We also saw new houses on empty lots of old streets such as Ethel, Andrews, etc. There were many old mansions on Lake Avenue. Lakewood's first big scandal occurred in one when a wealthy lady hired some one to feed her crippled husband poison which killed him. This was the famous "Kaber Murder Case."*

Marie Albers' "Memories of Early Lakewood" are reprinted here with her kind permission.

* See E. George Lindstrom, Story of Lakewood, Ohio for a discussion of this case.

FOCUS: Marie Albers

Born in December 1903, Marie Albers came to Lakewood with her family in 1906. Her father, T. H. Albers, was a bank director; when the bank closed during the Great Depression, he went to work for a wholesale millinery business. The family attended Pilgrim Lutheran Church, which Albers helped found in 1913. Pilgrim originated when some members of Saint Paul's Evangelical Lutheran Church sought to have services in English rather than in German. Marie's mother was active in the Ladies Aid Society at Pilgrim, while Marie joined the Camp Fire Girls and her brothers became Boy Scouts.

With her brothers Marie attended Lakewood schools. She was in the first class of the new Lakewood High School at Bunts and Franklin, when the influenza epidemic struck in the fall and winter of 1918. The epidemic caused the temporary closing of the high school. Wh[en] Lakewood Hospital proved too small [to] handle all the sick, the recently purchased Rhodes Estate handled the over[flow]. Despite considerable fear about catching the deadly disease, none of t[he] Albers became ill.

A member of the new National Ho[nor] Society chapter at Lakewood High School, Marie attended Cleveland Normal School and graduated in 1925. Miss Albers began teaching in Lakewood schools the following year. Dur[ing] the summers she attended Ohio State University to earn her bachelor's degr[ee]. In all, she taught in Lakewood for thir[ty] two years, spending two at McKinley and thirty at Madison School. In 1958 Marie retired and she currently lives in Cleveland.

Pictured here is the Albers family at home at 1356 Cook Avenue circa 1906, from left to right: Marie, Emma, Harold, and Theodore Albers.
Courtesy of Marie Albers

Marie remembers the itinerant photographer who came down her street one day and hoisted Spencer and Marie on the back of his donkey for this picture. The picture was taken on Cook Avenue circa 1911.
Courtesy of Marie Albers

FOCUS: Lakewood Schools

by the time Marie Albers began teaching in Lakewood, education was more [   ]ed. In the first years of settlement, [   ]ever, education was a luxury the [   ]munity could hardly afford. Formal [   ]cation in Lakewood dates to 1829 [   ]n Mars Wagar hired a teacher and [   ]ated a room in his house for classes. [   ]pite the building of a log school-[   ]se the following year, it took some [   ] before the farm community made a [   ]or effort to establish a school system. [   ]871, East Rockport residents voted to [   ]te a separate school district and [   ]ted officers to govern it. The new [   ]rd members quickly voted to assure [   ]er and decorum by forbidding "rude [   ]boisterous conduct," "the use of [   ]ane and improper language," and [   ]use of fireworks or tobacco in the [   ]ool house. For some years the school [   ]em raised money by selling apples [   ]n trees on school property. It also [   ]ed school land for pastures.

[   ]While the new board inherited three [   ]ools, they set about replacing them [   ]n newer buildings. West School (on [   ]site of McKinley School) opened in [   ]2, and a four-room building, East [   ]kport Central School on Warren [   ]d opened in 1879. East School occu-[   ]d the site of Garfield School. As [   ]ool enrollment quickly grew from [   ]in 1871 to almost 6,000 in 1919, the [   ]rd found itself involved in an exten-[   ]building program. Between 1900 [   ]1918, Lakewood constructed three [   ]rate high schools, the last at Frank-[   ]nd Bunts. From 1900 to 1927, the [   ]suburb produced a total of twelve [   ]school buildings; many required [   ]tions within a few years of construc-[   ]. Save for later additions, the city has [   ]ely retained the schools it built

during its early years as a suburb. The modern "Grant School" is the only entirely new building since 1927.

Lakewood residents have generally given strong support to the public school system. From 1934 to 1983, Lakewood citizens passed thirty-three out of forty-four tax levies and bond issues. Partly as a consequence of this support, Lakewood schools have ranked well in terms of student performance. In 1986, state evaluators found Lakewood public schools "outstanding." Today ten elementary schools, three middle schools, and a high school comprise the Lakewood Public Schools.

The Board of Education devised multiple curricula for the diverse school population. In the 1920s, the high school curriculum included five tracks: academic, commercial, home economics, scientific, and technical. Students could take a variety of electives such as cabinet making, millinery, or printing.

The Great Depression in the 1930s caused great hardship for both schools and teachers. In 1931, the teachers had to survive with a 3 percent pay cut; at the time many educators earned only about $2,425 per year. Nevertheless, teachers provided food and clothing to needy students and paid for their own supplies. By 1932 to 1933, conditions had worsened; twenty-six teachers were laid off and the board cut wages by 14 percent.

World War II and its aftermath meant a return to prosperity and continuing growth and change for the Lakewood schools. In 1946, the school board raised almost two million dollars in bonds to renovate aging school buildings. To accommodate the baby boom that followed World War II, Lakewood High School underwent a series of major additions.

As early as the 1940s, high school students raised money for the construction of a student center. The site for the "log cabin in the woods" was to be in the southwest corner of the school property. After the woods were removed for the new football stadium, the proposed center became a "cabin in the sky" to be placed on top of the high school. Finally, in 1953, after more than a decade of fund-raising, the long-awaited student center appeared in the form of the "L-Room." A new gym and

civic auditorium added to the school's amenities. In a few years the high school underwent even greater expansion and modernization. Recently, with the help of the Kiwanis Club, the outdoor athletic facilities were modernized.

Over the years women made up the vast majority of the teaching staff of Lakewood schools. Nevertheless, they did not always receive equal treatment. While male instructors who married could continue to teach, female teachers could not do so until 1956.

Lakewood schools continue to adapt to the changing needs of the community. Because of an increase in the number of dual working parents, by 1976 all elementary schools offered hot lunches for children whose parents work. In 1985, citizens passed a $12.6 million bond levy to remove asbestos, build five new gyms, and improve outdoor play areas. Lakewood schools also shifted from the junior high to high school arrangements of three years each, to a middle school and four-year high school configuration.

The city also has an extensive array of fine parochial schools. Elementary schools, include Roman Catholic (Saints Cyril and Methodius, Saint James, Saint Lukes, and Saint Clements); Lutheran (Saint Paul's); and a Seventh Day Adventist. From 1927 to the late 1960s, Saint Hedwig's School also provided elementary training. Saint Augustine Academy and Saint Edward High School offer grades nine through twelve. Saint Augustine Academy opened in 1925 at its current location on Lake Avenue. Saint Edward's grew out of Saint Theresa Elementary School at Robinwood and Detroit; it moved to its new facility on Detroit in 1951.

Old Grant School opened in 1899. Until 1904 when the new high school building opened on the east side of Warren Road (later Wilson School), Grant joined with the adjacent high school building on the west side of Warren Road (Board of Education building) to offer high school classes. After 1904, the old Grant School, pictured here in 1969, 1470 Victoria became an elementary school. In 1906 the adjacent high school building and Grant School were joined. The old Grant School served as an elementary school until 1969 when the new building across Victoria opened. When Marie Albers began school in Lakewood, she went to Grant.
Photograph by Fred Bottomer; courtesy of the Cleveland Press Library and Collections, Cleveland State University Libraries

In 1904, Lakewood opened its second separate high school to accommodate rapidly growing school-aged population. Located on the east side of Warren Road (site of the new post office), this building, shown here, served as the high school until an even larger building opened in 1918 at Franklin and Bunts. Named Wilson School, the older high school became an elementary and junior high school until 1942. During the war it served as the center of Lakewood's war effort and housed the Red Cross and the Ration Board. The building was demolished in 1947.
Courtesy of the Lakewood Public Library

Lakewood's third separate high school building, shown here in 1932, opened in 1918 on the corner of Bunts and Franklin. Shortly after it opened the influenza epidemic swept across Lakewood as well as the rest of the country forcing the temporary closing of the school. Today, only portions of the original facade of this building are visible; additions have largely altered the school's appearance.
Courtesy of the Cleveland Press Library and Collections, Cleveland State University Libraries

This aerial photograph of Lakewood High School was taken in 1948 by Butt Airphotos.
Courtesy of the Lakewood Historical Society

In 1953, the long awaited "Cabin in the Sky" materialized as the "L-Room" along with a new civic auditorium and gym. These changes brought a new look to the high school building. In 1970-1971, a 7.9 million dollar construction project altered the facade even more with the addition of an academic wing and library resources center and vocational educational building.
Courtesy of the Cleveland Press Library and Collections, Cleveland State University Libraries

"Wouldn't It Be Surprising, If" from the Lakewood High School Cinema, 1920, page 120.

The Memorial Fountain commemorated the "Lakewood High School boys who gave their lives in two wars for the American way and the American dream." Above the fountain, a plaque listed the names of seven men who gave their lives in World War I. After World War II, new plaques listed the names of one hundred and thirty students who died in the later war. The ceramic mural represented the Arts, Science, and Industry and was flanked by silk flags of the nation and the school. Located in the main hall opposite the entrance, the fountain was a favorite meeting spot for students. Here Natlan Bratton on the left and Phyllis Overbeke wait for friends to gather on April 28, 1932.
Courtesy of the Cleveland Press Library and Collections, Cleveland State University Libraries

kewood athletic teams long established a reputation for winning. As early 1907, Lakewood won the Cleveland championship in football; as part of Senate conference the chief rival East Tech. In 1917, Coach Corneal k over. By 1920, the team caught ention with its defeat of the highly pected Toledo Waite team. Working of a "66" formation, quarterback lly" Gribbens hit Len Reeves for a chdown in the early minutes of the me. In a few years, Coach Corneal ablished an even more impressive ord with the famed Golden Torna- es team who established seventeen

victories in a row between 1923 and 1924. In the latter year Lakewood won ten games including a City Championship, the Quad Championship, and the Northeast Ohio Championship. By 1924 Lakewood belonged to the Quad Conference of University School, Shaw, and Cleveland Heights. The Lakewood basketball team of 1920 shown here was equally strong. In 1924-1925, the basketball team suffered only three losses on its way to the state championship finals where they lost in a close 32 to 30 game to Springfield.
Courtesy of the Lakewood Public Schools

The children are having fun at the "Bedouin Bazaar" at Hayes School circa 1940.
Photograph by Gordon Conner, Madison Geddes Studio; courtesy of the Lakewood Public Schools

Saint Edward High School grew out of Saint Theresa Elementary School at Robinwood and Detroit. The new facilities that are shown here on Detroit between Nicholson and Elbur avenues opened in 1951. Saint Edward counts among its illustrious graduates TV celebrity Phil Donahue and U.S. Congressman Ed Feighan.
Photograph by Clayton Knipper; courtesy of the Cleveland Press Library and Collections, Cleveland State University Libraries

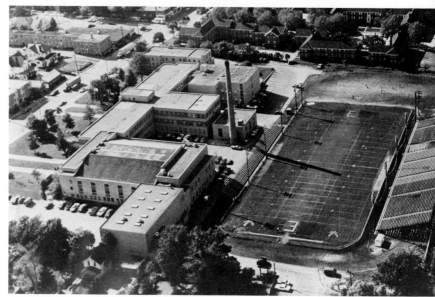

Saint Edward's Chris Williams runs against a Fairfield defender in the 1985 Championship game. In a short space of time Saint Edward's has established an impressive record in athletics. In recent years, the school has become the dominant school in wrestling in both the state and nation. Ten state wrestling titles attest to the quality of the program. Saint Edward's also holds two recent state championships in ice hockey. Williams, the school's all-time leading rusher, helped make the football team one of the most exciting teams to watch in the nation.
Photograph by Joe Glick; courtesy of Robert Budenski and Saint Edward High School

hapter 9

ocial and
ultural
ife of the
ew City:
)00 to 1930

*young suburbanites have been recreating something
[t]be tight-knit group of old. It is an achievement not to
[d]ismissed lightly. They have come together with many
[mor]e differences in religion, background, and expecta-
[tion]s. . . . the result bespeaks a pretty high quotient of kind-
[ne]ss and fundamental decency.*

William H. Whyte, Jr., *The Organization Man,* 1956

If Lakewood's record on education represented a
significant achievement, the community's efforts to carve
out social worlds as well as social and cultural organizations is equally impressive. As the emerging religious
landscape, social life and organizations reflected the
community's diversity; residents also introduced new
ways of life to the older settlement.

East Rockport and early Lakewood residents who
clustered along Detroit Avenue established an extensive
social life based on informal ties and entertaining at
home. As Lakewood's rapid growth during the first thirty
years of the new century exploded across the suburb, the
community's social and cultural life became at once both
more complex and more formal. While many traditional
aspects of nineteenth-century social life remained, new
institutions came to play an increasingly important role in
community life. World War I provided a common cause
that brought the diverse parts of Lakewood together; at
the same time the war also unleashed a mean-spirited
attack on some members of the community.

In contrast to early Rockport, Lakewood hamlet was
much more homogeneous. As the new century advanced,
however, the community again grew more heterogeneous.
This new diversity reflected differences in social class,
ethnic origin, and religion—but not in race. By 1930,
Lakewood claimed only 159 non-white residents out of a
total population of 70,509.

Social class, ethnicity, religion, and residential area
did not always overlap to produce discrete social worlds.
As his bakery business prospered, Stefan Lodzieski and his
family moved from the Village to middle Lakewood.
Morris and Sam Gold, Jewish immigrants from Eastern
Europe, located their grocery stores and homes in middle Lakewood, as did Slovak-born printer Jan Pankuch.
Nevertheless, many of middle Lakewood's middle-class
residents traced their ancestry to Western Europe and the
British Isles, while working-class Villagers had recently
migrated from Eastern Europe.

As with many new suburbs at the time, Lakewood
fashioned itself as a haven for native-born white citizens.
Nevertheless, by 1930 the foreign-born and their children
accounted for over 45 percent of the city's population.
Slovaks claimed almost one-third of all foreign-born in
Lakewood, while Germans, Irish, and Poles also accounted for significant numbers of this population.

Religious diversity grew as the young suburb developed. Protestant and Catholic (Roman and Orthodox)
churches peppered the city's landscape. Even here eth-

nicity influenced the development of churches; English, German, and Slovak Lutherans established separate churches, while Slovaks, Poles, and Galicians established separate Roman Catholic parishes only a block apart.

For today's "couch potatoes" it may be impossible to comprehend the first generation of suburban residents who likened themselves to "live wires." With seemingly endless energy, these new suburbanites engaged in continuous rounds of entertaining family, friends, and neighbors; they also began an incredible array of fraternal, social, religious, recreational, and civic organizations. In doing so they bridged the gap between the rural society of the nineteenth century and the urban world of the twentieth; many of their social customs drew on the former as they increasingly came to rely on the latter.

Not surprisingly, traditional practices exerted themselves at critical points in the life cycle: birth, marriage, and death. The home remained central to these key events. Many Lakewood mothers still gave birth at home. When Colette Sheehan Townsend was born in 1911, it was in the front bedroom of her family's home at 1471 Alameda. Two years later Alice Welfare Cotabish gave birth to her daughter Alice at the family's home on Lakeland. While a physician attended these births, midwives still presided at some Lakewood births. At least three served the city as late as 1930.

Although church weddings became increasingly common as the century advanced, many middle Lakewood couples still chose to be married at home. When D'Etta Brown, the daughter of Mr. and Mrs. George H. Brown of 15620 Detroit Avenue, married Marvin Dodge in 1917, they chose the Brown family's living room. In the same year, Inella Williams and Harvey Wagar, the son of Mr. and Mrs. Forrest R. Wagar of 1483 Elmwood, selected the old Wagar homestead at the corner of Detroit and Warren as the site of their wedding ceremony. While both weddings limited attendance to family only, the Williams-Wagar ceremony drew fifty guests for the seven o'clock affair. According to the Lakewood Press, the "bride wore a gown of royal blue satin and carried a shower bouquet of Ward roses." A supper followed the double-ring ceremony. In contrast, Slovak Catholic weddings in the Village generally took place on Saturdays in church; following a High Mass, the wedding party and guests adjourned to Mahall's or another hall for a festive party that could last well into Sunday.

In other ways the family home served as the locus of activities, ceremonial or social. Although Lakewood had several funeral homes, many residents continued to display their recently departed in their parlors. Nevertheless, the streetcar played an important role here; special rented funeral cars transported the casket and mourners to the cemetary.

Another important part of the city's social life involved home entertaining of friends, relatives, and neighbors. Suburban weeklies report a constant round of small

gatherings and parties throughout the year and for all ages. Husbands and wives surprised each other for birt days and anniversaries; together they hosted Hallowee and other parties for neighborhood children. These ac ties not only brought family, neighbors, and friends together, but they also linked their lives together into t social networks largely based on proximity.

Despite these extensive family-focused activities, residents participated in other activities as well. Lake-wood's weekly newspapers confirm the penchant of re dents for forming social organizations, an American phenomenon observed by many, including the noted French traveler, Alexis de Tocqueville.

Residents founded a number of neighborhood as ciations, including the Northland Avenue Residents As ciation, the South Side Improvement Club, and the Ros wood Club. These organizations represented residents City Hall and petitioned utilities to provide services promised. They also sponsored neighborhood parade and fairs as well as their own Fourth of July celebration

Of all these organizations, the Clifton Club stood out as the most impressive and long-lasting. The club i corporated in 1902 as a private social and recreational club for residents of Clifton Park. When the clubhouse opened in August, 1903, the Cleveland Leader reportec was "a delightful building of pleasing appearance." The first floor-housed a large reception hall while an "elaborately finished" ballroom occupied most of the second. A third story provided quarters for summer guests. By 1918 the Lakewood Press noted "the beau-tiful location of the club with the attraction of the yacht ing in the river, and the bathing on the beach as well as its facilities for entertainment in its ball room and dining room, has kept its membership filled up to abou 225." The club became the center of Clifton Park social life. Activities ranged from card parties to luncheons, wedding receptions, formal dinners and balls. Club membership also bestowed important social con-siderations since the club was one of Cleveland's elite social organizations.

Lakewood "live wires" also founded active chapte of the Odd Fellows (2), Knights of Malta, Knights of Pythias (3), Elks, Rosarians, Independent Order of Fore ters (3), Catholic Order of Foresters, Knights of the Maccabees (3), Knights of Columbus, Royal League, National Protective League, and the Masons (4). They a started chapters of major service organizations: Red Crc (1917), Kiwanis (1921), Rotary (1926), and Junior Chamber of Commerce (1929). Lakewood women also started local chapters of national organizations. While Rockporters founded a local chapter of the Women's Christian Temperance Union in 1879, the Lakewood chapter of the Daughters of the American Revolution began in 1927. They also founded a number of com-munity-based organizations including the Lakewood Woman's Club (1920), the South Lakewood Woman's b (1924), and College Club (1926). In 1928 these three ups joined with the Chamber of Commerce to rent eting rooms at Warren Road and Detroit. Other men's organizations included the Lakewood Business Professional Women's Club (1927), Florence Critten- Circle, Amity Club, Helping Hand Sewing Club, Ladies endly Club, Book and Thimble Club, and the Worth ile Sewing Circle. Children joined the Camp Fire Girls, Scouts (1914), Girl Scouts, and YWCA (1913), YMCA 21). Aficionados of homing pigeons founded the ewood Pigeon Club while rifle enthusiasts started the e Club; in 1908 residents founded the Lakewood nis Club and ten years later a baseball club. Affluent ting enthusiasts could choose between the Lakewood ht Club (later named the Cleveland Yacht Club) and Lakewood Boat Club.

Church lodges and organizations, of course, played ior roles in Lakewood social life. Regular rounds of rch bazaars and plays raised money for church build- s. At a time when few suburban families went to restau- s, bazaars provided an opportunity for families to eat and to socialize.

These were not the only diversions available. A iety of organizations, such as the Suburban Club, ered monthly dances. Nor were these soirees limited to ekends. New suburbanites seemed to be engaged in a nstant round of private parties at home while tripping light fantastic at Compton's, Gilbert's Academy, the sonic Temple or another of Lakewood's elegant lrooms.

Just thirty minutes away by streetcar, Cleveland also ered many attractions. However, suburbanites did not ve to travel far for movies, vaudeville shows, or amuse- nt parks. Several theaters in or near Lakewood provided deville performances, while seven motion-picture aters served the city in 1927. Lakewood also claimed amusement park close by. For many years Scenic Park Rocky River Valley attracted west siders. In 1906 Lincoln k replaced it; the park remained open until 1917. ewood offered other "big city" entertainment. Al- ough "dry" since 1905, the city also had its own speak- sies. When national Prohibition took effect in 1920, al entrepreneurs and amateurs alike produced bathtub and other illegal alcoholic products for profit and mestic consumption.

f Lakewood residents seemed excessively involved in cial activities and organizations, they did not neglect her their cultural or civic responsibilities. These new urbanites may have left the city but they retained their erest in the cultural and intellectual life of the big city. ey supported a plethora of organizations and schools advance culture and the arts. In 1918, the Lakewood ess reported the founding of the Lakewood Art Society a group of "artists, sculptors, lyric singers, writers, and linists." Thousands of suburban children took lessons he numerous private music schools in Lakewood and

Cleveland. Every year these young musicians who studied at the Lakewood Academy of Music, with Alvirda E. Fleming, or with another music teacher, entertained family and friends with recitals.

Lakewood women played key roles in the promo- tion of the arts in the new suburb. In 1919 nine young women founded the Three Arts Club to promote the per- forming arts of music, drama, and dance. Within four years the organization claimed seventy-five active and one-hundred-and-fifty associate members. The club held monthly recitals at the Clifton Club and eventually offered a series of scholarship grants for arts students living on Cleveland's west side.

New suburbanites continued to show an interest in the discussion of current issues. Churches, public schools, and other organizations sponsored public speakers on topics of significance to the community. For several years beginning in 1913, the Lakewood Tennis Club offered a Lyceum Herald featuring popular lectures and performers. In 1917-1918, the Masonic Temple presented a series of eight lyceum programs; performers included Loseff's Russian Quartet.

Residents could hear a range of views presented at community forums. In 1918, the Pilgrim Lutheran Church sponsored a lecture on the ideas of social reformer Henry George and his single tax plan. George had called for a single tax on land as a means to control the excesses of capitalism. In the same year Rev. Russell H. Conwell spoke at the Congregational Church. One of the most popular speakers of the day, Conwell frequently told his audiences that gaining wealth "is an honorable ambi- tion…money is power [and] every good man and woman ought to strive for power, to do good with it when obtained."

Although Lakewood's annual Chautauqua Week did not survive the 1920s, it also indicated the community's interest in serious entertainment, popular education, and political oratory. Modeled after the programs of the Chautauqua Institute in western New York, tent Chautau- qua, as it came to be known, provided a week of concerts, dramatic productions, and lectures on current topics. In the Cleveland area, the Coit-Alber Bureau, well known for its lyceum programs, operated tent Chautauquas. Despite initial successes, however, weak programming produced a precipitous drop in attendance that ultimately doomed this important cultural institution.

Lakewood offered its first tent Chautauqua in 1914. The program usually took place in June on the old high school grounds (Wilson School) at Warren Road near Detroit. Adults paid two dollars for the full week and chil- dren, one dollar. Morning sessions involved youths in rehearsals for a presentation later in the week. Afternoon programs usually featured a concert; in 1918, Lakewood's Chautauquans listened to the Welsh Glee Quartet, the Tchaikovsky Quartet, Ralph Dunbar's Royal Dragoons Band, and the Castle Court Singers. The Crawford Adams

Company also performed a concert of sacred music. Evening features included lectures on topics of current interest and concern. In 1918, while World War I was ravaging much of Europe, the lectures considered "New Ways of Feeding the World," and "Gassing the Mind of the World," while a noted war correspondent discussed "My Recent Experience on the Fighting Front in France and Flanders." That year Chautauquans also watched a production of William Shakespeare's *Comedy of Errors.*

More than any other event, the founding of a public library indicated the community's commitment to cultural life. Initiated in 1913 by Belle Graber and Bernice Pyke, members of the Board of Education, the library opened in May 1916 at its current site at Detroit and Arthur. It quickly attracted patrons; within the first year over five thousand residents borrowed from the collection's ten thousand books. Nevertheless, many Lakewood residents continued to patronize local book stores as well as commercial lending libraries operated by Bernice Pyke's Book Store and Burrows Brothers' Store.

Finally, while the Parent-Teacher Associations served a variety of functions for the public schools, they played an important role in supplementing the schools' cultural resources. Begun initially as "Mothers' clubs" at Madison School in 1912, and at Garfield in 1913, the organizations raised money for pianos, record players, and books. In 1919 the Mothers' Clubs joined together in the Lakewood Federated Parent-Teacher Association.

Lakewood residents also took active part in civic affairs. Begun in 1911, the Chamber of Commerce became an important fixture in the community. It set out "to promote and protect the moral, social, business, and civil interests of the City of Lakewood: to acquire and diffuse such information as will best serve such purposes and to provide entertainment for its members." Drawing on many of Lakewood's leading citizens, the chamber promoted the city and served as a forum on community issues; it also helped set the agenda for city government. In the latter case, the chamber played an instrumental role in the 1918 acquisition of the Rhodes estate for Lakewood Park. During World War I, members directed war bond sales efforts. In 1926, the chamber failed to convince residents of the efficacy of the city manager form of government. Lakewood voters overwhelmingly rejected the measure.

These organizations, social, cultural, and civic, did not draw equally on all sections of Lakewood. With important exceptions, many members came from middle Lakewood but Clifton Park residents often played key leadership roles. Nor did all Lakewood residents, even in middle Lakewood, partake of some or all these organizations. However the plethora of activities and groups touched the lives of many, while some "live wires" remained active in a wide range of organizations.

The Great War brought many of these groups and all of Lakewood's landscapes together to work for a common cause. Despite the relatively short duration of the United

States' involvement in the war and the relatively small number of casualties (more Americans died from the influenza epidemic of 1918 than died in the war), it touched the lives of all Lakewood residents. In ways th could not have been anticipated, the war also introduc important changes. Women not only gained the right to vote but for the first time began to move into traditiona male jobs. The war also produced a new interest in and concern for working-class residents. Ironically, the sam enthusiasm that produced unity in the war effort also u leashed a nativist attack on loyal Americans.

It is difficult to appreciate how quickly and completely World War I engulfed the new suburb; the war effort became a community crusade that enlisted the ai of almost every church, social organization, and individual. In these efforts women played a key role. Early i 1918, the newly-elected chair of the Lakewood's Woma Suffrage Party, Mrs. W. G. Waitt, urged women to "do ou part in making the world safe for democracy." Speaking before the Chamber of Commerce, a former Indiana governor made the same point: "this is a woman's war; is different from other wars; it must be won by our women who have taken up gloriously the spirit of conservation, the banding together of Red Cross units to se and knit, to hardships and privation as nurses, to take th place of our men in many walks in life."

Lakewood women needed little encouragement; they enlisted in Red Cross campaigns to raise money, make bandages, conserve food, tend war gardens, care the wounded, and cheer the troops. In the spring of 191 the Lakewood Red Cross branch reported that its work i the year included 2,810 shirts, 776 pajamas, 3,227 nighti gales (a one-piece hospital gown), 500 gowns, 589 bed socks, 586 bathrobes, 280 pairs of French underwear, 9: bed spreads, 4,469 socks, 3,116 sweaters, 415 wristlets, and 26 trench blankets. Virtually every women's organiza tion contributed to the Red Cross drives; meetings foun members knitting sweaters or socks for the Sammies (U soldiers), while the "Ladies of Clifton Club" gave a dinr for officers and crews of submarine chasers.

Lakewood residents also contributed heavily to the Liberty Loan campaigns. In the third campaign the com munity raised over one million dollars, more than doub its goal. These campaigns enlisted the aid of school chil dren as well as adults. The Lakewood Slovak Political Cl also contributed to the War Fund, while fraternal organi: tions donated money for the construction of social hous to provide member recruits in basic training with center for recreation and relaxation.

World War I permeated the entire social life of the new community. Virtually every organization found a wa to participate in the war effort; few social events escaped military and patriotic trappings. Lakewood members of the United Daughters of the Confederacy staged a danc to raise money to "endow" a bed in the American milita hospital in Neuilly, France. Lakewood's Rifle League trained potential recruits on the proper use of fire arms,

ile Suburban Club members danced the "Trench One
)."

Residents contributed to the war effort in other ways.
ing men served in the military; some gave their lives
ile others returned handicapped by shells or gas. Sgt.
ward Woodford may well have been Lakewood's first
casualty. Before the United States entered the war, he
isted with the Royal Canadian regiment; he died in
on in France on March 10, 1918. Some died even
ore they saw service; Capt. Harrison Wall died during
operation for appendicitis at Camp Custer, Michigan.

Many Lakewood men and, increasingly, women con-
uted to the effort through war work. Both Winton and
nplar automobile plants shifted to war work while
rkers constructed submarine chasers in Rocky River
ley. As men left their jobs to go to war, women replaced
m often at jobs they had never been permitted to per-
n. While many of these jobs were in factories, most
ewood residents noticed the change in other places.
tie Goodell pumped gas at Sinclair Oil Company's
ling Station" at Sloane and Edanola avenues; she
nd the work "much better than working in a store or
ce." Similarly, Carrie and Gizella Fuch took over their
ther's Northland Grocery Store at Madison and North-
d, when he went to war. Gizella handled the cashier,
okkeeping, and sales duties while Carrie took orders
l drove the delivery truck. The business thrived as
er before.

Slowly the war began to change society. To a con-
erable extent, Lakewood women won the municipal
nchise because of their war work; American women
ilarly won the right to vote by constitutional amend-
nt because of their major contributions to the war.
ese changes opened new doors for women in politics,
ousiness, and in industry. While the door was never
en wide or for long, these events intensified the pro-
s of change that has affected gender roles ever since.

The war also produced a growing concern about
migrants' loyalty to the United States. To respond to this
oblem the public schools sponsored evening citizen-
p and English language classes. Villagers already
ongly supported the war, but for those who were not
citizens, the classes provided the necessary vehicle.

As an unintended consequence of these efforts,
ders of the newly founded Parent-Teacher Association
A) became aware that many young children in the
age remained at home unattended while their parents
rked. While the PTA did not seek to redress the low
ges that required both parents to work, they did found
Lakewood Day Nursery at 12203 Plover Street. Aided
funds from the National Carbon Company and money
sed from four Cleveland Orchestra concerts in Lake-
od, the nursery, which opened in 1921, provided day
e for young children under the guidance of a regis-
ed nurse. Parents paid a fee of ten cents for the first
ld and five cents for each additional child at the center.
1925, the nursery moved to its present location at 2070
Dowd Street.

The war also produced a less benign reaction. Nativist
organizations had already established a base in the young
suburb. The National Protective League, which had a Lakewood chapter, was an anti-Catholic organization. However, the Allied war propaganda and the super-patriotism
that resulted from the war effort brought on a wave of
xenophobia that swept the nation. Drawing on Allied
propaganda which painted Germans as uncivilized "huns"
and Allies as the saviors of civilization, the Lakewood
Press editorialized that "all Germany [is] guilty of capital
crimes, every adult man and woman of the German
people. The only good German is a dead one. Germany
must be destroyed." The newspaper also carried full page
drawings depicting evil "huns" or the Kaiser.

German-Americans nationally and locally became
targets for these attacks. In clear violation of the Constitu-
tion, some Lakewood residents called on city council to
ban the use of German in city churches. The Lakewood
Press accused a high school teacher of promoting socialist
and pacifist doctrines. While it apologized later for its mis-
leading and incorrect story, it refused to back down from
its stand that "a lack of patriotism cannot be tolerated."

Nor were these the only results of hysteria. Some
Lakewoodites called for the elimination of German
language classes from the high school. Within weeks the
school board capitulated and immediately cancelled
German classes. In May 1918, Lakewood High School
students burned "every German textbook in a huge bon-
fire on the school grounds." Like a contagious disease, the
burning quickly spread to the Waechter und Anzieger, a
Cleveland German-language daily newspaper. Lakewood
Boy Scouts appropriated bundles of the paper and set
them afire. Henry Calvert, a justice of the peace, announced that no arrests would be made because he felt
there was no room for a German language paper in the
community. The Lakewood City Council then proceeded
to pass a resolution opposing circulation of the newspaper in Lakewood.

German-Americans were not the only ones to suffer
from this hysteria. Racism also surfaced when some
Lakewood residents protested the housing of three
hundred African-American war workers at Berea Road and
West 117th. In a letter to Lakewood's Mayor Clayton Tyler,
the president of the Lakewood Engineering Company
warned that "the class of people in such a settlement will
be most undesirable for the City of Lakewood." The letter
expressed special concern for the thirty young women
who had to pass the area to get to the streetcar. Nevertheless, black workers joined whites at the National Carbon
Company for at least the duration of the war.

Ironically, just as Lakewood residents seemed to
come together across different ethnic, class, and
religious boundaries in common support of and sacrifice
for the war effort, barriers arose again and a new wave of
intolerance ensued. Only a depression and another war
would restore that sense of unity.

The view looking west on Detroit Avenue from Warren Road is pictured here. Life in the young suburb came to a halt for three days in November 1913. A driving snowstorm propelled by winds clocked at over seventy miles-an-hour dropped about twenty inches on the Cleveland area. The storm downed power lines and stopped streetcars in their tracks. Courtesy of the Lakewood Historical Society

Children whose parents have recently moved into Lakewood are shown here with Geneva Tarr their teacher on September 9, 1924. As Lakewood's population swelled in the 1920s so too did its schools and classrooms. This group of somewhat eager scholars was replicated across the young suburb.
Courtesy of the Cleveland Press Library and Collections, Cleveland State University Libraries

Weddings continued to be an important ritual in the young suburb. The Jancik wedding took place at Saints Cyril and Methodius Church in 1910. In addition to Anna and Andrew Jancik, the bride and groom, seated, the party included from left to right: unknown, Emma Smoka, and John and Catherine Slavik. The Slaviks owned Lakewood Dairy. Courtesy of Mary Jacko

An Irish-American wedding, the bride, Patricia Nolan, and groom, Henry Erhardt, are from Lakewood. Their mothers, both from Ireland, joined them for this picture in 1947 which was taken on Elmwood Avenue. Their wedding took place at Saint Clement's Church. Courtesy of Joan Erhardt

...y residents of the new suburb
...inued to give birth at home rather
... in a hospital. Baby Alice, the daugh-
...f Joseph and Alice Cotabish was one
...ose home births in 1913. Her uncle,
...on Cotabish, had recently stepped
...n as Lakewood's mayor.
...rtesy of Alice Cotabish

Funeral streetcars such as this one from
the Cleveland Railway Company, circa
1920 were first introduced onto Cleveland streets late in 1899. Before the
widespread use of automobiles they
provided a means to take the casket and
funeral party from the site of the service
to the cemetery.
Courtesy of James McGorray

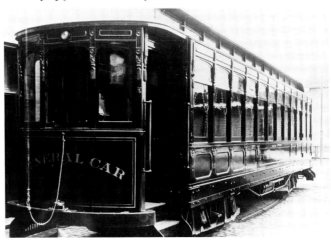

...ewood residents engaged in regular
...nds of entertaining friends, neigh-
..., and relatives. Children's birthday
...ties were common features of the
...v suburban landscape. The Auker-
...n twins, Eulslia and Mapril, at the
...d of the table on the left, celebrate
...h their friends in May 1918 including
...rlyn Meeker (Irwin) standing on far

...urtesy of Carlyn Irwin

Shown here is the Northland Avenue
Residents' Association's Fourth Celebration Program for Tuesday, July 4, 1916.
New suburbanites frequently organized
neighborhood associations that sponsored a variety of activities including
their own holiday celebrations. "Live-
wires" on Wagar Avenue sponsored
their own Fourth of July picnic.
Courtesy of the Lakewood Public Library

This is probably another Fourth of July celebration organized by the Rosewood-Orchard Grove-Westwood Civic Association in the early 1900s. These events frequently took place in addition to those sponsored by the city in Lakewood Park after 1917. All residents were invited to the neighborhood fairs. Many neighborhood events included a parade, booths, athletic events, a band concert, and fireworks.
Courtesy of the Lakewood Public Library

This Fourth of July parade was probably sponsored by the Lakeland Avenue Association in 1911. Despite all the effort that the children and parents apparently put into it, it appears to have attracted more participants than spectators.
Courtesy of the Lakewood Historical Society

Fraternal organizations such as the Lakewood Masonic Lodge Number 601, circa 1936, played an important role in Lakewood's social and civic life. Judge Donald Lybarger is seated in the center of the picture.
Courtesy of the Western Reserve Historical Society

Lakewood women also formed a large number of associations, both local and chapters of national organizations. The Lakewood chapter of the Daughters of the American Revolution formed in 1927 to promote interest in history, education, and patriotism. Dressed in

historical costumes are left to right: Mabel Harmon Kaiser, Clarabyrde Loomis, and Mrs. Hugh K. Dawson circ 1936.
Courtesy of the Cleveland Press Library and Collections, Cleveland State University Libraries

Clifton Club at 17886 Lake Road is
tured here on September 1, 1931. It
s the center of social life in Clifton
rk and hosted a wide range of lunch-
s, dinners, card parties, and dances
well as some community activities.
 building opened in 1903. It was
troyed by fire on January 11, 1942.
he time of the fire the Club had 175
mbers. Shortages in building materials
 result of the war delayed construc-
n of a new club building until after
war.
rtesy of the Cleveland Press Library
d Collections, Cleveland State
iversity Libraries

Shown here are the characters in a play
about a Slovak wedding at Mahall's Hall,
circa 1926. Ethnic organizations kept
alive traditions and values through plays
and musicals as well as courses on native languages and cultures. Lakewood
Slovaks formed a number of dramatic
and musical organizations. Some of
these plays were held at Mahall's in the
hall above the bowling alley. The hall was
also the site for wedding receptions and
dances.
Courtesy of Mary Jacko

unded in 1921, the YMCA took over
 former home of Mathew Hall, shown
re at 16718 Detroit Avenue, for their
adquarters in about 1938. Previously
 YMCA occupied a store front office
 Belle at Detroit. They vacated the
use thirty years later for the new
ilding shared with the YWCA. The
WCA was founded in 1913 and oper-
ed out of small store-fronts on Detroit
enue until they joined with the YMCA
 building a new structure.
rtesy of the Lakewood YMCA

The new uniform for Girl Scouts, circa
1929, when a more feminine dress of
soft green replaced the original boyish
khaki. Lakewood children also participated in a wide range of organizations.
By the 1940s there were thirty Girl Scout
troops. Alice Heise, of Troop 102, and
1316 Sloane Avenue models the new
uniform adopted by the Girl Scouts.
*Courtesy of the Cleveland Press Library
and Collections, Cleveland State
University Libraries*

137

The Parent-Teacher Association grew
out of Mothers' Clubs at Madison School
and Garfield School. The formation of
the Lakewood Federated Parent-Teacher
Clubs demonstrated residents' concern
for the quality of education in the
community. Through their efforts the
PTA supplemented the resources of
schools and provided a link between
parents and the school system, such as
this PTA party for teachers at the Lake
Shore Hotel in May 1940.
Photograph by Madison Geddes;
courtesy of the Lakewood Public Schools

Shown here is the Lakewood Day Nursery at 2070 Dowd Street. In 1922, the
Parent-Teacher Association (PTA),
organized the Lakewood Day Nursery to
aid working families in the Village.
National Carbon Company donated
money and a building while the PTA
supplied matching funds. By 1940 the
nursery cared for fifty children ranging
in age from two to ten years. Parents
paid small fees for the day care service.
Courtesy of Dan Chabek

Not quite ready for the Bolshoi Ballet
but. . . . Many Lakewood parents supplemented their children's education
with music, drama, and dance lessons.
One of the schools available was Vida
Cotabish's Dance School operated out of
the family home at Detroit and Cohassett. Vida was the daughter of Lakewood
mayor Nelson Cotabish. Vida's cousin,
Alice Cotabish, is on the left circa 1910.
Courtesy of Alice Cotabish

This is a program from one of the "tent"
Chautauqua productions held each
summer in Lakewood from 1914 until
the early 1920s. For one week Lakewood
residents could enjoy a wide range of
entertainment and cultural activities.
Courtesy of the Lakewood Public Library

igned by Charles W. Hopkinson, the
bitect for the Board of Education, the
 library opened on May 19, 1916.
 building shown here was located at
present site at Detroit and Arthur
nues. According to Margaret Butler,
library opened its first branch "in a
ted second floor dance hall at the
ner of Madison and Newman avenues
921." In 1929, a permanent building
 constructed next to Madison Park.
 library also maintained collections
 many of the schools as well as at
ewood hospital.
rtesy of the Cleveland Press Library
 Collections, Cleveland State
iversity Libraries

Shown here is the main building interior
of Lakewood Public Library. This may
be the opening day of the library, May
19, 1916.
Courtesy of the Lakewood Public Library

kewood had a number of fine ball
oms and "live wires" often had an
portunity of attending more than one
nce on any night of the week. Frater-
l organizations often rented these
lls for dances while the owners pro-
ded dance lessons during the week.
lbert's Dance Hall, at 14623 Detroit
enue is pictured here on November 9,
25.
urtesy of the Cleveland Press Library
d Collections, Cleveland State
niversity Libraries

Many Lakewood residents spent warm
summer days bathing at Edgewater
Park. The bandstand at the park also
featured concerts and other programs
while some fraternal organizations held
regular outings there. Shown here is the
Edgewater Bathing Pavillion, circa 1927.
Courtesy of the Cleveland Press Library
and Collections, Cleveland State
University Libraries

As in later years, Lakewood residents also participated in a wide range of athletic activities. Here is the Individual Wet Wash team, the Lakewood Muny Class A Champions in 1931.
Photograph by the Miller Studio; courtesy of the Cleveland Press Library and Collections, Cleveland State University Libraries

Although Templar Motors Corporation at Templar Park continued to produce automobiles during the war, its major effort shifted to producing 155 millimeter (6 inch) artillery shells for the World War I effort. The piles of shell castings are to be machined in the factory. To maintain automobile production, Templar added two additional floors on its plant. The ground floor contained the heavy machinery for finishing shells while automobile production moved to the upper floors.
Courtesy of the Western Reserve Historical Society

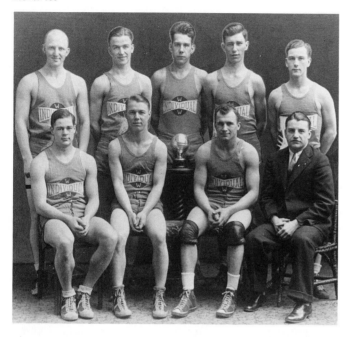

"Having passed through the factory, they come out at the other end, bored, milled, ground, polished and varnished, ready for inspection." from Templar Topics. During the war Templar employed nearly one thousand workers. The company projected their production at two thousand shells per day.
Courtesy of the Western Reserve Historical Society

Although the United States was not in World War I long before the war ended, the experience for American "Sammies" was far from easy. Troops were given only minimum training and then were thrown into trench warfare. The experience included poison gas, constant shelling, and trench living. During World War I Walter Hooks served in a balloon

company of the U.S. Army. He fought in France and Germany and returned to the United States in 1919. He is pictured here in his uniform circa 1918. Until his recent death, Walter Hooks was an active member of the Lakewood Barracks, an organization of World War I veterans.
Courtesy of Zoe Hooks Harper

FOCUS: Lakewood Theaters

Before television began glowing in family living rooms in the late 1940s, neighborhood movie theaters provided low cost entertainment. Many Americans went to the movies once or even several times every week to see features, short subjects, and newsreels.

By the late 1920s almost every section and neighborhood in Lakewood had a theater within walking distance. In the early years of the Great Depression of the 1930s when many unemployed Americans had more time than money, inexpensive entertainment such as motion pictures, and miniature golf courses became very popular. Nevertheless, Lakewood theaters experienced considerable difficulty as the Depression advanced. Some closed their doors permanently while others reopened under new names or after prosperity returned. By the 1950s the automobile and television brought new competition, and Lakewood theaters again experienced difficulties. By 1989 only one motion picture theater, the Detroit Theater, continued to show films.

Lakewood's first motion picture house appeared in 1912 (The Lakewood). Although several theaters were short-lived, within four years the city claimed five movie houses. In 1927, the last new theater building opened (Hilliard Square). At its high point in 1929, seven theaters served the city while Cleveland and Rocky River had movie houses close-by. In all, Lakewood produced eleven different motion picture theater buildings.

Lakewood moviegoers thrilled to the films and stars of the day. Until the late 1920s, films were silent while color movies appeared just before World War II. In 1918 the Homestead Theater featured William S. Hart in the *Wolves of the Rail*, and Mabel Normand in *The Floor Below*, while U-NO patrons watched Charlie Chaplin in *The Rink*, Harry Cary in *The Marked Man*, and Sarah Bernhardt in *Mothers in France*. Many films provided entertainment and escape from the cares of the day. Goldwyn Pictures advertised the plot line of *The Cinderella Man*, as "She was rich, and He was poor, Nothing between them but six tin roofs covered with snow—How in the world will we get them together?"

To attract customers Lakewood theaters provided a range of entertainment. Before the Depression, some mixed vaudeville shows with films, as did many of the downtown theaters. Some residents recall vaudeville shows at the Melba Theater (11728 Detroit) while several blocks away in Cleveland, the elegant Granada also mixed vaudeville with "moving pictures." During and after the Depression theaters attracted patrons with a variety of new devices. The U-NO Theater (12224 Madison) held an amateur night every Friday night. The Homestead Theater featured Zippo, a game which awarded prizes, while on Wednesday night they offered Bingo. Many theaters held "Plate Night" once a week. The Janciks regularly attended the U-NO on those nights. Over the years they accumulated twenty-four place settings of attractive gold-rimmed floral dishes which Mary Jancik Jacko now owns.

At matinees every Saturday afternoon, thousands of Lakewood youth crammed theaters across the city to munch on popcorn or Baby Ruth bars and scream for their favorite cowboys and cowgirls: Tom Mix, Bob Keane, Gene Autrey, Roy Rogers, and Dale Evans. Each week children also rushed back to see the latest episode of the current serial featuring twenty-first century space traveler Buck Rogers or Captain Marvel, as well as Bugs Bunny, Mickey Mouse, or Felix the Cat cartoons. Prices for these matinees went up over the years. In the 1920s Marie Albers and her brother Spencer went to the Lakewood Theater nearly every Saturday for a nickel each. Eventually Spencer earned free admission by distributing flyers in their Cook Avenue neighborhood. By the late 1940s and 1950s the Saturday afternoon shows cost an outrageous ten cents; by the end of the 1950s matinees cost twenty-five cents. A box of popcorn cost another

Lakewood Theaters

Theater	Address	Dates
Lakewood Theater	15013 Detroit Avenue	1912 to 1922 1924 to 1930
Highland Square Theater Pastime Theater	11920 Madison Avenue	1913 1917
Melba Theater	11728 Detroit Avenue	1915 to 1917
St. Charles Theater	14625 Detroit Avenue	1915 to 1916
Homestead Theater Last Picture Show	11806 Detroit Avenue	1916 to 1974 1976
Lucier Theater Lakewood Little Theater	17825 Detroit Avenue	1916 to 1938
U-NO Theater Royal Theater	12224 Madison Avenue	1918 to 1930 1931 to 1952
Lakeside Theater?*	15012 Detroit Avenue?	1923 to 1924?
Detroit Theater	16407 Detroit Avenue	1924 to 1933 1938 to present
Lincoln Theater	15504 Madison Avenue	1924 to 1950
Hilliard Square Theater Westwood Art Theater Hilliard Square Theater	16409 Hilliard Road	1927 to 1961 1962 to 1986? 1988

* It is unclear from city directories if this theater actually existed or reflects a misprint in the directory.

ten to twenty-five cents.

Lakewood theaters were neighborhood theaters. They lacked the elegance of the Palace, Hippodrome, State, and Ohio theaters downtown or even the nearby Granada with its Spanish-inspired architecture, and murals of painted stars and clouds. Nevertheless, in comparison with today's shopping center mini-theater complexes, Lakewood theaters were both impressive and immense. When the Lincoln Theater (15504 Madison Avenue at Arthur) opened on August 20, 1923, it contained one thousand seats. The Hilliard Square Theater (16409 Hilliard), which opened in 1927, contained about twelve hundred seats. In addition to the arcade which linked Madison and Hilliard, the theater came equipped for live theater including catwalks, a greenroom, and three basement levels.

By 1954, Lakewood theaters had passed their peak. Just three were left, the Detroit, Hilliard Square, and Homestead. In the 1960s and 1970s theaters continued to struggle. The Homestead closed about 1974 only to re-emerge under a new marquee, The Last Picture Show, which remained open only a short time. Today the Homestead houses rock concerts. The Hilliard Square closed in 1961 but reopened as the Westwood Art Theater the following year. For several years the theater featured foreign films but shifted to porno movies when the attendance declined. Recently new management brought a return to the foreign film format but it proved unsuccessful. The theater is now up for sale. Only the Detroit survives, but it has recently remodeled to provide two smaller theaters.

It is difficult to fix the precise dates of Lakewood theaters. The preceding list is based on city directory listings. Since this source is not entirely accurate, the dates must be considered as approximate.

According to city directories, the Lakewood Theater was open from 1912 to 1922. Apparently it re-opened in 1924 and then closed for a final time in 1930.
Photograph by Paul Corell; courtesy of the Lakewood Historical Society

The U-NO theater at 12224 Madison Avenue, was open from 1918 to 1930. It is pictured here circa 1920.
Courtesy of Amelia Bendik Cotter

The Royal Theater at 12224 Madison Avenue, is shown here in the 1930s or 1940s. The Royal took over the U-NO theater. It opened in 1931 and remained open until 1952.
Courtesy of Home Federal Savings Bank

Lakewood's lone surviving motion picture theater, the Detroit first opened in 1924. Like other theaters it experienced difficulty during the worst years of the Great Depression and closed its doors in 1933. As the Depression came to an end the Detroit Theater reopened and has remained open. It is pictured here circa 1950. In 1988 the theater was divided into two smaller auditoriums.
Photograph by James Thomas; courtesy of the Cleveland Press Library and Collections, Cleveland State University Libraries

A typical youthful Saturday matinee audience glued to the screen at the Hilliard Square Theater in 1948. Photograph by James Thomas; courtesy of the Cleveland Press Library and Collections, Cleveland State University Libraries

Chapter 10
VIGNETTE
Herbert Gold, Fathers

Hard times were not unknown in the young suburb. The depression in late 1920 badly hurt the local automobile industry. Winton and Templar Motors suffered from the downturn. Their closings in 1924 threw employees out of work and, at least in the case of Templar, left stock holders with huge losses. In contrast, the Great Depression had an even more powerful impact. Some Lakewood residents lost their jobs and eventually their homes; desertion rates increased.

As the economic collapse rippled across industrial Cleveland and into the suburbs, merchants began to feel the crunch; soon survival came to be associated with success. For Sam Gold, owner of a grocery store on Detroit at West 117th as with many other shopkeepers, survival required sacrifice and long hours. It also necessitated a family effort. Sam's son, Herbert, drew on his family's experiences during the Depression to provide the base for his impressionistic book, *Fathers*, "a novel in the form of a memoir." The following excerpts suggest the Depression's impact touched all parts of Lakewood.

Caruso the Truck Driver used to toss me up, up, up toward the ceiling of our house, toward the starry, inpenetrable sky of Lakewood, Ohio, and that's how it wa before bedtime on Fridays in 1934. . . . On those Friday nights my mother kept an improvised boardinghouse fo the odd crew that worked weekends nearly around the clock in my father's store. Girls and men, they shucked corn on the back porch; they flirted with each other whil dropping yellow silk in baskets and pots; they bedded down on all corners of the house after my mother's grand meals served on paper plates. Like explorers, they dropped to sleep whenever they found a congenial moment. . . .

Work began at three in the morning during the spring and summer months; Caruso and my father and boy rolled through the predawn streets toward the marke to load up the truck with the earliest, choicest produce; b the time they rolled back from downtown Cleveland, top heavy with crates of crisp greens, bursting reds, juice dripping from corners of crates, Caruso singing and m father planning, the others had got the store in order, the displays ready, the doors cleared for the onrush of Depre sion bargain hunters. . . .

Caruso lifted me into the cab and proudly conducted me around the block. He drove the truck to the produce market empty, and then returned heaped high. He also delivered orders to the lonely and telephoning ric in their Great Lakes Antique mansions with the captain's turrets along Lake Avenue. They gave him dimes; gloomy butlers gave him dimes. And he transported the group of boarders who slept under my mother's wing on Friday nights. . . .

He was often paid at the store in "script," promises k bankrupt Cuyahoga County to hungry sewer workers, or I.O.U.'s from wolfish Black Legionnaires, or genuine Canadian Scotch with cherry pits floating in it (bootlegge eat too), or post-dated checks by little ladies in electric car who then asked: "Would you plug into me for an hour or two?"*

"What?"

"The battery needs just a little juice to get me home, Mr. Gold, and since you have already proven yourself such a gentleman—"

"Chrisamighty. Drive around to the back and tell the man to get out the extension cord."

And relief checks. And church funds. And ahoy the touch from old friends recently out of business. . . .

The farmers were famished amid so much food; the

 `le of the city went hungry; only the rats, spiders,
`dchucks, silverfish, and swooping black dawn birds
` no afterthoughts about the agonies of distribution in
`ne of waste and displeasure. Overhead, the market
`on dimmed into day. All over the city of Cleveland,
`a who had no work sat up, switched on the light,
`embered, groaned, and put out the light again. They
`` no work; they could try sleeping curved into the
`mth of their wives' bodies. They twitched back into
`b. There was great weakness abroad in those days.

*But my father wrestled the thickly evasive element of
e in the wind. He put both hands firmly upon the
*ds. He would make his business work, he would make
*'s Market pay, he would squirt the juice out of spoiling
*atoes—"MAKE GOOD SOUP!"; he wallowed with fat
* in the appetite of insecurity, showing his gold tooth for
*. "Who knows if the berries will keep over Labor Day?
*s anybody know? What if there's one bad berry
aked in underneath? Well, put in the cooler, We'll see."

*No fatalist, but a speculator, he did not examine
*h berry personally. He merely cast his eyes over the
*kets and scared them. His crocodile gaze deterred
d, stopped rot, mitigated fruit rust. . . .

*Through the week, my brothers and cousins and I,
*eldest, we all stayed late on the playground of Taft
*ool in Lakewood, Ohio. Home was dark, silent, empty;
` mother and father worked all day. . . .

*We found the slow freight which ran from Cleveland
*`ittsburgh and Cleveland to Toledo. The Nickel Freight
*`ins were covered with a crawling, clinging live weight,
* weight of homeless men, and we watched them with
*zzlement. . . . why did they stare at us without expres-
`n from the tops of their boxcars?

Reprinted from Herbert Gold, *Fathers*, 77-9, 83-4,
2, 94, 96, 98, 143, by permission of the author.

Black Legion" Gold refers to the Black Legion else-
vhere in *Fathers* as having "haunted the countryside
around Cleveland. It made contact with the Klan in
Parma and the Bund in Lakewood. . . ." It was a terrorist
organization that was virulently anti-Catholic, anti-
Semitic, and anti-Black.

Sam and Frieda Gold, the parents of novelist Herbert Gold, came to the United States at an early age. Pushed by the growing anti-Semitism in Russia and Eastern Europe and pulled by the promise of opportunity in the United States, Samuel S. Gold and Frieda Volk Frankel eventually ended up in Cleveland. Sam and Frieda married in 1923.

With his brothers, Sam worked variously as a commission merchant and operated a series of fruit and vegetable stores, most on Cleveland's west side. In 1923, Sam and his brother opened their first Lakewood store at 11721 Detroit Avenue. Within a few years the brothers had three stores in Lakewood. Although the location of some of these stores changed from year to year, Sam took over the store at 11721 Detroit while Morris ran the store at 15100 Detroit (at Gladys); they operated these stores until the early 1940s when both brothers began new careers in real estate.

In June 1927, Sam and Frieda Gold purchased the store site they had operated for four years. The onset of the Depression only added to the difficulties of running a small business. For the Golds survival meant long hours and hard work. At the same time Gold's Market evolved from a fruit and vegetable store into a grocery; with "self-service" shopping, it became one of Lakewood's first "master markets." Frieda Gold recalls that the business survived because they had the lowest prices. Saturday was the biggest shopping day and required additional clerks. Local customers brought wagons to carry their groceries home while some came to Gold's Market from as far away as Rocky River and Bay Village.

In 1925, both Sam and Morris moved

their families to Lakewood to be closer to their stores. Two years later, Sam and Frieda built a double house at 1229 Hathaway, while Morris and Anna Gold bought a double at 1252/54 Hathaway. Both families remained on Hathaway until the early 1940s. The children attended Taft and Emerson. Two of Sam and Frieda's sons, Sidney and Herbert went to Lakewood High—Herbert, the oldest, graduated in January 1942.

At Lakewood High School, Herbert was active in "Ping Pong, Hi-Forum, Speakers [along with twins Don and Doug Geiger], Honor Society, and English Council." He also served as *High Times* editor and "Editor Emeritus." The paper sought to be "the organ of scholastic freedom: truthful, pertinent, liberal" and cost less than three cents a copy to produce.

With a prolific and much-honored writing career, Herbert Gold easily ranks as the best writer to come from Lakewood; critics rate him as one of the foremost literary chroniclers of life in modern America. Gold has produced twenty-four novels, four volumes of short stories, two works of non-fiction, and numerous articles. His many awards include the PEN American Center West Special Achievement Award for Body of Work presented to him in 1988. The recipient of prestigious Guggenheim and Ford Foundation fellowships, Gold has taught at Harvard, Cornell, Western Reserve, Stanford, and the University of California. In 1987, he was inducted into the Lakewood High School Hall of Fame.

Herbert Gold, second from left, was editor of the Lakewood High Times from 1940 to 1941. With him are, left to right: Fisher, Gold, Hawthorne, and Ellstrom. With the Depression largely over and the United States not yet at war, the early 1940s were good ones for Lakewood High School. In 1940 to 1941, the football team won the league title; the basketball team, "using a fast breaking, ball-hawking attack" went all the way to the state finals. The following year the High Times garnered two national awards; the football team was again league champion; the swimming team placed third in the state; and Harry Figgie pitched a no-hitter for the baseball team. [Harry Figgie is now president of Figgie International, Incorporated, a very large holding company that includes Rawlings Sporting Goods]. From the

Sam and Frieda Gold with two of their four sons, Robert on the left and Sidney on the right are pictured here in front of the Colonial Motel on Euclid Avenue in Cleveland in September 1964. Following the closing of their respective businesses in the early 1940s, Sam and his broth Morris each began new careers in re estate. The Colonial Motel represente one of Sam's ventures.
Courtesy of Frieda Gold

By the time this photograph was taken around 1933, Gold's Market at 11721 Detroit Avenue evolved from its origins as a fruit and vegetable store into a grocery. Advertisements in the store window indicate a wide range of items, from ham at twenty-two cents per pound to pot roast at fourteen cents per pound, eggs at twenty-one cents a dozen, Rinso, Oxydol, and Ginger Ale Stacked watermelons dominated half the store's windows. Here passersby vi vegetables and fruits in the window while a clerk waits on a customer. The Lakewood Bakery is to the left.
Courtesy of Ann Buscho

Lakewood High School Cinema, 1941, page 51.

*...hor Herbert Gold is portrayed here
...bout a beard on June 19, 1962,
...en* Fathers *was published. In 1968,
...ers received the California Litera-
...e Medal; earlier Gold's* The Man Who
...s Not with It *received the Ohioana
...k Award. In 1988 Gold received an
...orary doctoral degree from the City
...iversity of New York and won the
...N American Center West Special
...ievement Award for Body of Work.
...is the author of twenty-four novels
...d numerous other works.
...rtesy of the Cleveland Press Library
...d Collections, Cleveland State
...iversity Libraries*

*In addition to Herbert Gold, Lakewood
has produced a number of fine artists.
Although Burgess Meredith did not live
in the city long, he did begin his acting
career here. He dated that beginning to
his appearance as a soloist at the Lakewood Methodist Church. The Merediths
moved to Lakewood when Burgess was
about nine years old. The son of a
physician, Meredith attended Lincoln
School and in 1918 he participated in
the Gaston Allen Masonic Lodge annual
children's party. Even at a young age
Meredith, dressed in a navy suit, attracted attention when his picture was
featured in the Lakewood* Press. *After
several years, the Meredith family moved
back east. He returned to Cleveland
after a brief stay at Amherst College.
With his brother he started a haberdashery store on Fairmount Boulevard
in Cleveland Heights. Within two months
the business went bankrupt. Over the
next few years Meredith worked at a
variety of jobs including seaman and
salesman. His acting career began in
earnest playing Tweedledee in* Alice in
Wonderland, *and went on to a distinguished career on Broadway. He also
established an impressive reputation as
a movie actor in such films as* True
Confessions, *and starred as "The
Penguin" in the TV series "Batman." He
is pictured here from* The Sentinel,
*around 1979.
Courtesy of the Cleveland Press Library
and Collections, Cleveland State
University Libraries*

*Actor Hal Holbrook is protrayed here in
the NBC Television Network series "The
Bold Ones." Holbrook moved to
Lakewood to live with his grandparents
(the A.V. Holbrooks) who lived at 17540
Lake Avenue. He graduated from Saint
Augustine Academy (elementary school)
in 1938. Holbrook remembered as a
child being rescued by the Lakewood
Fire Department when he and his sisters
became trapped on the shale cliff above
Lake Erie at the foot of Webb Road. He
also had fond memories of his years at
Saint Augustine. After he graduated
from Saint Augustine's, Holbrook
attended Culver Academy, and later
Denison University. He began his acting
career at Cain Park Theater in 1942. his
film career includes roles in such movies
as* The Great White Hope, The Group,
Julia, *and* All the President's Men. *He
also did a five-year stint on the television
soap opera, "A Brighter Day." The
photograph was taken in October 1970.
Courtesy of the Cleveland Press Library
and Collections, Cleveland State
University Libraries*

Shown here is Sammy Kaye on the "Sunday Serenade" at NBC Radio on Sundays at 2:00 PM, circa 1947. Big band leader Sammy Kaye was born in Lakewood and grew up in the Village and nearby. His family came to the United States from Czechoslovakia. He attended Ohio University on a track scholarship and studied civil engineering; he was active in extracurricular activities, especially musical ones. After graduation he opened the Campus Inn, a gathering spot for college students. Kaye's band gained national attention when it broadcast coast to coast on the NBC network from the Cleveland Country Club. The band had established a national following when it debuted in New York City in 1938. The Sammy Kaye Orchestra had a series of hit records including "Rosalie," "Love Walked In," "All Ashore," "Hurry Home," "Penny Serenade," "Drean Valley," "Daddy," "Remember Pearl Harbor," "I Left My Heart on the Stage Door Ca teen," "Chickery Chick," "I'm a Big G Now," "The Gypsy," "That's My Desire "Serenade of the Bells," "Careless Hands," and "Harbor Lights." The ba which played under the slogan of "Su and Sway with Sammy Kaye," was known as one of the "sweet bands" the swing band era. They played at th inaugural balls for both Presidents Nixon and Reagan. According to the New York Times, Kaye "good-humore chastised himself for having worked s hard to disguise his foreign ancestry" after Lawrence Welk had become po lar. Kaye died in 1987 at the age of 7 Photograph by NBC Photo Service; courtesy of the Cleveland Press Librar and Collections, Cleveland State University Libraries

The comic strip, "The Born Loser," is the creation of Lakewood cartoonist Art Sansom. The strip won the Reuben Award for the best humor cartoon strip of 1988. This cartoon is a self-caricature of the artist. He presented it to his son, Chip, as a present. Chip is now a co-artist with his father.

hapter 11
)epression,
ransition, and
Iaturity:
)30 to 1960

could feel the Depression deepen, but you could not
out the window and see it. Men who lost their jobs
pped out of sight. They were quiet, and you had to
w just when and where to find them.
  Caroline Bird, *The Invisible Scar*, 1966

By the late 1920s Lakewood had come into its own. As Cleveland's "second city," Lakewood also ranked as one of the larger cities in the state. With a wide range of community organizations, a hospital, and a thriving social and cultural life, Lakewood stood out as one of the area's best places to live. Lakewood public schools established a solid reputation for scholarship, while the high school's athletic programs regularly produced top quality teams in a variety of sports.

Ironically, just as the community reached its peak of success and population, the bottom fell out. The Great Depression helped change the fate of the rising new community. The glow and optimism that so marked the "live wires" of the first thirty years of the century disappeared as the community struggled just to survive. From 1930 on, the city's population began a long, slow decline while a new generation of community leaders confronted problems never anticipated by its founders. World War II and to a lesser extent the Korean war also demanded heavy community involvement; in turn these efforts continued the processes of change that World War I helped initiate. If post-World War II Lakewood fell short of the promise it held in the 1920s, the community could still bask in its accomplishments while a new generation of suburbanites began to make their own imprint on the city.

Just as the 1929 stock market crash announced the Great Depression's coming, the sharp economic downturn made clear its arrival. When local industry cut back on production and laid off workers, other businesses responded with cut-backs in employees, wages, and hours. These actions then caused a series of further cuts as the economy spiraled downward. Reduced wages began to affect other areas. Across metropolitan Cleveland home-buyers confronted the possibility of foreclosure and savings institutions faced bankruptcy, while cities experienced sharp declines in revenue. All of the forces that had combined to make suburb-building possible in the first thirty years of the new century now seemed to conspire to undo what had been done.

As early as April 1930 Lakewood city government reported a 24 percent decline in tax collections. A. I. Kauffman, the finance director and soon-to-be mayor, noted the precipitous decline in the real estate market: "you almost have to give land away." Between 1930 and 1933, real estate valuation in the city plummeted by sixty million dollars; by 1934 city revenues from property taxes declined by nearly one-half of that in 1930. Then in 1933, the city lost part of its funds when the Union and Guardian Trust Banks collapsed.

While revenues declined, the need for city services grew dramatically. Between 1931 and 1933, the city's relief expenditures quadrupled. Much of this relief went for groceries, fuel, rent, room and board, and medical services for needy Lakewood residents. Nevertheless, city efforts fell short of the community's needs. In his 1933 annual report Mayor Kauffman noted that "more relief work could have been done were it not for the fact that the funds did not permit…the big item in the relief work was the purchase of groceries and other commodities for those out of employment."

To make ends meet, city council voted for 20 percent pay cuts for most employees; administrators received smaller cuts while the mayor and council promised to "voluntarily" rebate a portion of their salaries back to the city. In 1935, most employees received small "raises" while full restoration did not take place until 1938. Other public employees received sharp cuts; in 1932, teachers experienced a 10 to 15 percent pay cut, while library employees went three months without pay.

Besides city relief efforts, the community fought back on a series of fronts. Some churches, including Grace Presbyterian, took up collections for a "fund against which members, caught without ready cash, may borrow for necessities." In 1932, the Lakewood Sewing Circle, and the First Church of Christ, Scientist began a program to collect milk from the Ohio Farmers Milk Service and bread from the Spang and General Baking Companies. Under the direction of Mr. and Mrs. Charles Gibson, the group distributed food to Lakewood's hungry from election booths on Warren Road, and the Madison Park Shelter House. In 1933, about 750 Lakewood families received food daily from these centers. Mayor Kauffman noted that this work was "a God-send to many many unemployed people."

Finally, in the fall of 1932, as "unemployment became more and more prevalent," the city established its own employment bureau. While the bureau placed many unemployed men and women, most positions were temporary and part time. Many of these jobs were with the city since the shattered economy provided few permanent or full-time jobs. As late as January 1938, Lakewood's relief roles still contained 181 families.

The Depression did not affect everyone to the same extent and in the same ways. Some barely felt its impact, although they could see others around them struggling. When their tenants proved unable to pay rent, Henry Burton Townsend lost much of his family's (Beach) extensive land holdings in Lakewood; he died shortly after. To make ends meet, some drug stores sold illegal gin to customers; one resident recalls that as a young delivery boy he regularly took pint bottles to some of Lakewood's larger lakefront homes. (The recipe for this gin included half a pint each of alcohol and water with several drops of glycerin to sweeten it and a drop of oil of juniper berries).

Out of disaster some fresh hopes arose. For the

Geiger family the Depression brought a shattering end successful chain of thirteen clothing stores across Clev land. Undaunted, in 1932 Charlie Geiger, Sr., opened a new store at the corner of Warren Road and Detroit. Fo years later they moved nearby to their current location and soon became a Lakewood institution. The Depress offered the Schermer Brothers Department Store an op portunity to expand. Unable to find a business tenant f their property at 15607 Madison, they operated their ov Lakewood Department Store for several years. At the sa time Cleveland's Bailey Department Store opened its branch store at Warren Road and Detroit.

Ironically, the Depression brought Lakewood fam lies and neighbors closer together. When young adults lost their jobs or experienced cutbacks, they frequently moved back home to save money; elderly parents also moved in with their children. With limited resources, many families found new, less expensive diversions. Josephine Angelo recalled her family often played gam together. Clifton Park residents also felt the Depression pinch. Blythe Gehring noted that young married reside of Clifton Park started the Park One Hundred Club in th fall of 1930 to maintain their active social life. Since "th Depression years left little money for entertainment," c members pooled their resources. Gehring remembere Guy Lombardo's Orchestra playing at dances during the 1930s, while the "keynote was elegance."

The Depression's impact could be seen in other ways. Carl Dryer recalled that "most of us married later than kids do now; by 1935 things were stabilizing and people started marrying." The city's health department also chronicled changes in Lakewood's social life; although childbirths increasingly took place in hospitals, many families delayed starting families until their finan situation stabilized, and then they had fewer children. T health department also noted that the pressures created by the Depression produced an increased death rate.

Fortunately, the city did not have to fight the Depr sion alone. With Franklin D. Roosevelt's election as pres dent and the institution of his "New Deal," Lakewood benefited substantially both in employment and civic improvements. In an effort to put the unemployed back to work as a means of boosting the economy, the Roose velt administration proposed a series of programs to fur local public works projects. Under the Civil Works Administration (CWA) and the Federal Works Progress Administration (WPA) Lakewood received funding for major capital improvements, including widening and re paving streets, maintenance work on public buildings, and construction of water mains, storm sewers, a new sewage disposal plant, tennis courts at Lakewood, Madison, and Wagar Parks; a bandstand and comfort station i Lakewood Park, a municipal garage, and a breakwater to provide a dumpsite for twenty-five years. The latter even tually added five acres to Lakewood Park. While measur ably improving the city, these projects also gave work to ny unemployed workers.

If the Depression brought families and the community closer together to confront common problems, crisis also unleashed other forces. A number of hate organizations appeared across the region that targeted other Americans for attack. Because their organizations were often secret, it is difficult to know their influence or impact on Lakewood residents. Nevertheless, groups like the Ku Klux Klan, the Black Legion, the German-American Bund, and the followers of Detroit radio priest, Father Charles Coughlin, had a presence both on the west side generally and in Lakewood. Most of these groups singled out Catholics, African-, and Jewish-Americans.

With the onset of World War II, Lakewood residents again had a confrontation with a world-wide conflagration. As with the First World War, the Second elicited great sacrifice from Lakewood residents; it also speeded changes introduced by the first war.

Once again, young and not so young Lakewood men and women volunteered for service for their country. This war, however, would last longer and claim an even greater toll in life and injury. As with World War I, all sections of Lakewood contributed to military service and acted behind the war effort; they also felt the pain and anguish of loss. On October 24, 1944, the Cleveland *Plain Dealer* reported the deaths of two Lakewood flyers. Lieut. Charles Parmalee, an ace pilot credited with shooting down five German planes, was shot down and killed over Belgium. Lieut. Milan Mikulec died when his bomber crashed during a training flight in South Dakota.

At home the war also meant sacrifice as the domestic economy geared up for the war effort. Wilson School on Warren Road housed Lakewood's "war effort." Here the draft board decided who would be drafted and whose work was essential to the war industry. Nearby, Carlyn Irwin ran the Lakewood Ration Board that issued stamps for everything from sugar and coffee to gasoline and automobile tires. The Red Cross also made its contribution from its offices in the old school building. Once again Lakewood women made bandages and other items to support the war effort. Across the city, school children purchased stamps and war bonds to make their contribution to the war effort. Older Lakewoodites dusted off their "victory gardens" once again. Even more than in World War I, Lakewood residents cut back, observing meatless days and trying to find palatable ways to cook untried parts of animal anatomy. They carefully saved metal and tin cans for city special collections to help the war effort. As it turned out these programs aimed more at domestic morale than recycling material for the war effort.

While some Lakewood women, especially those in the Village, had worked in factories well before the war, World War II provided even greater opportunities for industrial employment. Josephine Angelo, who had not worked since her marriage in 1921, recalled why she went to work at the bomber plant in Berea: "since my son was fighting for our country, I wanted to help out in some way, too." For about forty cents an hour she inspected bombs.

Other changes became apparent; some held great importance for the post war period. As war completed the return to prosperity, Lakewood youth once again began to marry at a younger age; although the baby boom awaited the end of the war and the return of the troops, the birth rate also began to rise during the war. By 1950, Lakewood schools would again confront an overabundance of school-aged children, as they had in the 1920s.

From the end of World War II to the beginning of the 1960s, Lakewood finally began to enjoy the benefits of an earlier generation's efforts at community-building. Both the Depression and the War brought significant changes. The sharp contrasts between the five landscapes diminished, as did some of the tension between them. Moreover, residents continued to build on the community's social and cultural life by introducing new organizations and programs. Lakewood finally began to emerge as a mature community with an impressive record and a growing self-consciousness about its past.

While Lakewood's population declined by over four thousand between 1930 and 1960, even more significant changes took place. This period witnessed a major transformation of lakefront estates. Well before the Great Depression, many of Lakewood's wealthiest residents had either died or moved away. In 1918, the Rhodes estate reverted to public land. The opening of Edgewater Drive from Wilbert to Lakewood Park bisected the property of lakefront estates. Subdivision of this land produced greater density housing although the attractive Georgian revival houses designed by architect Clarence Mack proved to be quite distinctive. In 1925 the Wintons moved to Clifton Park; by 1961, Roseneath was a boarding house. Theodor Kuntz's mansion remained intact after his death in 1937, and millionaire Robert R. Morrow maintained the house for some years after. In 1961, developers removed Kundtz' marvelous "castle" and replaced it with sixteen homes packed together along the new Kirtland Lane.

The lakefront landscape was not the only area to undergo changes. While Clifton Park escaped the developer's wrecking ball, it no longer claimed as many eminent or well-placed Clevelanders as it once had. At the other end of the city, Village residents began to experience considerable job mobility. In its early years nearly 85 percent of residents held unskilled jobs. By 1940, only 15 percent had such positions while most were semi- and skilled workers. Many Villagers had already moved out to other parts of Lakewood and suburban Cleveland.

While the Depression profoundly affected individual businesses, Lakewood's commercial landscape remained relatively intact to the 1950s. The two most significant changes involved dramatic growth in the numbers of gas stations and taverns. The latter came with the end of Prohibition in the 1930s; by 1950 neighborhood bars were ubiquitous. The widespread growth of gas stations reflected the growing reliance on the automobile rather than the streetcar or bus. In contrast, small grocery stores, especially those that specialized in meats, fruits, and vegetables, experienced great difficulties; as with Gold's Market few survived to 1960.

Nevertheless, important changes in transportation during the period augured major changes for social life and commercial enterprise. The decline of the streetcar profoundly affected the nature of life in the streetcar suburb. By the late 1920s, high overhead and competition from automobiles began to erode the streetcar's base. After World War II the situation became untenable. Service on the Clifton line ended in 1947, while the Detroit and Madison lines terminated in 1951 and 1954 respectively. Buses replaced streetcars and the private Lakewood Rapid Transit Company provided service to Cleveland's Public Square (1937-1954). Nevertheless, many riders had already deserted mass transit for automobiles.

While suburban life in the 1950s shared much with that of the 1920s, there were important changes. Electric refrigerators, gas and oil furnaces ended regular visits from ice and coal dealers. Increasingly, home delivery of goods such as bread and milk declined, as did the numbers of street vendors. Nevertheless, bakeries, grocery stores, beauty shops, and druggists remained within walking distance of most city residents.

If the young suburb had clearly sought to develop the cultural life of the community, a number of areas remained undeveloped. During the 1930s and 1940s, a new generation sought to fill these gaps by founding theatrical and musical groups. While these amateur ventures could not compete with Cleveland's professional companies, they provided residents with opportunities to participate in the community's cultural life.

Growing out of a Junior Chamber of Commerce production in 1930, a small group of thespians formed the Guild of the Masques. Initially they performed in rented halls, at churches, and in public schools. Renamed the Lakewood Little Theatre in 1933, within five years they established a more permanent home at the Lucier motion picture theater at 17823 Detroit. By 1947, they purchased the theater and within ten years they owned the building outright.

Undaunted by difficult conditions in the early years, these avid theater buffs rehearsed wherever they could find a room. During World War II they selected plays that contained more female parts to circumvent the shortage of male thespians. In later years Lakewood Little Theatre regularly offered eight productions per year. Founded shortly after the Theatre, the Lakewood Civic Chorus and the Light Opera Company greatly expanded the community's cultural offerings.

As the community matured, it also grew more interested in its past. Three years before the city's semi-centennial celebration, two books appeared that reflected this new found historical interest. Under the guidance of Mrs. Milton McIntyre, the Lakewood Chapter of the Daughters of the American Revolution published their studious volume entitled *The Early Days of Lakewood.* the same time E. George Lindstrom, a journalist and writer, produced his chatty *Story of Lakewood, Ohio.* The multiple events of the 1939 semi-centennial also helped focus attention on the community. Through its historical pageant, "Wagons West," many residents either participated directly or attended one of the four performances.

Nevertheless, it was Margaret Butler who single-handedly led a campaign to foster interest in Lakewood history. Highlighted by the publication of *The Lakewood Story* in 1949, she regularly produced newspaper columns about the community's past. In addition, she chaired Lakewood's Golden Anniversary History Pageant committee in 1961, revived the Lakewood Historical Society 1952, and led a successful campaign to preserve and relocate the "Oldest Stone House" as a museum in Lakewood Park.

Lakewood had come into its own in other ways as well. While it is more difficult to evaluate accurately the quality of the educational system, Lakewood Schools ranked high in the state on the basis of test scores on standardized exams and on the number of graduates who went on to college. In athletics, Lakewood also stood out. When the Cleveland *Press* published a review of Ohio high school athletic programs in 1957, it ranked Lakewood High School second only to "all sports leader" Canton McKinley, based on how schools placed overall in state meets since 1920. When the *Press* compared the number of state championship teams in all sports since 1920, Lakewood again came in second, this time to Cleveland's East Tech. Not surprisingly, Lakewood held strong positions in several individual sports: first in cross-country, second in track and field, third in swimming, fourth in tennis, and tenth in wrestling. Lakewood's cross-town streetcar rivals, Shaw and Cleveland Heights barely made the *Press* list.

By the end of the 1950s, the city experienced a major building boom; part of this took place in the public sector as new leadership sought to expand the limited public landscape. The city had already acquired the hospital in the early 1930s. In 1959, it finally replaced its aging city hall in Lakewood Park with a new municipal building on the site of Memorial Park, at Detroit and Alameda. Major programs also upgraded and expanded public school buildings, including the construction of the "L-Room," a new gymnasium and an impressive civic auditorium. New recreational facilities included swimming pools at Lakewood and Madison Parks. Nor was the city the only active group here. In 1950, Clifton Club members celebrated the opening of a new club house; in 1942 a fire had destroyed the previous building.

This outpouring of energy and construction helped the city win national recognition. In 1960, *Look* magazine the National Municipal League named Lakewood a runner-up" in their "All American City" contest. Despite award and the deserved acclaim for other projects, wever, all was not well in the city. While its population wly declined; nearby Parma grew rapidly and by 1960 laced Lakewood as the county's "second city." As the city grew older, so too did its housing stock and public buildings. Older industries also began to experience increasing difficulties while newer homes in more distant suburbs attracted some Lakewoodites away. These events produced problems for the city's treasury and cast a long shadow on its future.

The Cleveland Press on February 27, 1933 announces the growing difficulty with banks as the Depression reaches near the bottom.
Courtesy of the Cleveland Press Library and Collections, Cleveland State University Libraries

The Great Depression was hard on small businesses. Despite the large number of small "fruit and vegetable" stores like Gold's Market and Lakewood Fruit Company, shown here circa 1930, many survived the hard times. Frank Sinagra's Lakewood Fruit Company is remarkable in its ability to survive until 1981. Frank "Nate" Sinagra, who migrated from Messina, Sicily, purchased his store at 16924 Detroit Avenue from Charles Fazio in 1925.
Courtesy of Anthony Sinagra

The interior of Sinagra's Market, at 16924 Detroit Avenue is shown here circa 1940.
Courtesy of Anthony Sinagra

The Lakewood American Legion Mounted Troops are pictured here participating in the Memorial Day Parade in 1936.
Courtesy of the Western Reserve Historical Society

Shown here is a South Lakewood bus to Rocky River circa 1937. For a time Lakewood even had its own private transit company. According to a 1939 Suburban News and Herald *advertisement, "thirty minutes and one-and-a-half cents per mile is all it costs in time and money when you ride the luxurious coaches of the Lakewood Rapid Transit to and from downtown Cleveland." Cleveland Transit System purchased the bus line in 1954.*
Photograph by Byron Filkins; courtesy of the Cleveland Press Library and Collections, Cleveland State University Libraries

Downtown Lakewood appears bustling with traffic and shoppers. From the Lakewood High School *Cinema, 1938, page 164.*

Begun in the early 1930s, Lakewood Little Theater took over the Lucier motion picture theater (17823 Detroit) in 1933. They regularly provided amateur theater productions for the community through the war despite some difficulty finding enough men to play parts.
Courtesy of Beck Center

Shown here is Battery B's new Lakewood Armory nearing completion on June 8, 1939. In 1949 the armory was expanded and garages added. The city purchased the armory in 1982 and sold it to the Beck Center the following year.
Photograph by Kenneth D. Newell; courtesy of the Cleveland Press Library and Collections, Cleveland State University Libraries

The community's first soldiers of tomorrow are back home from Camp [Sh]elby, Mississippi, on holiday leave," [i]s the quote from the Cleveland Press [of] December 28, 1940, page 9. Even [bef]ore the United States entered World [Wa]r II, Lakewood residents had begun [to v]olunteer for service. From left to right [are] Corp. Frank Krasman, Corp. Michael [G]rilla, Pvt. Steve Polansky, Pvt. Frank [Ca]sor, and First Sgt. John Karbovanecz. [Eve]n more than the First World War, the [Sec]ond World War claimed the lives of

many Lakewood residents; many others found their lives dramatically changed. In 1942, Lakewood resident Lt. Richard Lehr, a pilot in the 431st Bombardment Squadron was reported missing in action on the first day of the Battle of the Solomons. Earlier he had been cited for gallantry in battle during the Battle of Midway. His loss extended to his friends as well as his parents and his aunt, Ruth Lehr, who helped raise him.
Courtesy of Dan Chabek

The Starettes—women bakery truck drivers from Star Bakery, were photographed by G. Zahn in 1943. World War II changed the lives of both men and women. To aid the war effort many American women went to work at nontraditional jobs. Driving a home delivery bakery truck was one of those. Justine Swan and Catherine Schroeder of 2085 Wascana Avenue pitched in to work as Starettes for the Star Baking Company.
Courtesy of the Cleveland Press Library and Collections, Cleveland State University Libraries

[Dr.] Antonio Longoria and furry friend [ar]e pictured in his laboratory at 11802 [Ed]gewater Drive, circa 1941, now the [Sh]oreham Apartments. Dr. Longoria was [bo]rn and educated in Madrid, Spain. [Du]ring the war he lived in the Traymore [Ap]artment Building at Donald and [Cl]ifton. His research focused on new [we]lding techniques, electricity, and [ca]ncer. His invention of a new welding [te]chnique brought him considerable [in]come. At the time, however, neighbors [we]re unsure of his research and thought [th]e worst. These stories grew immea-

surably when Dr. Longoria told reporters he was working on a "death ray." The neighborhood had earlier experienced mysterious scientists. From about the time of World War I to 1930, Arthur Bullock operated a laboratory at 12027 Lake Avenue. Although he did research on magnesium, Bullock refused to comment about his work leaving neighbors to imagine strange experiments.
Photographed by James Thomas; courtesy of the Cleveland Press Library and Collections, Cleveland State University Libraries

Aiding the war effort included a wide range of activities including keeping a Victory garden; having meatless days; recycling metal, newspapers, and lard; and in this case sharing one's automobile with others so as to conserve on the nation's resources. These six young men, all from Lakewood, show off their recently acquired "Share The Ride" buttons on May 29, 1942.
Courtesy of the Cleveland Press Library and Collections, Cleveland State University Libraries

War efforts enlisted students as well. Classrooms competed against classrooms, schools against schools, and city against city to raise money for the war effort. Each week school children would purchase war stamps with their savings and then paste the stamps into a book. When the stamp book was filled it could be traded in for a United States Savings Bond. The teacher here may be Miss Celia Garley circa 1944.
Courtesy of the Lakewood Public Schools

Another part of the war effort required the rationing of vital materials. This included everything from food to gasoline and automobile tires. The Ration Board, located in Wilson School, issued each person, adult or child, a ration book. Without ration stamps you could not buy those items that were controlled. That required families to combine their stamps together and to save them for some time before they could make a purchase for some items.
Courtesy of Miriam Borchert

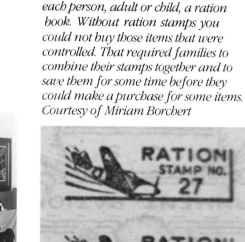

Lakewood women joined Lakewood men in the military. As often happened with the military, equipment assigned did not always fit. Elinor Jacko's Army issue boots were size 12, six sizes too large for her, as pictured here on December 15, 1943.
Courtesy of Mary Jacko

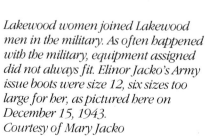

For many Lakewood residents, as elsewhere in the country, the end of the w seemed never to come. At last families long separated could come together again, and fathers could get acquaint with children they had not seen for several years. V-E Day, May 8, 1945, u the day Germany surrendered as V-J Day, September 2, 1945, was the day Japan surrendered to the Allies. Show here are some children parading dow Clifton Boulevard in Lakewood.
Courtesy of the Cleveland Press Librar and Collections, Cleveland State University Libraries

The end of the war brought difficult housing conditions. Few new houses had been built during the Depression or World War II and now there was a great demand for homes by couples and families that could now afford a home. Lakewood's Memorial Park shown here on May 20, 1947, provided temporary housing for veterans and their families. Memorial Park is the site of City Hall. Courtesy of the Cleveland Press Library and Collections, Cleveland State University Libraries

On April 11, 1946, General Dwight David Eisenhower, later U.S. president, came to Lakewood High School to honor his personal pilot, Maj. Lawrence Hansen, who served Eisenhower during World War II. Hansen graduated from L.H.S. in 1937. The Cinema noted that "a tremendous ovation greeted the general as he joined the faculty and student representatives on the platform surrounded by a special guard of honor of veterans." From Lakewood High School Cinema—1946, page 155.

o sooner was World War II over than e Cold War began. In 1958 school ildren across the country such as nnie Smith, shown here, were issued "og tags" so their bodies could be entified in the event of a nuclear ·ack. The Civil Defense agency set up mb shelters in schools and other public ildings while school children learned "duck and cover" in case of a ·uclear attack. At the same time, volun- ·rs, equipped with binoculars, climbed op tall buildings to scan the skies for ·ssible enemy bombers. Undaunted, ·hool children exchanged their dog tags

as a sign they were "going steady." Photograph by Byron Filkins; courtesy of the Cleveland Press Library and Collections, Cleveland State University Libraries

On bitterly cold January 11, 1942 a devastating fire completely destroyed the Clifton Club. The local press noted that it was the city's most disastrous fire in twenty years and represented a loss of seventy-five thousand dollars. Fortunately the Club's nine employees escaped unharmed. Photograph by Phototechnics, Inc.; courtesy of the Cleveland Press Library and Collections, Cleveland State University Libraries

Members of the Clifton Club regrouped after the fire and the new club house opened formally on June 3, 1950. The club celebrated its fiftieth anniversary in June 1952.
Photograph by Bernie Noble; courtesy of the Cleveland Press Library and Collections, Cleveland State University Libraries

The formal lounge of the new Clifton Club is pictured here in 1950. Photograph by Fred Bottomer; courtesy of the Cleveland Press Library and Collections, Cleveland State University Libraries

Founded in 1921, the Lakewood Kiwanis Club counted many of Lakewood's leading citizens among its charter members including Rev. A. J. Wright of Lakewood Presbyterian Church, Lakewood Press editor Capt. Walter Pagan, Justice of the Peace Henry Calvert, automobile dealer H. B. Townsend, and funeral directors William R. Daniels and Fred Branch. By 1929, the Kiwanis regularly attracted about eighty members to meetings. Within its first nine years, the club raised over thirteen thousand dollars for charities including nearly six thousand dollars for Lorain tornado victims and five thousand dollars for the Boys' Lodge. During the Great Depression Kiwanians collected

clothes for the needy for six consecutive years from 1930 to 1936. Following World War II, Lakewood civic and fraternal organizations including the Kiwanis Club redoubled their efforts. Kiwanians instituted a Scholarship Foundation in 1954 that has grown over the years; they also provided major funding for the Open Pavilion in Lakewood Park in 1971. The photograph here is cropped; only one-third of the members attending the outing are shown here on their annual outing on August 1, 1945. Mayor Amos Kaufman is on the far left in the second row. Photograph by Miller Ertter Studios; courtesy of James McGorray

Maj. Gen. Curtis Le May, a World War hero is flanked by Judge Donald Lyba ger on the right, at the Masonic Lodge Installation, circa 1945. Le May was named "Man of the Year" by the Lakewood Merchants Association. Courtesy of the Lakewood Historical Society

After President Harry Truman removed Gen. Douglas MacArthur from his command of U.S. forces during the Korean War, MacArthur toured the country, including Lakewood, as part of a triumphal return. In Lakewood, huge crowds lined the route of the motorcade along Detroit in September 1951. At the end of his tour he addressed Congress and issued his famous line that "old soldiers never die; they just fade away." Courtesy of the Cleveland Press Library and Collections, Cleveland State University Libraries

Margaret Butler (1898-1971) shows off her new book, A Pictorial History of the Western Reserve, circa 1965. Margaret Butler was born in Cleveland and graduated from Smith College. She helped organize the Smith College Alumnae Club in Lakewood and founded the Lakewood Historical Society. For five years she wrote a regular column for the Lakewood Post on Lakewood history. She then converted that work into two books: The Lakewood Story (1949) and Romance in Lakewood Streets (1962). Her third book, the pictorial history of the Western Reserve won the first award for pictorial histories of Americana. In 1949 Lakewood named her its outstanding citizen for her community activities and her writing. She was responsible for saving the "oldest stone house" and having it removed to Lakewood Park where it serves as the home of the Lakewood Historical Society. To help the project, she borrowed over three thousand dollars on her own home. In 1961, the Cleveland branch of the American Institute of Architects honored her and Lakewood for preserving the house. Photograph by Herman Seid; Cleveland Press Library and Collections, Cleveland State University Libraries

By 1953, downtown Lakewood bustled with daytime shoppers. However, the streetcar that had appeared in many earlier photographs was missing from the landscape. The automobile, and traffic jams, became more common. Photograph by Bernie Noble; courtesy of the Cleveland Press Library and Collections, Cleveland State University Libraries

159

In the post-war period, grocery stores became "super markets." Nevertheless, at least one store was well within walking distance of almost every home. Here an A. & P. and a Fisher Brothers store compete circa 1940. The new shopping center, a strip development with parking in front and the rear, began to reflect the growing impact of the automobile on the streetcar suburb. Nevertheless, streetcar tracks and brick pavement still present on Detroit.
Courtesy of the Cleveland Press Library and Collections, Cleveland State University Libraries

Exemplary of the status Lakewood had acquired by the 1950s, Lakewood Park tennis courts hosted the International Pro Tennis Tournament in 1951 and 1952. In the latter year, Francisco (Little Pancho) Segura shown here circa 1953, defeated Richard (Big Pancho) Gonzales for the championship. At the time Pancho Gonzales was the indoor world champion. In 1951, Frank Kovacs upset Segura in a two-and-one-half hour match.
Photograph by Fred Bottomer; courtesy of the Cleveland Press Library and Collections, Cleveland State University Libraries

Lakewood residents continued to be active sports enthusiasts despite the success of Cleveland's professional baseball and football teams in the late 1940s and early 1950s. For many years the lighted Elks baseball field drew large numbers of spectators on summer nights, while during the day a full schedule of baseball was also played. In the 1950s, the King and his Court (a four-man team) would challenge Lakewood's finest softball players. League championships would be decided on the same night. Elks Field was originally the site The Lakewood Tennis Club. In 1918 Lakewood Lodge of the Elks purchase the clubhouse site and named the ten court area "Elks Square." The courts became the baseball field shown here 1936. A Finast Supermarket now occpies the site, while the Elks headquarte remains at 14018 Detroit.
Photograph by E. W. Koster; courtesy of the Cleveland Press Library and Collections, Cleveland State University Libraries

During the 1950s Lakewood added two large outdoor pools to its recreational facilities. The pool in Lakewood park opened in 1954 while Madison Park pool opened in 1958. Shown here is Lakewood Municipal Pool, Lakewood Park, circa 1957.
Photograph by James Thomas; courtesy of the Cleveland Press Library and Collections, Cleveland State University Libraries

In 1959, Lakewood replaced the old city hall in Lakewood Park and its Municipal Court and Police Department buildings with a new, single center on Detroit Avenue. Funded by a $1,750,000 bond issue in 1957, the new building housed administrative offices, the police department, municipal court, and a service garage. The council chambers and auditorium could seat six hundred people. The building is on the site of Memorial Park.
Photograph by Glenn Zahn; courtesy of the Cleveland Press Library and Collections, Cleveland State University Libraries

While all seemed to be going well for Lakewood in the early 1950s, the massive gas explosion that ripped up West 117th Street from Berea Road to Lake brought death and destruction to the Lakewood border in September 1953. Huge sections of concrete were thrown up and automobiles like the one in the foreground overturned. The view here is north on West 117th, toward the railroad tracks and Clifton Boulevard.
Courtesy of the Lakewood Historical Society

FOCUS: Lakewood's Department Stores

Along with the nearly seven hundred retail stores that lined Detroit and Madison avenues in 1930, Lakewood also contained two important department stores. Both stores, Schermer Brothers (1919-1962-1970) and Baileys (1930-1965), fit well into the two to three-story retail landscapes. They provided new suburbanites with easy access to a wide range of merchandise. Virtually every Lakewood resident could reach one of these stores on foot or by a short streetcar ride. Such amenities were a necessity for the city's young, growing families who needed to shop regularly but often lacked the time to go downtown on a regular basis.

The Schermer Brothers Department Store at 12201 Madison Avenue was one of the first suburban department stores in Cleveland and Lakewood's first. It began as a clothing store. In March 1906 Abe and Gussie Greenwald purchased a parcel of land at the corner of Madison and Magee avenues from the Pleasant Hill Land Company. Schermer family members remember Abe as an itinerant peddler who emigrated from Vishna Olyka, Hungary (Czechoslovakia). Soon after, the Abraham Greenwald Clothing Store opened for business at 12201 Madison Avenue.

Apparently, the Greenwalds sent to Hungary for their nephews, Isadore and Joseph Schermer, to help them with the store. By 1917, Joseph was president. The following year, the brothers took over the store and renamed it Schermer Brothers Department Store. Within two years they purchased an adjoining lot, expanded the store, and sent for brothers Sol and Harry to join them. Soon after, their widowed mother, Molly

Greenwald Schermer arrived with her children Elaine, Helen, Leo, and Jack. Molly and the children moved into the first floor of a double house at 1595 Winchester Avenue while Harry's family lived upstairs. The Winchester home served as the center of family activity; the brothers frequently took their breakfast and lunches there.

Schermer Brothers main store was a two-story building with an impressive white terra cotta facade. It contained three floors of merchandise. The basement held toys, hardware, and appliances, except during Christmas season when the toy department with Santa Claus took over half of the area. Clothing and dry goods occupied the ground floor while the second contained furniture and carpeting, including oriental rugs. Because the store was open seven days a week from nine in the morning until nine at night, and open halfdays on Wednesdays and Sundays, the store served Lakewood residents who worked long hours in nearby factories as well as the west side generally. In addition to their long hours, the Schermers' ability to speak a variety of languages made them readily accessible to other new immigrants. In varying degrees they were fluent in Hungarian, Slovak, Russian, German, Polish, Yiddish, and English.

In 1960, forty-one years after the Schermers took over their uncle's store, only three brothers, Sol, Harry, and Jack, remained in the business. On August 16, 1962, a devastating fire completely destroyed the store. The Schermers operated a smaller store at a neighboring site until 1970.

In contrast to Schermers' store, the Bailey Company was a branch of a major Cleveland department store. Built in 1930, the store was one of the nation's first suburban branch department stores; its location at Warren Road and Detroit greatly strengthened that location as the retail center of the new community. Within walking distance of many Lakewood residents, the Detroit streetcar line also provided easy access to the store.

Following World War II, the rapid growth of suburbs to the west, the increased use of automobiles to shop, and the development of Westgate Shopping Center, undermined Lakewood's depart-

ment stores that drew their business from pedestrian and streetcar shopp Lacking extensive free parking, the older stores found it more difficult t compete with the new shopping cer

Baileys fought back by expanding remodeling the store. In 1954 Bailey reorganized its main floor to facilita self-service shopping and added gra to the first floor facade. Ten years lat Baileys expanded and modernized t building. A new, modern facade of p cast concrete covered the old facade brick and glass on the upper two flo Despite these efforts, Baileys sold th store to Nevilles, Incorporated. A yea later the new owners optimistically p posed expansion into the INA build then under construction next door. However, in 1968, the store went ba rupt. A division of Control Data Corp tion now occupies the former Bailey building.

Thus, within the span of several ye Lakewood lost both of its departmer stores. Regular customers and emplo ees, many of whom lived in Lakewoo lost important city institutions.

A. Greenwald Dry Goods Store, 1220 Madison Avenue at Magee Avenue, circa 1906 to 1918, began as a cloth store. Under the Schermer Brothers it emerged as a department store. Whi the six brothers—Joseph, Isadore, Sol, Harry, Jack and Leo—all worked in store at one time or another, other family members, including their siste also helped out. Jack's daughter, Nea remembers that one of the treats for working in the store was lunch at Mi or Asiatic Gardens at 11725 Detroit. 1931, the brothers expanded their bu ness with a branch store at 15607 M son Avenue; the Lakewood Departm Store remained open for several year Courtesy of Dr. Marvin Schermer

Lakewood Fire Department arrived to fight the Schermer Brothers Department Store fire on August 16, 1962. The fire broke out before 3 A.M. and took twelve hours for firefighters to bring it under control. In the process three firefighters suffered injury and the building sustained an estimated three hundred thousand dollars in damage. Four days later a 110 mile per hour wind blew down the store's east wall.
Photograph by Clayton Knipper; courtesy of the Cleveland Press Library and Collections, Cleveland State University Libraries

Jack Schermer inspects the ruins of the Schermer Brothers Department Store, 12201 Madison Avenue on August 16, 1962. Despite the devastating fire, the Schermers opened a new, smaller store at 12221 Madison Avenue. The Schermer Brothers Discount Store stayed in business until 1970. An apartment building now occupies the site of the original department store.
Photograph by Herman Seid; courtesy of the Cleveland Press Library and Collections, Cleveland State University Libraries

This April 23, 1949, photograph shows the original facade of the Bailey Company Store at Detroit Avenue and Warren Road. Although Baileys advertised as "Lakewood's Complete Department Store," it served the west side generally. Until the 1950s the streetcar brought customers to the front door. Buses continued service after the streetcar service ended.
Photograph by Deming Photo Service; courtesy of the Cleveland Press Library and Collections, Cleveland State University Libraries

Lakewood high school students try on coats at Bailey Company's Lakewood store. From its opening in 1930, Baileys competed with the Schermer Brothers store as well as with the Sears, Roebuck store at West 110th and Lorain. The opening of Westgate Shopping Center in Fairview Park challenged all three of these stores, and eventually all three closed. Baileys sought to compete by providing free parking and evening hours two days a week. Only the Schermer Brothers offered shopping seven days a week. From an advertisement in the Lakewood High School Cinema—1942, page 144.

Shindledecker, Furst, and Wilk are being shown new station wagon coats at the Bailey Company's Lakewood Store ● They know that they can depend upon Bailey's for quality and reliability in merchandise and service

The BAILEY
Company

"Lakewood's Own Department Store"

163

FOCUS: Lakewood Bakery

For nearly seventy years Lakewood Bakery was an important community business. Its origins trace back to 1896 when Judd's Bakery opened at 11717 Detroit Avenue. Four years later Edward Rupp purchased the store and renamed it Lakewood Bakery. Rupp operated the business until 1921 when he sold it to Stefan Lodzieski. Under Lodzieski's direction the business grew rapidly; at its peak Lakewood Bakery employed over one hundred workers in twenty-three outlets in Cuyahoga County and beyond.

As with many other successful Lakewood businessmen, Stefan Lodzieski (1882-1951) was an immigrant. While his business expanded across Lakewood and into the metropolitan area, Lodzieski also played an important role in the community's civic life; at the same time he gained national prominence for his work with Polish-American organizations.

Born in Wierzbno, Poland, Stefan Lodzieski came to the United States at the age of twenty. He learned the craft of baking after migrating. About 1911, he purchased the Puritan Bakery at the corner of Plover and Robin (12318 Plover). Two years earlier Stefan had married Victoria Twarogowska (1887-1950); she had come to the United States from Rypin, Poland, at the age of eighteen. The Lodzieski family moved into a house next to the bakery. In addition to bread and pastries, they also provided a baking service for the neighborhood. This was especially true for festivals and weddings, when patrons would bring their own meats and other foods to be cooked in the bakery's large ovens.

About 1922, the Lodzieskis sold Puritan Bakery and purchased the Lakewood Bakery at 11717 Detroit Avenue; the building contained both bakery and shop. Several years later a fire destroyed the original frame structure; Stefan replaced it with an attractive brick and white terra cotta building. While they sold baked goods from the store, the bakery in the rear became the production center for a chain of outlets throughout Lakewood, Rocky River, Parma, and elsewhere in Cuhahoga County and beyond. On the eve of World War II, the Lodzieskis had four additional stores in Lakewood: at 14895 Detroit, and at 12422, 13343, and 14811 Madison Avenue. By 1952, Lakewood Bakery had fifteen stores concentrated in Lakewood and the west side. In later years the Lodzieski children took an active role in the business, with Edwin serving as president and treasurer and Elizabeth Sliwinski as vice president and secretary. They sold the business in 1960; eventually Davis Bakery took over some of the stores. Lakewood Bakery provided a wide range of baked goods but specialized in Danish pastry (made with butter), pastry novelties, and individualized wedding cakes.

Stefan Lodzieski was active in Lakewood's organizational life. He was a member of the Lakewood Elks, Kiwanis, and Chamber of Commerce. He also played a major role in the Polish-American community. Lodzieski helped found the National Committee of Americans of Polish Descent and served as its presdent as well as the president of the Joseph Pilsudski Institute of Modern History (a research institute based in New York City). During World War I, Stefan supported Poland and continu to aid Polish relief, the Polish Nationa Committee, and other organizations. Victoria also took an active role in Pol American organizations; she served a president of the Polish Welfare Association.

The Lodzieskis remained importar participants in Lakewood community life. They attended Saint Hedwig's Catholic Church and lived at 1426 Woodward until their deaths. Their children graduated from Lakewood High School and Edwin worked in th business; Elizabeth married Stefan Sliwinski, a captain in the Polish arm Saint Hegwig's first night wedding. T Sliwinskis lived in Europe for over te years. During World War II, Stefan wa captured and sentenced to death as a political prisoner; liberated by the U.S Army, he returned to the United State in 1946. Elizabeth continues to live ir Lakewood as do her two children, Ka Anthony, a teacher, and Christine Sey litz. Christine is executive director of Broadway School of Music and the Ar

Shown here is the Lakewood Bakery Building with the Detroiter Restaurant on the first floor at 11711 Detroit Avenue in 1988. The name "Lakewood Bakery" remains on the building that formerly housed the bakery. Now a restaurant, the building also retains the attractive white terra cotta facade. Th interior was also handsomely decorat with marble halls and brass railings. Gold's Market was to the right of the bakery.
Photograph by Jim Borchert

Stefan Lodziewski stands near the fifteen hundred pound cake made by Lakewood Bakery, circa 1939. Stefan's daughter Elizabeth Sliwinski believes this cake commemorated an important community event, perhaps for the Chamber of Commerce, the Kiwanis, or Lakewood's Semi-Centennial. It may have been on display at the Reidy Furniture Store on Detroit Avenue at Hird across the street from Lakewood Bakery. Courtesy of the Western Reserve Historical Society

FOCUS: Lakewood Athletes

Lakewood has been home to many professional and amateur athletes. Over years a number of Cleveland Indians, Browns, and Barons have lived in the area. Lakewood has also produced many fine athletes and athletic teams. The Recreation Department has offered many opportunities for youths and adults to participate in athletic activities. It is impossible to identify every great or near great athlete; the following provide a sample of Lakewood's athletic prowess.

During the 1920s and 1930s, heavyweight prize fighter Johnny Risko (1902-1953), thrilled Cleveland fight fans with his victories over future world heavyweight champions Jack Sharkey and Max Baer. In November, 1925, Risko lost a close fight to Gene Tunney, and in 1929, Max Schmeling knocked him out. An aggressive fighter with a devastating punch and a big heart, Risko fought in 59 amateur and 137 profes-

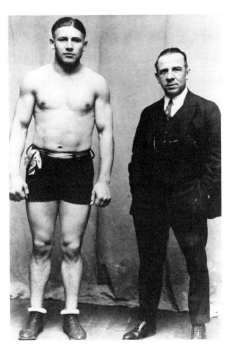

sional fights. During the early 1920s if not earlier, Johnny's parents and family moved to the Village. From 1923 to 1925, Johnny lived at 2038 Quail; the city directory lists his occupation as "pugilist." Of Slovak ancestry, Johnny had many friends and fans in the neighborhood, and Lakewood generally. Although he trained at a gym in Cleveland, he occasionally worked out in the second floor gym at the Lakewood Athletic Club on Plover. He is pictured here on the left with his manager Danny Dunn in a June 23, 1925 News-Bee photograph.
Courtesy of the Cleveland Press Library and Collections, Cleveland State University Libraries

Paul Graebner poses during the Press Junior Tennis championships in June 1934. Graebner played on the Lakewood High School tennis team in the mid-1930s. He won the Ohio high school singles championship in 1935 and teamed up to win the doubles in 1933 and 1934. His son, Clark, later won three state championships making them the only father-son combination to win Ohio scholastic tennis championships. The elder Graebner practiced dentistry. Courtesy of the Cleveland Press Library and Collections, Cleveland State University Libraries

Clark Graebner swings at the ball on January 13, 1959. Following in his father's footsteps, Clark won three straight Ohio scholastic tennis championships (1959-1961). At the time he was only the second in state history to do so; Cincinnati Walnut Hill's star, Tony Trabert, was the first (1946-1948). In college, Graebner starred on Northwestern University's tennis team. From 1965 to 1968, Graebner established a 16-4 record in Davis Cup competition. Save for 1965, he was listed in the top ten of the U.S. Lawn Tennis Association rankings every year from 1964 to 1972; in 1968 he was second ranked. Over the years he won singles titles in U.S. Indoor, Clay Courts, and Hard Courts as well as six national doubles titles. In 1974, along with his spouse Carole, Clark joined the Cleveland Nets professional team in the World Tennis league; he also served as player-coach for the Nets.
Courtesy of the Cleveland Press Library and Collections, Cleveland State University Libraries

Jeannette McClincey of 2036 Lark Street, the Press marbles champion is showing Lakewood Kiwanis president Arlo Graber of 1633 Onondaga, her winning form, circa 1952. Eleven years old when she won the Press championship, the freckled and redheaded Jeannette McClincey went on to place second in the National Marbles Tournament at Asbury Park, New Jersey. Jeannette also won many other marble championships and placed second in the national championships four consecutive years. Her athletic career extended well beyond marbles, however. She played on championship soccer and baseball teams at Harding Junior High School. A 1956 graduate from Lakewood High School where she was active in sports, Jeanette went on to star in baseball and basketball. Known as "Pinky McClincey," she took an enviable pitching record of 12-0 into the World Women's Softball Tournament after winning the regional championship for the Sheffield Bronze team. She also played forward on the Shaw Lanes basketball team that won the Lake Erie AAU women's district basketball championship. Named foul shooting champ, she also made the tournament's all star squad.
Courtesy of the Cleveland Press Library and Collections, Cleveland State University Libraries

Marie Walther practices at Lakewood High School in 1962. Lakewood High School produced several fine women gymnasts. In 1959, Betty Jean Maycock was a winner at a National Gymnastic meet. Marie Walther, who graduated in 1962, was a Junior National Women Champion. Walther was on the U.S. gymnastics team in the 1964 World Olympics in Tokyo where she participated in the balance beam, floor exercise, horse vault, and uneven parallel bars. The U.S. team finished ninth in the competition.
Courtesy of Lakewood High School Alumni Association and Anthony DiBiasio, Jr.

Dave Mills of the Lakewood High School Track Team starts a race in March 1959. Mills, a 1958 Lakewood High School graduate, broke nearly every track record in the 440-yard run. In his senior year he set a national scholastic mark of 46.6 seconds for the run, only a second off the world record time. He also went on to win the state championship in the 100- and 220-yard dashes; Mills was only the second runner in Ohio scholastic history to win all three sprints. Over his three-year career, he won five state championships. Mills went on to run at Purdue University and participated in the Pan-American Games.
Courtesy of the Cleveland Press Library and Collections, Cleveland State University Libraries

IGNETTE
akewood at Fifty:
he 1939
emi-Centennial

With the Depression not yet a memory, Lakewood residents organized a massive celebration for the community's fiftieth anniversary. The semi-centennial drew participants and organizations from all parts of Lakewood; it tapped a wide range of religious, fraternal, civic, educational, and community organizations. While organizers of earlier patriotic parades and events had sought to represent a broad cross section of the city, the semi-centennial probably went further than any previous effort. As such, the anniversary celebration represented a high point in community unity and cooperation.

The celebration focused on the week of July 16 through 22, 1939. The city's three newspapers, the *Courier,* the *Suburban News and Herald,* and the *Post,* commemorated the event with special sections on Lakewood history. Events included church services, an historical exhibit at the public library, an "anniversary parade," the Seventh Annual Merchants' Community Picnic at Lakewood Park, and the coronation of "Miss Lakewood." It also included four performances of a historical pageant entitled "Wagons West," at Lakewood High School Stadium.

"Wagons West" traced the history of Lakewood from its creation to the future; it reflected a sense of drama and pageantry typical of the 1930s. With a cast of over one thousand performers, the production drew heavily on Lakewood churches, fraternal, civic, educational, and community organizations for support. More than sixty-five organizations participated, including the Orders of the Eastern Star of Lakewood, scout troops, Lakewood Junior Chamber of Commerce, American Legion Post No. 66 and Clifton Post 421, the Clifton Masonic Lodge, Catholic Daughters of America, Women's Welsh Club of America, the Lakewood Pioneers, Townsend Clubs, the PTA, Lakewood Congregational Church, South Lakewood Woman's Club, and the Lakewood Fire Department.

The pageant presented eighteen episodes tracing Lakewood history from the "Ballet of Creation" which symbolized "the first appearance of living things upon the earth with the creation of land, sky and flowers," to a finale involving more than a thousand people forming "the Wheel of Progress" of twelve spokes symbolizing united effort. The program also portrayed the "arrival of the Pony Express and the collection of tolls from those using the plank road," "the incorporation of Lakewood fifty years ago with the reading of the original minutes and comments of that meeting," as well as "The Melting Pot," and a "World War Memorial." The following photographs illustrate various groups that took part in the parade and the "Wagons West" pageant.

Lakewood Kiwanis and First Slovak Catholic Union marchers line up for Lakewood's Semi-Centennial Parade July 18, 1939. According to the Cleveland Plain Dealer, *the parade had nearly seventy-five hundred participants while crowds of over seventy-fi[ve] thousand lined the parade route alon[g] Detroit and Madison avenues. The tu[o] mile-long parade included over twen[ty] five bands, numerous floats, and rep[re] sentatives of fraternal, veterans', and[o] civic organizations.*
Courtesy of the Western Reserve Historical Society

The Slovak family float passes by in the Lakewood Semi-Centennial Parade on July 18, 1939. Celebrating both their ethnic ancestry and Lakewood citizenship, Lakewood Slovaks donned traditional clothing. Behind this float came a large contingent of Slovak-Americans, also in traditional dress and carrying American flags. Other marchers included the Saints Cyril and Methodius Church Band, the Modern Woodmen of America, the Sons and Daughters of Ireland, the Knights of Malta, the Letter Carriers' Band, and Saint Catherine's Sokol and Girls Auxiliary.
Courtesy of the Western Reserve Historical Society

This photograph probably illustrates th[e] pageant finale, "Wheels of Progress" presented at the Lakewood High Schoo[l] Stadium, July 19 through 22, 1939. Pr[o] duced by John B. Rogers and directed [by] Wayne Lemmon, "Wagons West" demonstrated both the depression era'[s] interest in dramatic documentary history and its strong belief in progress. "As with the parade, the pageant's inclusio[n] of groups from all of Lakewood also reflects the strength of the period's democratic spirit.
Courtesy of the Western Reserve Historical Society

This is probably a photograph of "Forests" from Episode 2: "The Ballet of Creation." The "Ballet" included twenty-two young women as "rivers," seventeen as "creation," and thirty-three as "forests." Other episodes portrayed a "typical" Indian camp, the first white men, Lakewood pioneers, the first church, Dr. Kirtland, the first school, an early wedding, the Rocky River Railroad, and "Lakewood's Achievement" (a recognition of the U.S. Chamber of Commerce national award for superior fire prevention in 1930).
Courtesy of the Western Reserve Historical Society

Dressed in traditional Slovak dress, performers for the "Melting Pot" episode included the Chuck Lecki Dance Band who are kneeling in front. Lecki is behind the accordian. The group standing behind the band were dancers. The program for "Wagons West" noted that Episode 13 "brings. . .the colorful and authentic dances of our Slovak and Polish citizens." Msgr. F. J. Dubosh of Saints Cyril and Methodius Church served as advisor for "The Melting Pot" and co-chaired the Religious Observance Committee. Charles Schreiber presided over the Semi-Centennial's executive committee.
Courtesy of the Western Reserve Historical Society

These are probably the "Gay Nineties Bathing Beauties" who competed in a mock contest; "the daring girl showing her ankles" won. Sponsored by the South Lakewood Woman's Club and the American Legion Post 66, the "Gay Nineties" episode evoked the greatest laughter when, according to the Lakewood Post, "women in bustles and men in frock coats and mustaches showed a typical busy street. . .high wheels and tandem bikes, early automobiles chugged around the huge stage."
Courtesy of the Western Reserve Historical Society

FOCUS: Louis B. Seltzer

Louis Seltzer (1897-1980) gained prominence as editor of the Cleveland *Press*; as a community leader his optimism reflected the booster spirit prevalent in the first three quarters of the twentieth century. To Clevelanders and Lakewood neighbors, Seltzer embodied the Horatio Alger ideal. Born to a poor, near-west-side family, he dropped out of school at age thirteen to go to work as an office boy at the Cleveland *Leader*. He quickly rose up the ladder to news reporter. In 1914 he joined the *Press* and within two years became city editor. At the young age of nineteen Seltzer became the paper's editor; after three months he decided he needed more experience for the position and stepped down to become political editor. In 1928 he again took the reins as editor, a position he held unt[il] retirement in 1966. Under his leaders[hip] the *Press* gained a national reputation and became one of the flagship pape[rs] of the Scripps-Howard newspaper cha[in].

Louis Seltzer married Mary Elizabet[h] Champlin in 1915; their marriage last[ed] until her death in 1965. The Seltzers lived in Clifton Park for many years, an[d] Louis became a popular speaker for Lakewood meetings and commemora[tions]. As editor he gained great respec[t] from his staff. His sense of humor and love of practical jokes kept the *Press* reporters on their toes; they readily reciprocated with similar pranks. In th[e] end the *Press* established an esprit de corps that became the envy of rival newspapers.

Louis B. Seltzer snapped at his retirement party reading a special Cleveland Press *edition in July 1958. Photograph by Frank Aleksandrowicz; courtesy of the Cleveland Press Library and Collections, Cleveland State University Libraries*

FOCUS: Carlyn Irwin

As happened in World War I, the Second World War drew more women, especially wives and mothers, into the workplace. Carlyn Irwin's life reflects these changes. Although a wife, mother, and community volunteer before World War II, she soon took on added responsibilities. Along with many women she returned to domestic duties after the war, but she continued her active involvement in community life. Nevertheless, volunteer activities proved an insufficient outlet for Carlyn's energy, so she eventually returned to public service full time.

Carlyn Meeker was born in 1904 and came to Lakewood with her family fou[r] years later. After graduating from Lakewood High School in 1922, she attende[d] Mount Ida College. A family illness required her to drop out and find a job. She worked as a secretary until she ma[r]ried Fred Irwin in 1929. Fred was self-employed and worked on the develo[p]ment of neon lighting.

Fred had served in World War I and both Fred and Carlyn were active in the Lakewood World War I Veterans' Organization. As with many middle-class women of that era, Carlyn was busy wit[h]

ng a son and participating in civic
nizations such as the Lakewood
nen's Club and the League of
nen Voters.

the beginning of World War II,
or Amos Kauffman selected Carlyn
ead Lakewood's War, Price, and
oning Board. The Second World War
iired rationing of practically every
modity, including food, gasoline,
tires. Carlyn's agency oversaw the
ribution of stamps to Lakewood
ilies.

though Carlyn returned to domestic
res following the war, she also
ked to provide Clevelanders and
ers with a broader perspective on
ld affairs. She helped organized trips
nigh school students to Washington,
. In 1952 she organized a trip to the
ted Nations, (U.N.) headquarters in
v York for leaders of local women's
inizations. The latter became a
del for Scripps-Howard Newspapers
ch sponsored similar trips in other
es. In 1953, with *Press* sponsorship,
lyn took eighteen Cleveland women
a study trip to Latin America. She also
an a Letters Abroad Program, which
ame the People to People Program
ler the Eisenhower administration,
l actively supported the United Na-
ns. In 1964 she was honored for this
rk along with Adlai Stevenson, then
. Ambassador to the U.N., and Dr.
njamin Spock.

eventually Carlyn's volunteer work
l her back to a full-time career. She
ned the Cuyahoga County Welfare
partment, where she worked as Pub-
Information Director until her
rement in 1973. Now in her eighties
l still living in Lakewood, Carlyn
unteers in senior citizens' activities
l continues to speak out about
unteerism and world affairs.

Chief Clerk of the Lakewood Ration Board at Wilson School, Carlyn Irwin, is standing by the flag in this 1943 photograph. The ration board allocated

stamps for the purchase of scarce goods during World War II.
Courtesy of Carlyn Irwin

Carlyn Irwin continued to be active in civic affairs. She won the Cleveland Mayor's Committee for the United Nations award, on October 2, 1964, for her efforts to educate Clevelanders about the United Nations and about Latin America. Her co-winners here include

famous physician-writer-activist Benjamin Spock of Cleveland and Adlai Stevenson, former governor of Illinois, two-time presidential candidate (1952 and 1956), and U.N. Ambassador.
Courtesy of Carlyn Irwin

Chapter 13
Satellite City: City in Transition, 1960 to 1989

Suburbia was supposed to be an alternative to the city, an antidote to all the things that were going wrong in urban America—or at least an escape from them. But now suburbanites are experiencing what they thought they had left behind.

William Severini Kowinski, New York *Times Magazine*, 1980

If the previous thirty years of Lakewood history ended in a period of relative prosperity and maturity fo the streetcar suburb, the next thirty years produced a series of challenges even greater than those of the Gre Depression. As the community aged, both its reputatio and its well-being faced strong tests.

Many of these changes came from outside. Buffet by economic forces and governmental decisions beyor the community's control, the once self-confident city tl had controlled its own destiny now seemed a mere pa The needs of newer suburbs to the west seemed to gai precedence. The first assaults came in the form of high ways designed to speed traffic through Lakewood. The plans threatened the spatial integrity of several key neig borhoods. Next, a sharp decline in the region's industr also hit the city. With the rest of the metropolitan area, Lakewood underwent major shifts in population, land-scapes, social life, and economic activity. Even mother nature turned her wrath on the city by unleashing a devastating, deadly wind storm that swept through Lakewood Park during the 1969 July Fourth celebration

The embattled city responded. Although Lakewoc had always sought to avoid Cleveland's problems by distancing itself from the metropolis, by the 1980s man of the community's problems mirrored those of the big city. On the other hand, Lakewood expanded its social and cultural programs far beyond those available to it ir the past.

As with much of the Cleveland metropolitan area, Lakewood's population experienced decline. While La wood regained some of its lost population during the 1960s, the next decade produced a sharp drop. With 61,963 residents in 1980, Lakewood ranked third in the county only slightly ahead of Euclid and Cleveland Heights, while the 1980s promised an even more precip tous decline. Although projections vary, the most pessi-mistic anticipated a further loss of ten thousand by 1990 If these estimates are accurate, Lakewood's 1990 popula tion will be about 70 percent of its population in 1930.

By 1980, Lakewood's population was older, more likely to be single and less affluent. While the communi aged, so did its population; seniors headed about one o of every ten households. At the same time more residen lived alone, while average household size declined. Wh newer homes in more distant suburbs drew some Lake-wood residents away, changes in the region's economy

...ted the incomes and even livelihoods of others. Al-
...gh Lakewood continued to be home to many profes-
...als and other well paid workers, these changes helped
...e the city from near the top of the county's wealth-
...cities. By 1980 Lakewood ranked twenty-ninth of the
...nty's thirty-three cities.

This decline reflected important changes in the city.
...he end of the 1980s, nearly 10 percent of Lakewood's
...ulation fell below the poverty line. In part, Lake-
...od's growing poverty reflected the aging of the city and
...economic disruptions that produced layoffs and shut-
...ns. It also reflected the growing number of women
...children among the poor. According to the Lakewood
...lic Schools, in 1986, single-parent families headed
...rly one-third of families with children in public ele-
...ntary schools. Nearly 40 percent of elementary school
...dents qualitifed for free or reduced cost lunches.

While the city's ethnic base remained largely the
...e, new groups added to the diversity. People with
...e German ancestry made up about one-third of the
...'s population, while those with some Irish, English,
...Slovak ancestry also accounted for major population
...ups. Nor had Lakewood abandoned its role as a home
...immigrants. If less than 10 percent came from outside
...United States, nearly 20 percent of the city indicated it
...difficulty speaking English. Although immigrants con-
...ed to arrive from Europe, Lakewood increasingly at-
...ted immigrants from Puerto Rico, Mexico, Asia, and
...Middle East. The city also became home to gays and a
...nber of gay-owned businesses.

The legacy of past exclusionary efforts and ongoing
...ctices continued to discourage potential African-
...erican residents. By 1980, African-Americans made up
...s than 1 percent of the city's population. Ironically
...ewood's black families had incomes well above the
...average. Throughout the period landlords violated
...law by refusing to rent to African-Americans. In 1967,
...new owner of the Mayflower Apartments told a pros-
...tive tenant, "You're Colored, No, Not Here, Never!"
...e year later, the Ohio Civil Rights Commission had to
...ervene for a black applicant at the Edgewater Towers.
...1987, a Lakewood landlord refused to rent his duplex
...Clarence Bolden, a lawyer and the newly appointed
...ector of the Cuyahoga Plan's Discrimination Complaint
...vice. In all three cases the landlords relented when
...ed with legal action, but such activities had a chilling

effect on many African-American families.

The city's record on minority hiring proved equally
discouraging. In 1987, a U.S. District Court judge ordered
Lakewood to change its criteria for hiring police and fire
department employees. At that time the city had no African-American safety workers and other city departments
had equally poor records; Lakewood Hospital alone accounted for thirty-two of the city's thirty-six minority
employees. To correct these problems, city officials began
working with the Cuyahoga Plan to improve employee
recruiting and to attract minority residents to the
community.

One of the major causes of Lakewood's growing
sense of impotence emerged from its battles to stop state
highway construction within its borders. As new suburbs
emerged to the west, Lakewood increasingly became a
community through which many others passed. Since
these new suburbs historically lacked streetcar connections with downtown Cleveland, residents relied heavily
on automobiles to get to work. As more and more western
suburbs stacked up along the lake, Lakewood's two
bridges over Rocky River experienced major traffic jams.

In the late 1950s the state proposed extending
Clifton Boulevard through Clifton Park, and by bridge to
Rocky River. Ironically, a former Lakewoodite, County
Engineer Albert Porter, proved to be one of the key pro-
ponents of this project. The city delayed the bridge
through court appeals, but in 1960 the Ohio Supreme
Court ruled against the city. The bridge opened in January
1964. The project removed eight homes and parts of fifteen other properties, while the road bisected Clifton Park
with a six-lane highway.

The second project followed closely on the heels of
the Clifton Boulevard bridge. Originally called the Northwest Freeway, planners intended I-90 to be even more
effective at speeding automobile traffic through inner
suburbs and the city. Again Lakewood fought with delay-
ing actions in the courts. When the freeway opened in the
early 1970s, a huge trench divided parts of south Lakewood from the rest of the city. Construction removed
130 houses.

Although the I-90 trough presented a more significant intrusion, the Clifton bridge also adversely affected
Clifton Park. Sensing a changed environment in the park,
developers proposed both high rise apartments and
cluster housing. While the city rejected the former, one

cluster project did gain approval. Developers proved more successful with higher-density single-family homes. In 1965 Clifton Park Lane with four houses on it, replaced Mabel Hanna Parson's thirty-six room mansion at 17896 Beach Road. Four years later the former home of shipping magnate Harry Coulby, on 17896 Lake Avenue, faced destruction.

Although not directly related to bridge and freeway development, lakefront estates also suffered at the hands of the developer's wrecking ball. In the 1960s, the adjacent Lake Avenue estates of Alexander Winton and stockbroker Roland Meacham became sites for high-rise apartment buildings, while Kirtland Lane, with sixteen new houses on it replaced the Theodor Kundtz/Robert R. Morrow estate at 13826 Edgewater Drive.

Lakewood's prominence and maturity in the 1950s masked more than population declines. While the demand for services increased to serve an older, less affluent population, the city's aging building stock required repair or replacement. At the same time the tax base eroded. Politicians confronted the need for more services at the very time its resources began to dry up.

In 1956, Frank Celeste inherited these problems from Amos Kauffman. Celeste, the city's first Democratic mayor, drew on past solutions of development and growth to pattern his "Operation Lakewood." The program sought to increase the tax base through new construction and to revive existing structures through strict code enforcement. With the city largely built upon, new development largely came at the expense of older structures and produced greater densities for those properties. In his two terms of office, Celeste strongly promoted apartment development throughout the city. When Republican Robert Lawther became mayor in 1964, he continued Celeste's program of development but sought to exercise more control over the projects. Through "Project Pride" he also promoted a strict code enforcement program.

By the end of Lakewood's first century the results of these policies reverberated across most of the city's landscapes. Between 1940 and 1980 the number of new housing units constructed equalled 33 percent of the previous housing units. Before 1930, single- and double-family houses dominated the landscape, accounting for 75 percent of the city's housing stock. By 1980 multi-family housing made up a major share of the residential landscape. Apartments of three or more units accounted for 43 percent of all units. Larger units of ten or more made up 33 percent of the housing stock.

No section of Lakewood escaped the apartment mania. Developers crammed apartment buildings into almost every conceivable site, often with little regard for the surrounding area or for parking. As Celeste critics noted, many buildings covered nearly the entire lot leaving little setback from the street or room for parking. While these developments helped the tax base, few apart-

ment buildings had the character or fine decorative features of those built before the Great Depression.

Larger parcels of land gave developers more room both for profits and amenities. In 1959 speculators purchased the eight-acre site of the Detroit car barns for $155,000; a year later they sold the property to develop for more than a 100 percent profit.

The Gold Coast developments, however, stand o as the best projects completed during the period. Whi apartment construction along Edgewater, Lake, and Cl anticipated the Gold Coast, construction of the luxury Lake Shore Hotel in the late 1920s served as a direct precursor. Edgewater Towers started the post-war deve ment; with its building permit dating to 1950, the 205 ten-story, brick-facade building opened four years late The Berkshire followed shortly after. Gold Coast const tion began in earnest in the late 1950s with permits iss for the Lake House (1958), the Shoreham (1959), Mar Towers East (1960), Winton Place (1961), Marine Tow West (1963), 12000 Edgewater (1963), Imperial House (1964), the Carlyle (1968), the Meridian (1971) and th Waterford (1972). In 1971 Celeste converted the Lake Shore Hotel into the Lake Shore Towers apartments, w in 1964 the Envoy Apartments went up on the south si of Lake Avenue.

Unsure that they could attract Clevelanders to live high rise buildings, developers of the first Gold Coast projects produced conservative structures. Although much wider and taller than neighboring apartments, th first buildings blended into the existing apartment land scape. With unadorned red brick facades and no bal conies, the Berkshire and Edgewater Towers reflected traditional apartment facades and emphasized solidity and safety.

By 1961, developers no longer had to convince tenants about the efficacy of high rise living; a new con fidence, ostentatiousness and even arrogance crept int the designs. The newer structures became signboards t attract potential tenants; the Winton Place went one ste further by placing its large blue logo on the roof for all see. While older high rise apartment buildings followe Lakewood's utilitarian pattern of hugging close to the street, both Winton Place and the Carlyle broke from th to emulate the wealthy lakefront estates they had come occupy. The deep grassy setbacks provided a perspecti to show off the monumental structures.

The Winton Place stands out as the Coast's largest and most interesting structure. Designed by Loebl, Schlossman and Bennett, the building rises thirty storie into the sky. The designers made it appear even taller w bold vertical lines emphasized by thin reinforced con crete support structure and narrow frontage. Glass wall and extended balconies make the building "float," in contrast to its boxy brick neighbors. As a result, the Winton Place dominates the city's skyscape.

Drawing on the successful Gold Coast developments, the city launched a "Silver Strip" program in 1966
counter the growing numbers of empty stores along
Madison Avenue. The plan called for high rise apartments
alternated with revitalized retail businesses. Although
several medium height apartment buildings went up near
the Avenue, new projects increasingly faced community
opposition. A proposal for an eleven-story condominium
Northland and Madison ran into neighborhood
opposition. Other projects, as Stephen Babin's Detroit
Avenue Castlewood Apartments suffered from
construction delays that eventually threw the developer
into default. By 1975, when Robert Lawther won election
his fourth mayoral term, development had slowed
considerably.

Lakewood's commercial landscape also experienced
profound changes. With the streetcar, Detroit and Madison
rail businesses survived into the 1950s. The increased
of the automobile profoundly affected both while the
rapid growth of shopping centers and large chain stores
further undermined Lakewood's small business environment. The construction of large supermarkets on Warren,
Detroit, and Bunts played important roles in this
transformation.

The magnitude of the change is striking. By 1970
Lakewood's two department stores had closed. In 1950,
city had forty-nine bakery stores; by 1970 there were
only five. Drug and grocery stores declined by half, while
meat stores and confectioners almost disappeared entirely. More than two-thirds of the hardware stores disappeared between 1940 and 1970, while motion picture
theaters fell from a high of seven in 1930 to three in 1970
and one in 1989. Since 1960, "mom and pop" grocery
stores virtually became extinct even in the Village. In their
place appeared the ubiquitous "convenience" chain store.
Only a few businesses that made up the neighborhood
commercial landscape survived, most notably bars, barber,
and beauty shops. Some commercial institutions persisted,
however, such as Charlie Geigers.

Nor were these the only changes in Lakewood's
commercial landscape. As small stores and shops closed
down along Detroit and Madison, the city grew increasingly concerned both for the loss of businesses and its
declining tax base. Development again seemed the solu-
tion as the city government largely backed private efforts
renew Lakewood center. By the 1980s, high-rise office
buildings transformed downtown Lakewood from a
commercial center to an office center. Increasingly, Lakewood's downtown became like that of Cleveland and
other large cities. After 5:00 P.M. the daytime workers
depart leaving the once-bustling evening streets empty.

Although many played important roles in these
changes and support from city hall proved helpful, much
of the work was the inspiration of one man. The son of a
Detroit Avenue fur store owner, Stephen Babin began to
transform Lakewood center (which came to be known as
"Babinwood") in 1948 when he remodeled the second
floor of his father's business at 14700 Detroit. The following year he converted the Community Center Building at
Saint Charles and Detroit into an office building. In 1961,
he purchased the former Baileys Department Store building for his own department store, Nevilles. Five years later
Babin's company, Marwood, Incorporated, began construction on the seven-story I.N.A. building next door. In
1970 Babin produced his most ambitious project, Lakewood Center North, at Belle and Detroit. The fifteen story
office building occupied much of the block that had
housed such Lakewood institutions as the Shanty Auto
Parts store, the state liquor store, and Rozi's Wine store.
Several years later Babin began plans for the seven-story
Medical Building across the street. By 1975 his holdings
included nearly all of center Lakewood including the
Warren and the Detroit Warren Medical Buildings.

Within the year, however, his empire began to come
apart. Another project, the Castlewood Apartment building, fell into foreclosure and required sale. Babin soon
confronted financial problems at Lakewood Center North.
Nevertheless, Babin's legacy remains an important center-
piece in Lakewood's transformation. The office buildings
persist while Bailey's/Nevilles Building eventually became
home to a division of Control Data Corporation.

Changes in Lakewood's physical landscapes reflected
and influenced changes in the community's social life.
Shopping increasingly necessitated an automobile. En-
capsulated in automobiles, neighbors interacted less
frequently. As local theaters closed down, residents faced
longer drives for entertainment facilities. As more and
more family members acquired their own automobiles,
the narrow streets of the trolley suburb became choked
with parked cars, adding a physical barrier between
neighbors.

As more women entered the workplace to help supplement family incomes, family life also changed. With
more dual-income families and fewer children, husbands
began to share more household duties, although their
spouses still shouldered the brunt of the work. In contrast
to early suburbanites, families began to eat out more
frequently. This shift has benefited the whole restaurant
industry, including the most expensive as the Pier W and
The Dock, the moderately-priced Millers and Senels, and
the inexpensive, fast-food chains. The numbers of restaurants represent a visible measure of the suburb's changed
lifestyles.

Changes in the workplace have also affected community life. As more women joined the workplace, Lakewood's great volunteer army slowly dwindled. While older
housewives carried on the work, fewer young women
joined them.

Fraternal, religious, recreational, and civic organizations also experienced these losses. Younger generations

increasingly moved away or chose either not to join or to be less active than their parents. The Kiwanis Club, whose active membership has grown, represents one of the few exceptions. Some of Lakewood's mainline churches also experienced declining memberships. Lakewood Presbyterian church membership declined from a high of 2,300 in 1950 to only 834 in 1988.

With membership declines many organizations experienced reduced activity and vitality. If most of the city's social organizations continued to function and play an important role, their central place in the community atrophied. Suburbanites in the early years of the century collectively focused their energy into shared organizational activities. By the end of the century residents' activities seemed less focused, more privatized, and individualistic. While the presence of TVs and VCRs may help account for the shift from "live wire" to "couch potato," many Lakewoodites today appear to have traded involvement in social, fraternal, and religious organizations for educational and self-fulfillment programs.

The dramatic growth of apartments presaged other important community changes. Ironically, while Lakewood lost nearly nine-thousand residents since 1930, it added nearly seven thousand housing units. As with the rest of the nation, household size declined sharply. On the Gold Coast, new high rises introduced both condominium living and a new method of social stratification. While the first buildings offered moderate rents for all units, later buildings included elaborate and expensive penthouse apartments along with more moderately priced units on lower floors. Rather than the horizontal distribution of wealth that characterized Lakewood years ago when wealth increased as one moved from southeast to north and northwest, the new arrangement is vertical.

In spite of the problems and disruptions of the last thirty years, Lakewood residents made important additions to the community's quality of life, and in the process earned considerable acclaim for the city. The city established an impressive record developing services and facilities for its aging population. In 1963, with help from federal loans, the first Westerly building opened and a second followed in 1969. Other components included the Barton Center, which provides meeting and activity rooms, the Landmark building (converted in 1980 from the Lakewood Storage building), and additional Westerly housing, the last of which will open in 1989.

Closeby, Lakewood Hospital underwent a series of costly expansions, additions, and modernizations. Unfortunately, growing medical costs increasingly created problems. In 1961 the city council voted to sell the hospital but could find no appropriate buyer. In the late 1980s, after more than fifty years of public operation, the city finally decided to privatize the operation. This followed a pattern adopted by many other area hospitals.

Lakewood also expanded its recreation facilities.

After years of turning its back on the lake, the city close its Lakewood Park landfill and effectively landscaped th area to provide both visual and physical access to the l; For winter recreation the city purchased Winterhurst Ic Rink from City Ice and Fuel in 1961. In 1975 Lakewood opened a major skating complex on the site. A progran of modernization and expansion also produced new gyms at most Lakewood schools while Lakewood High School's athletic complex underwent major renovatior and improvement.

Lakewood's cultural life also experienced conside able growth and expansion. Each summer from 1962 to 1981, Lakewood played host to the Great Lakes Shakespeare Festival. Held in Lakewood Civic Auditorium, the festival served as a major attraction for the entire metropolitan area. However, the most important addition to Lakewood's cultural landscape was the completion of Kenneth C. Beck Center for the Cultural Arts in 1976.

If by the end of Lakewood's first century, resident: seemed less like the social "live wires" of the beginnin of the century, they also could claim to be involved in f more recreational, educational, and cultural activities, a programs than were their forbears. By 1989, the city of "joiners" had became a city of "do-it-yourselfers," profe sional and amateur sports fans, and adult students strug gling to gain advanced degrees. While the city's traditio ethnic differences began to blur together and its class differences diminished, three of its residential landscap remain distinct. If the commercial landscape and that o elite lakefront estates have undergone major change an transformation, enough outcroppings persist to remind one of their presence.

While Lakewood now offers a wide range of cultu and recreational offerings never before available in the community, the city's homes remain its greatest attractic With a strong code enforcement program widely envied by other communities, Lakewood has been able to mai tain its housing stock. Moreover, the city contains an un usually wide range of housing. The Gold Coast offers moderately priced apartments and expensive penthous units. Along the lakefront and in Clifton Park one can fir large, attractive houses with broad, deep lots and many amenities. Most common are modest three- and four-bedroom houses in a variety of styles, including bungalows, four-squares, colonials, homesteads and an occasional Queen Anne. Cleveland doubles, terraces, an a wide variety of apartment buildings also dot the landscape.

The city also remains a safe place in which to live while its commercial arteries have grown even more attractive. Lakewood gained national recognition for its fire prevention and fire-fighting abilities. By 1973, Lakewood had won thirteen national awards for fire safety. In the same year, *Esquire* magazine selected it as "America Safest City." To improve the visual quality of commercial

ts the city introduced a sign ordinance. Strong en-
ement reduced the visual clutter that had marked both
ison and Detroit and greatly improved the aesthetic
lities of both streets.

By the end of the first century Lakewood continued
e an attractive suburb, but it also offered residents
ortant urban amenities. The most telling aspect of the
sformation from suburb to satellite city can be seen
he skyline. In 1889 trees dominated the skyscape; by
church steeples joined this skyline. Fifty-nine years
, the high-rise office buildings at center Lakewood,
residential spires on the Gold Coast and Detroit tower
r the surrounding area. Despite a smaller population,
suburb appears more like a city than at any time in its
ory. As the number of office buildings increased, more
more Lakewood residents found they could live and

work in the same community. By 1980 nearly one-fifth of
all employed Lakewood residents worked in the city;
more worked in Lakewood than in downtown Cleveland.

Over the years the city has proven to be amazingly
resilient. It has survived the pains of adolescence and
middle age. As Lakewood begins its second century,
important problems persist and others lurk in the wings.
However, the city seems to have grown more comfortable
with itself and its place in the sun. It seems to be more
tolerant of those who are different and new. As Margaret
Butler concluded forty years ago in *The Lakewood Story*,
"today Lakewood is a good place in which to raise a
family." But she also warned that "it will not remain that
way by allowing nature to take its course. If we value its
good things we must work to preserve them, and we must
begin TODAY."

*In 1948 Lakewood's landscape and
skyscape remained dominated by trees.
Only Saint James and several other large
buildings on Detroit and the beginnings
of the Gold Coast suggest the sharp
changes to come. Only three bridges cross
the Rocky River while Clifton Park
remained intact.*
*Photograph by Clyde Butler; courtesy of
the Lakewood Historical Society*

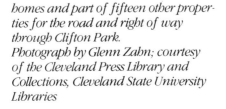

*During the Fourth of July 1969 festivi-
ties at Lakewood Park a deadly squall
line swept across Lakewood. The storm
uprooted trees and sent them thunder-
ing down on houses, cars, and people.
While the only loss of life occurred in
Lakewood Park, property destruction
was widespread across the city.*
*Photograph by Herman Seid; courtesy
of the Cleveland Press Library and
Collections, Cleveland State University
Libraries*

wn here is the "Clifton Road bridge
roach construction through the
mer quiet of Lakewood's wealthy
'ton Park section" on April 14, 1963.
ewood fought the proposed bridge
roach to the Ohio Supreme Court
ore construction began in 1962.
nstruction removed a total of eight

homes and part of fifteen other properties for the road and right of way
through Clifton Park.
*Photograph by Glenn Zahn; courtesy
of the Cleveland Press Library and
Collections, Cleveland State University
Libraries*

This is the Northwest Freeway (I-90) looking west through Lakewood on August 17, 1972. With increasing population to the west, new road construction was necessary to speed traffic downtown. Construction on I-90 began in the county in 1965. The completed freeway opened November 4, 1978. Construction for I-90 removed 130 houses and left a huge ditch running through part of south Lakewood. The freeway split up neighborhoods and isolated part of south Lakewood. Photograph by Van Dillard; courtesy of the Cleveland Press Library and Collections, Cleveland State University Libraries

After many years under Republican Amos Kauffman, Lakewood elected Democrat Frank Celeste (1907-1988 office. Celeste attacked the declining base by encouraging apartment dev ment; these efforts added thirty milli dollars to the tax base. He also promo a strong code enforcement program maintain Lakewood's housing stock. Born in Cerisano, Italy, Celeste came the United States with his parents whe he was only ten months old. A gradu of Wooster College and Western Rese University Law School, he previously worked in a steel mill and waited tab to pay for his college tuition. Celeste re-election in 1959. He is being swor by Appellate Judge Joy Seth Hurd in December 1955. Photograph by Herman Seid; courtes of the Cleveland Press Library and Collections, Cleveland State Universit Libraries

"Richard Celeste, Lakewood mayor's son working as a garbage man" on July 11, 1956. The future governor of Ohio, Yale graduate, Rhodes Scholar, and former director of the Peace Corp learned government from the bottom-up. Courtesy of the Cleveland Press Library and Collections, Cleveland State University Libraries

While planning and construction for the first high-rise apartments on the Gold Coast began in the early 1950s, the major share of construction took place during the 1960s. By the time of this photograph June 4, 1971, building was nearly complete; only the Waterford remained to be built. These developments added greatly to the city's tax base. They also changed the city's skyline and brought many new residents to Lakewood. Photograph by Bill Nehez; courtesy of the Cleveland Press Library and Collections, Cleveland State University Libraries

Designed by the Chicago architects Loebl, Schlossman and Bennett, the Winton Place was advertised when it opened in 1963 as the tallest apartment building between New York and Chicago. With its glass walls and thin structural supports the building soars in contrast to the older brick apartments on the Gold Coast. Photograph by Frank Alecksandrowicz in 1967, courtesy of the Cleveland Press Library and Collections, Cleveland State University Libraries

C. Stephen Babin, president of Marwood, Incorporated, third from left and just to the right of Mayor Robert Lawther, nearly single-handedly transformed downtown Lakewood with the construction of the I.N.A. Building, Lakewood Center North, and the Medical Building for which ground is being broken here in August 1973. Courtesy of the Cleveland Press Library and Collections, Cleveland State University Libraries

the 1960s downtown Lakewood gan to change. The I.N.A. Building on right was Stephen Babin's first major oject shown here at Detroit and Saint arles avenues looking east in 1964. lier he had remodeled several buildings located at this intersection. However, future developments would remove entire block of stores on both sides of etroit from Saint Charles to Belle. The ell Gas Station, The Shanty, Rozi's ine Store, and the State Liquor Store ould be removed for the Lakewood nter North complex while the Medical uilding removed the Sohio gas station d the florist shop on the south side of etroit. urtesy of Lakewood Historical Society

abinwood," three of Stephen Babin's ajor projects in center Lakewood inude the seven-story I.N.A. Building, left ar; the seven-story Medical Building in e foreground, and the Lakewood nter North tower on the right pictured re in February 1978. urtesy of the Cleveland Press rary and Collections, Cleveland ate University Libraries

Chartered in 1911 as Orol Federal Savings and Loan Association, Home Federal Savings Bank represents a Village institution that has grown to serve all of Lakewood and the western suburbs. After many years at 12511 Madison, Home Federal moved to a new building at 12218 Madison; in 1961 they acquired adjacent property on Madison for parking. In the same year the bank celebrated its fiftieth birthday. In the next twenty-eight years Home Federal opened a branch office on Detroit at Victoria and recently moved its headquarters to downtown Lakewood at 14650 Detroit Avenue. Secretary-Treasurer Joseph P. Derba cuts the cake on April 25, 1961, as President George E. Fedor looks on.
Photograph by Rebman Photos; courtesy of the Cleveland Press Library and Collections, Cleveland State University Libraries

While many retail stores on Detroit found it increasingly difficult to compete with new shopping centers, some businesses have survived and prosper Founded in the depths of the Great Depression, Charley Geiger's Haberdashery shown here in 1936, h become an institution in downtown Lakewood. Originally located on the northwest corner at Warren Road an Detroit, they moved quickly to their present site just down the street. Over years, Geiger's has sponsored a wide range of amateur sports activities an teams in Lakewood.
Courtesy of Charlie Geiger, Jr.

Since the 1950s, a few large supermarkets surrounded by parking lots increasingly replaced the many smaller grocery stores that had once marked the streetcar suburb. By 1989 only a few grocery stores remained, requiring many Lakewood residents to drive to do food shopping. Even the Fisher Foods store shown here circa 1950 on Warren

failed to survive the decline in grocery stores; in 1989, this building became the new Post Office. Before construction of this store, Wilson School occupied the site.
Photograph by Bill Nehez; courtesy of the Cleveland Press Library and Collections, Cleveland State University Libraries

"Who'll buy my cookies?" asks Cheryl Ann Anson, 7, pocket-sized charmer from Brownie Troop 1442. Cheryl was second-grader at Lakewood's Hayes School in March 1959.
Photograph by Frank Reed; courtesy of the Cleveland Press Library and Collections, Cleveland State University Libraries

In addition to older service organizations, several new ones have emerged in recent years. Founded in 1980 as a nonprofit organization, and run largely by volunteers, the One World Shoppe at 14549 Madison Avenue pictured here in 1988 provides a retail outlet for craftspeople in underdeveloped areas to market their products. The store features crafts from numerous Third World countries as well as economically depressed areas in the United States. The store also promotes alternative forms of holiday celebrations. Over its first nine years of operation, the Shoppe has sold over four hundred thousand dollars worth of merchandise for these craftspeople.
Courtesy of the One World Shoppe

...ith Lakewood's service organiza-
...s: the Rotary, the Junior Chamber of
...merce, the Kiwanis, and others, the
...ewood Lions Club has greatly bene-
...d the larger community. Founded in
...1, the Lions supported efforts to
...ide school children with eyeglasses,
...the blind, and contribute to the work
...he Cuyahoga Sight Saving Council.
...y have also sponsored amateur sports
...vities. Here Lakewood Lions Club
...nbers pack light bulbs for their
...d-raiser.
...tograph by Herman Seid; courtesy
...he Cleveland Press Library and
...ections, Cleveland State University
...aries

...e city's population aged, Lakewood
...dents developed a series of programs
...rvice the needs of seniors. Con-
...ed about senior housing problems,
...rv Barton founded an organiza-
...s to focus on these needs. These
...rts led to the construction of the first
...sterly" apartment building which
...ned in 1963. Additions followed in
...9, 1974, 1980, and 1989. Barton
...helped establish the Senior Center in
...4 which is now named for him. A
...ner executive for Music Corporation
...merica, Barton was active in a
...nber of Lakewood organizations
...uding the Lakewood Rotary Club. In
...8, he was honored by the Veterans
...oreign Wars as Lakewood's "Man of
...Year." In addition to the Westerly
...rtments and the Barton Center, Lake-
...d established a series of neighbor-
...d centers for seniors. Directed by
...by Lawther, the Office on Aging pro-
...s a wide range of programs. The
...ton Center Chorus provided a Christ-
...s serenade on December 18, 1968.
...tograph by Fred Bottomer; courtesy
...he Cleveland Press Library and
...ections, Cleveland State University
...aries

Responding to the growing needs of Lakewood residents for help, the Lakewood Christian Service Center opened in the fall of 1982 as a counseling and food center. The following year they added a job placement service. Initially sponsored and founded by twelve Lakewood churches, the Center now receives the backing of twenty-six churches. Pictured here in 1988, Hazel Balogh on the left, and Harriet Irwin are bagging food for needy families. Formerly located at 14201 Madison Avenue, the Center recently moved to Marlowe Avenue near Detroit. The Service Center added to the work begun earlier with the establishment of the Garret Shop in 1946.
Courtesy of the Lakewood Christian Service Center

Winter recreation has long included ice skating. For many year Lakewood residents risked the ice on Rocky River to enjoy this sport; since 1918 residents have also had the pond at Lakewood Park. These teenagers are playing "Crack the Whip" at Lakewood Park ice pond in December 1969.
Photograph by Fred Bottomer; courtesy of the Cleveland Press Library and Collections, Cleveland State University Libraries

Long an institution in Lakewood, C Ice and Fuel's Winterhurst Ice Rink a major center for winter recreatio Opened in 1930, Winterhurst was t largest outdoor artificial rink in the country. Pictured here in 1960, the purchased Winterhurst the next yea 1975 the city opened the new skatin complex which cost over three millio dollars to build.
Photograph by Paul Toppelstein; courtesy of the Cleveland Press Libra and Collections, Cleveland State University Libraries

In 1962 the Recreation Department held their first Silver Skates Derby at Winterhurst Municipal Rink. Amateur skaters from around the state could compete by age and gender.
Photograph by Paul Toppelstein; courtesy of the Cleveland Press Library and Collections, Cleveland State University Libraries

While many recreational pursuits have remained the same, residents have added a number of new ones to their repertoire. Lacking the great swells of distant oceans, Lakewood youth have taken up "sidewalk surfing" in a big way. These young "hotdoggers" are well prepared for an encounter with "sidewalk surf."
Courtesy of the Lakewood Public Schools

A summer tradition in Lakewood Park, Lakewood residents listen to the "Star Spangled Banner," at the Home Town Concert in June 1968.

Photograph by Ted Schneider, Jr.; Cleveland Press Library and Collectio Cleveland State University Libraries

A 1965 graduate of Saint Edward High School, Ed Feighan on the left, attended Loyola University and Cleveland Marshall School of Law. Although unsuccessful in his bid for Cleveland mayor, Feighan, now a Lakewood resident, is in his fourth term as a U.S. Congressman. He previously served as a state representative and a county commissioner. Tom Campbell, on the right, taught at the Ohio State University campus in Lakewood until Cleveland State University opened. He is currently a professor of history at C.S.U. They are shown here as mayoral candidates during the campaign in Cleveland in July 1977.
Photograph by Larry Nighswander; courtesy of the Cleveland Press Library and Collections, Cleveland State University Libraries

The Great Lakes Shakespeare Festival opened on June 30, 1964. Lakewood's role as a cultural center for the entire metropolitan area was highlighted by the establishment of the Festival at the Civic Auditorium. Every summer from 1962 to 1981, the city hosted the festival. Special buses operated from Shaker Square to the Civic Center to bring east-siders to the programs. In 1982, the Festival moved to Loew's Ohio Theater on Playhouse Square.
Photograph by Frank Reed; courtesy of the Cleveland Press Library and Collections, Cleveland State University Libraries

FOCUS: Beck Center

The development of the Kenneth C. Beck Center for the Cultural Arts in '74 represented a major addition to Lakewood's cultural offerings. It also demonstrated the extent to which Lakewood had become a satellite center that served the entire western portion of Cuyahoga County. In the process, westsiders generally demonstrated their commitment and support the arts.

The Center emerged from an offer made by Kenneth Beck to the city of Lakewood for an art museum to be built in Lakewood Park. When the city proved unable to match the proposal, Beck turned to the board of the Lakewood Little Theater. He proposed to donate three hundred thousand dollars the community could match it. Westsiders came up with six hundred thousand dollars. Five savings and loan institutions pooled their resources to provide a mortgage. The forty-seven thousand square foot arts center cost about ten million dollars and is the only community theater in Ohio that contains a full arts center.

By setting the Center back from the street and providing a grassy area in front, architect Fred Toguchi broke the monotony of Detroit Avenue and provided a frame for his building. The Center's diverse facilities include a five hundred seat theater, a studio theater for experimental productions and a galleria which features the work of local artists and serves as an exhibit site for the collections of the Cleveland Museum of Art and the Cleveland Institute of Art. The Center also provides classes in the arts, dance, and theater, children's theater, teen theater, and meeting spaces. Its various activities attract two hundred thousand people each year.

By the end of Lakewood's first hundred years the wilderness that changed successively from orchard to suburb, had become a satellite city for the metropolitan area. With a major cultural center, an impressive center for major concerts, a well-equipped hospital, and extensive recreational facilities, Lakewood provided amenities often found in larger cities. The development of an office center in downtown Lakewood increasingly has made the city an employment center as well as a residential community. Its 1976 skyline, marked by high-rise office towers and apartment buildings, also resembles that of a large city.
Photograph by Bill Nehez; courtesy of the Cleveland Press Library and Collections, Cleveland State University Libraries

While the Great Lakes Shakespeare Festival temporarily established Lakewood as a regional arts center, the founding of the Kenneth C. Beck Center for the Cultural Arts gave Lakewood a permanent institution to serve the metropolitan area. Inspired by Kenneth C. Beck, the Center emerged as a product of public and private efforts.
Photograph by Frank Reed; courtesy of the Cleveland Press Library and Collections, Cleveland State University Libraries

"Chorus Line" proved to be the most popular production in Lakewood Little Theater's long history. This rehearsal scene is from the 1985-1986 season.
Photograph by Humbert Studio; courtesy of the Beck Center

FOCUS: Bonne Bell

The growth of Bonne Bell, the well-known cosmetics company, reflects the growth of light industry in Lakewood as well as the continuation of a long-standing family business. Started by Jesse Grover Bell in the basement of his Cleveland house, Bonne Bell moved to an east side factory in 1927. Two years later when his business again outgrew his facilities, Bell moved his fledgling company to Lakewood. Since that time, Bonne Bell has had three locations in Lakewood: Detroit and Giel, Detroit and Spring Garden, and then to its current location at Detroit and Graber avenues. In 1969, the Bell family redeveloped an entire block at the latter site for their corporate headquarters. The Georgetown house facade brought a distinctive look to the neighborhood. In 1989, the Lakewood facility employed about one hundred workers.

Bonne Bell has always been a family business. When Jesse Sr. stepped down in the 1960s, he passed the reins on to his son, Jesse Jr., and daughter, Bonne Bell Eckert. The third generation James and Jesse Bell, III, are now being groomed for future leadership.

Bonne Bell is well known for its healthy skin care image; its major mar[ket] initially was teenagers. The company developed a market niche for a health[y] and athletic look. They serve as corpo[r]ate sponsor for 10K marathons, the outward bound program, charity runs, and multiple events for the growing number of women athletes, including tennis, skiing, biking, hiking, white water canoeing, and mountain climbi[ng].

Bonne Bell has also implemented f[it]ness and good health programs for the employees. Their facilities at Westlake of a track, tennis courts, and health clu[b] are available to employees. The company encourages employees to maintain moderate weight and forego smoking.

The new Bonne Bell Company building is shown here at Graber Drive and Detroit Avenue, circa 1969.
Photograph by Fred Bottomer; courtesy of the Cleveland Press Library and Collections, Cleveland State University Libraries

Chapter 14

VIGNETTE

Still Diverse After All These Years

From its founding as a pioneer outpost in the early years of the nineteenth century to the present, Lakewood has attracted a diverse population. As a frontier society it housed the majority of the county's African-American population. At the beginning of the twentieth century, Lakewood drew significant numbers of immigrants from western, central, and eastern Europe as well as from the British Isles. It also attracted native-born Americans. The origins and nature of Lakewood's diversity have changed over the years while the city continues to attract new peoples. Newcomers brought new perspectives and a penchant for founding institutions and businesses. Some of Lakewood's greatest success stories come from the ranks of its immigrant population. Newcomers renewed the city and added the cosmopolitan touch that has made it a far more interesting and enjoyable place to live.

The following families and businesses represent a sampling of Lakewood's newer residents. Some have been here for over ten years, while others have arrived more recently.

The Huang Family

Anne En-Hwa and Jang Huang each came to the United States from Taiwan. They met in New Jersey while they both worked for a Chinese-American family that owned a restaurant. After marrying and working at a variety of jobs, they settled on the restaurant business.

They learned the business by working for a number of Chinese restaurants. In 1983, they opened a small restaurant, Szechwan Garden, on Detroit at Gladys. When the building was slated to be torn down to make way for Burger King, they moved to larger quarters at 13800 Detroit. During this time their family grew with the birth of three children.

To survive and prosper, the Huangs have worked very long hours. Their efforts have been rewarded by excellent reviews and a regular clientele. Many consider Szechwan Garden to be one of Cleveland's best Chinese restaurants. As with many family businesses in the past, such as the Golds, Schermers, Lodziewskis, and Pankuchs, Anne and Jang have drawn on their extended family. Anne's parents emigrated from Taiwan to help. Her father works in the kitchen while her mother looks after the three children. A success story, the Huangs now own three restaurants and employ twenty-five people.

The Jackson Family

As the Huang family, the Jackson family also reflects hard work and the growing racial diversity in Lakewood. The Jacksons moved to Lakewood in 1978 when Jerome Jackson's employer transferred him from Los Angeles. They decided to live on the Gold Coast. Several years afterwards they bought Margaret Butler's house on Edgewater Drive. Mrs. Jackson moved back to the Gold Coast with her youngest child, Eric, after she was widowed and her daughters left for college.

The Jacksons were attracted to Lakewood by the affordable housing, good schools, and proximity to the airport. Although Vernice Jackson was concerned about possible racial hostility to their children, the Jacksons found Lakewood friendly and family-oriented. An important contributor to community life, Vernice has served as president and as a board member of the Lakewood YWCA; she has also served on the board of the Lakewood Junior Women's Club. She has also volunteered at Lakewood Hospital. In addition to these activities she works in corporate training and development for Parker Hannifin

Corporation in Cleveland.

Mrs. Jackson has observed the increase in African Americans in Lakewood since their arrival. Her daughters may well have been Taft School's first black students. By the 1988 Christmas pageant at Taft, eleven black youngsters participated. She notes other blacks are now visible in the community.

The Saadi Family

The Saadis, Hussein and Najwa, came to the United States from Beirut, Lebanon, in June 1987. Hussein received a fellowship in endocrinology at Case Western Reserve University Medical School. In Beirut, Najwa worked as a chemistry teacher. They are Sunni Muslims.

The Saadis are very concerned about conditions in their native land and are unsure whether they will return. They miss family members very much, but Lebanon is war torn. When Najwa gave birth to twins, her mother, Mounira, came to help take of them. The Saadis chose to live in Lakewood because they already had friends living here and because they feel secure.

The Skorobatckyj Family

Irena and Wladimir Skorobatckyj both migrated to Lakewood from Poland. Wladimir came to the United States with his parents when he was a small boy. He met Irena some years later when he returned to Poland for a visit. When they met, Irena taught Polish and Russian. They married and came to the United States in 1974. Wladimir works as a computer programmer at Blue Cross. Irena could not find work as a language teacher and so she embarked on a new career. She is currently working in a dentist's office and studying to be an extended function dental assistant at Case Western Reserve University. Their son Andrew, a seventh grader at Saint Rose School, is actively involved with the Teen's Theater at Beck Center. The Skorobatchkyjs are an active family and can frequently be seen bicycling along Lake Avenue and in Lakewood Park.

Another State of Mind Book Store

Lakewood is home to a large lesbian and gay community many of whom are professionals or own their own businesses. Linda Malicki, who started the bookstore, gained business experience in her parents' meat market and other jobs such as managing a McDonald's restaurant. She became aware of the limited number of book stores in the city; she saw that none served the feminist or gay/lesbian communities.

She opened Another State of Mind bookstore on May 9, 1987. Business has been good with sales doubling since its founding. The bookstore also functions as a community resource, an information and referral center. Another State provides individualized attention to customers. Under the watchful eye of Sophie, the cat, customers may have a cup of tea and receive assistance finding the right book for themselves or as a gift.

Minh-Van Vietnamese Restaurant

The Tran family came to the United States from Vietnam in 1981. As with many other immigrant families depicted in this book, all seven family members work. Mrs. Tran, Phung Tu, and her daughter, Kim, run the restaurant, the only Vietnamese one in Lakewood. Kim dropped out of college in order to help her mother with the business since Phung Tu has not yet mastered English. The Trans purchased the restaurant from a previous Vietnamese owner in 1988. They specialize in hot beef soup, egg noodle soup, fried rice, and Vietnamese crepes.

A Taste of Thailand Restaurant

In 1981 Dr. Pradist Satayathum, a surgeon, opened A Taste of Thailand Restaurant at 14803 Madison Avenue. A Lakewood resident since 1963, he had previously owned The Continental Inn. As with many other family businesses in Lakewood, Taste of Thailand has involved a number of Dr. Satayahum's relatives; his brother, John, was the first manager, followed by Pradist's son, Mark, and now, Pradist's sister, Toi Tan. A cousin from Thailand is currently living with Toi and helps out in the restaurant. John's daughter Patti also works there.

As with the Huang family and their Szechwan Garden, the Satayathums' hard work has produced success. A Taste of Thailand now has two other locations in Cleveland in addition to the initial restaurant in Lakewood.

Szechwan Garden has earned a reputation for being one of the best Chinese restaurants in the Cleveland area. Jang and Anne Huang are the owners of this and two other restaurants in the metropolitan area. From left to right: Anne's cousin Connie; Anne's sister Angie; Ma En-Hwa, Anne's father; and Jang and Anne Huang are shown here in 1986. Courtesy of Anne Huang

*rnice Jackson and her son Eric at
ne in their Gold Coast condominium
1988.
urtesy of Vernice Jackson*

*The Saadi family at home in their Lake
Avenue apartment in 1988. From the
right are Najwa, Hussein, and Najwa's*

*mother, Mounira with the twins.
Courtesy of Najwa Saadi*

*Pictured here are Irena Skorobatckyj
and her son Andrew at Lakewood Park
in 1988.
Courtesy of Andrew Skorobatckyj*

*ictured here is the Another State of
lind Bookstore in 1988 at 16608*

*Madison Avenue.
Courtesy of Linda Malicki*

*The Minh-Van Restaurant at 12210
Madison Avenue is shown here in 1988.
Photograph by Jim Borchert*

*A Taste of Thailand Restaurant is at
14803 Madison Avenue shown here in
1988.
Photograph by Jim Borchert*

BIBLIOGRAPHY

Books:

Abbott, Virginia Clark. *The History of Woman Suffrage and the League of Woman Voters in Cuyahoga County, 1911-1945.* Cleveland: William Feather Co., 1949.

Avery, Elroy M. *A History of Cleveland and Its Environs.* 3 vols. Chicago: Lewis Publishing Co., 1918.

Butler, Margaret Manor. *The Lakewood Story.* New York: Stratford House, 1949.

———. "Lakewood College Club's Forty Years: 1926-1966." Lakewood: Lakewood College Club, 1966.

———. *Romance in Lakewood's Streets.* Cleveland: W. Feather Co., 1962.

Clark, Clifford Edward, Jr. *The American Family Home: 1800-1960.* Chapel Hill: University of North Carolina Press, 1986.

Christiansen, Harry. *Lake Shore Electric Railway: 1893-1938.* Cleveland: Harry Christiansen, 1963.

———. *Trolley Trails Through Greater Cleveland and Northern Ohio.* 2 vols. Cleveland: Western Reserve Historical Society, 1975.

Coates, William G. *A History of Cuyahoga County and the City of Cleveland.* Chicago: American Historical Society, 1924.

Cuyahoga County Archives. *Sacred Landmarks.* Cleveland: Board of Cuyahoga County Commissioners and the Cuyahoga County Archives, 1979.

Daughters of the American Revolution, Lakewood, Ohio Chapter, The Historical Research Committee. *Early Days of Lakewood.* Lakewood: Daughters of the American Revolution, 1936.

Davis, Russell H. *Black Americans in Cleveland.* Washington, D.C.: Associated Publishers, 1972.

Gehring, Blythe, Comp. *Vignettes of Clifton Park.* Cleveland: Penton Press-Private Printing, 1970.

Gold, Herbert. *Fathers.* New York: Arbor House, 1962.

———. *Family.* New York: Arbor House, 1981.

Green, Harvey. *The Light of the Home: An Intimate View of the Lives of Women in Victorian America.* New York: Pantheon Books, 1983.

Gregory, William M. *The Story of James Nicholson.* Lakewood: Lakewood Public Schools, 1953.

Handlin, David P. *The American Home: Architecture and Society, 1815-1915.* Boston: Little, Brown and Co., 1979.

Higham, John. *Strangers in the Land: Patterns of American Nativism, 1860-1925.* New York, Atheneum, 1965.

Hull, Robert. *All the Way Home: Lake Avenue Years and Related Memories.* n. p., private printing, n.d.

Jackson, Kenneth T. *Crabgrass Frontier: The Suburbanization of the United States.* New York: Oxford University Press, 1985.

Johannesen, Eric. *Cleveland Architecture: 1876-1976.* Cleveland: Western Reserve Historical Society, 1979.

Johnson, Crisfield, comp. *History of Cuyahoga County, Ohio.* Cleveland: D. W. Ensign and Co., 1879.

Kimes, Beverly Rae. *Standard Catalog of American Cars, 1805-1942.* Iola, Wisconsin: Krause Publications, 1985.

Knight, Thomas Arthur. *Beautiful Lakewood: Cleveland's West End.* (Lakewood?: T. A. Knight, 1902).

Lowing, Frank C. *A Chronological Statement of Facts Concerning the City of Lakewood from Its Inception, including Portraits and Biographical Sketches of Policemen, Firemen and City Officials, Past and Present.* Lakewood: Published for the Benefit of the Fire and Police Pension Fund, 1915.

Lindstrom, E. George. *The Story of Lakewood, Ohio.* edited by Lawrence J. Hawkins, Lakewood: Ohio, George E. Lindstrom, 1936.

Megles, Susi, Mark Stolarik, and Martina Tybor. *Slovak Americans and their Communities of Cleveland.* Cleveland: Cleveland State University, 1978.

Pankuch, Jan. *Dejiny Clevelandskych a Lakewoodskych Slovakov.* Cleveland: n.p., 1930.

Rehor, John A. *The Nickel Plate Story.* Milwaukee: Kalmbach Books, 1965.

Rose, William Ganson. *Cleveland: The Making of a City.* Cleveland: World Publishing Co., 1950.

Schauffler, Mary. *The Suburbs of Cleveland: A Field Study of the Metropolitan District outside the Administrative Area of the City.* Chicago: University of Chicago Press, 1945.

Siebert, Wilbur H. *The Underground Railroad from Slavery to Freedom.* New York: Arno Press, 1968.

Stevenson, Katherine Cole, and H. Ward Jandl. *Houses by Mail: A Guide to Houses from Sears, Roebuck and Company.* Washington, D.C.: National Trust for Historic Preservation, 1986.

Van Tassel, David D., and John J. Grabowski, eds. *The Encyclopedia of Cleveland History.* Bloomington: Indiana University Press, 1987.

Wager, Richard. *Golden Wheels: The Story of the Automobiles Made in Cleveland and Northeastern Ohio, 1892-1932.* Cleveland: Western Reserve Historical Society, 1986.

Warner, Sam Bass. *Streetcar Suburbs: The Process of Growth in Boston, 1870-1900.* 2nd ed., Cambridge: Harvard University Press, 1978.

Wheeler, Robert A. *". . . Pleasantly Situated on the West Side."* Cleveland: Western Reserve Historical Society, 1980.

Wickham, Mrs. Gertrude Van Rensselaer, ed. *Memorial to the Pioneer Women of the Western Reserve.* 2 vols., Cleveland: Woman's Department of the Cleveland Centennial Commission, 1896.

Wilson, Joseph and Eleanor Chidester, eds. and comp. *A Compilation of Histories: The Lakewood Public Schools.* Lakewood: Lakewood Public Schools, 1984.

Maps and Atlas:

Flynn, Thomas, Otto Barthel, R. H. Bunning, and Thomas Hassan. *Atlas of the Suburbs of Cleveland.* Philadelphia, A. H. Mueller and Co., 1898.

Hopkins, G. M., and Co. *Plat Books of the City of Cleveland and Suburbs.* Philadelphia: G. M. Hopkins, 1912-56.

Lake, D. J. *Atlas of Cuyahoga County.* Philadelphia: Titus, Simmons, and Titus, 1874.

Sanborn Map Publishing Company. *Insurance Maps of Cleveland.* New York: Sanborn Map Publishing Co., 1913-1929.

Institutional Histories:

"A Brief History of Lakewood Public Library." (Lakewood Public Library).

Butler, Margaret Manor. *Fifty Years of Service to Lakewood Children: A Brief History of the Lakewood Day Nursery, 1921-1971.* Flyer, n.c., n.p., n.d.

Cincik, Dr. Joseph. *SS. Cyril and Methodius Church—1949.* Lakewood: Saints Cyril and Methodius Church, 1949.

The Clifton Club: 75th Anniversary. n.c., Clifton Club, 1978.

The Clifton Park Land Improvement Company. Cleveland: Clifton Park Land and Improvement Company, n.d.

Fowerbaugh, Albert E. "The Church of the Ascension, Lakewood, Ohio: The First Hundred Years, 1875-1975." typescript, Church of the Ascension, 1975.

Gethsemane Evangelical Lutheran Church. *Twenty-Fifth Anniversary.* Lakewood: Gethsemane Evangelical Lutheran Church, 1973.

Lakewood Congregational Church. *Fortieth Anniversary.* Lakewood: Lakewood Congregational Church, 1945.

Lakewood Methodist Church. *A Living Centennial: 1876-1976.* Lakewood: Lakewood United Methodist Church, 1976.

Mecredy, Alice. *History of Lakewood Presbyterian Church.* Lakewood: Lakewood Presbyterian Church, 1982.

Memorial Booklet of the Fiftieth Anniversary of St. Lukes Parish, 1922-1972. n.c., Saint Lukes, 1972.

National Carbon Company, Inc. *Cleveland Works: Its History and Activities.* n.p., National Carbon Company, n.d.

———. *National Carbon Company: History, Products, Organization.* n.c., Union Carbide and Carbon Corporation, 1953.

Saint Clement's Parish. n.c., Saint Clement's Church, 1923.

Saint Clement's Church. *Respecting the Past We Look to the Future: 60th Anniversary, 1922-1982.* n.c., Saint Clement Church, 1982.

Saint James Community: 1908-1983. n.c., Saint James, 1983.

Saints Peter and Paul Lutheran Church. *Seventy-Fifth Anniversary—The Spirit of Christ '76.* Lakewood: Saints Peter and Paul, 1976.

Saints Cyril and Methodius Church. *Diamond Jubilee: 1903-1978.* Lakewood: Saints Cyril and Methodius Church, 1978.

Directories:

The Cleveland Directory: 1870-1974.

Cleveland West Suburban Directory: 1964-1976

Lakewood City Directory: 1949-1963.

Articles:

Albrecht, Carl W. "Profile: Jared Potter Kirtland." *Timeline,* 2 (April/May, 1985) 44-49.

Henry Alger. "The First Settlement of Rockport up to 1821." Cleveland *Morning Leader,* November 8, 1858, 1; November 9, 1858, 1.

‑tt, Timothy H. "An Introduction to Domestic Architecture in Cuyahoga ‑ounty with Emphasis on the Eclectic and Vernacular Styles." *Journal of ‑e Cuyahoga County Archives,* vol. 2 (1983), 9-46.

‑hert, James, and Susan. "The Bird's Nest: Making of an Ethnic Urban ‑illage." *The Gamut,* 21 (Summer, 1987), 4-13.

‑. Migrant Responses to the City: The Neighborhood, Case Studies in Black ‑nd White, 1870-1940." *Slovakia,* 31 (No. 57, 1984), 8-46.

‑ste, Frank P. "Lakewood, Ohio Blocks Urban Decay." *The American City* ‑August, 1958), 90.

‑man, Caren. "The West Side Jews." The Cleveland *Plain Dealer Magazine,* ‑ovember 2, 1975, 6-18.

‑t, H. Roger. "Interurban." *Timeline,* 3 (April/May, 1986), 14-33.

‑ill, Tom R. "Welfare in the Suburbs." *Cleveland Magazine,* 9 (September, ‑980), 56-63, 125-27.

‑bler, Sibley W. "Jared Kirtland and His Warbler." *The Gamut,* 23 (Summer, ‑988), 75-78.

‑ik, Frank. "The Crabgrass Empire." *Cleveland Magazine,* 10 (May, 1981), ‑1-88.

‑ Ten Safest Cities." *Esquire.* (December, 1973), 146-47.

‑man, John. "Fear and Loathing in Lakewood." *Cleveland Magazine,* 3 ‑November, 1974), 60-64.

‑ial Reports:

‑of Lakewood. *Annual Reports.*

‑erintendent and Clerk of Lakewood Schools. *Annual Reports.*

‑ies, Oral Histories and Reminiscences:

‑rs, Marie. "Memories of Lakewood." Lakewood Historical Society.

‑h, Emma J., Diaries: January 1-March 14, 1868; and 1891. Lakewood ‑listorical Society.

‑on, Jr., Wayne B. "How a Kid Survived the Great Depression." Lakewood ‑listorical Society.

‑ord, Sister Stanislaus. "Annals of the Congregation from the year 1851." ‑listers of Charity of Saint Augustine.

‑ic Women in Cleveland Oral History Project, Women's Comprehensive ‑rogram, Cleveland State University.

‑t, Sabrina, Diary (1843-1854). Lakewood Historical Society.

‑, Alfred M., Diary (1881-98?) Lakewood Historical Society.

‑, Mrs. Alfred M., Diary (1892). Lakewood Historical Society.

‑ublished Papers:

‑anic, Michael J. Jr. "The Slovak Community of Cleveland: Historiography ‑nd Sources." typescript, University of Akron, 1988.

‑. "Slovaks in Cleveland, 1870-1930: Neighborhoods, Politics and ‑Nationality Relations." typescript, University of Akron, 1988.

‑strom E. George, comp. "Unpublished Material of Lakewood History ‑Taken from Private Files of E. George Lindstrom." 2 vols. Lakewood: n.p., ‑940.

‑owell, James M. "Lakewood Churches: A Prolific Year." typescript, ‑Lakewood Historical Society Collection, 1980.

‑o Historical Records Survey Project, Service Division, Works Progress ‑Administration. "Historic Sites of Cleveland: Hotels and Taverns." ‑Columbus, Ohio: Ohio Historical Records Survey Project, 1942.

‑erka, Lucy Lang. "A History of Lakewood's World War I Veterans." typescript, ‑Lakewood Historical Society Collection, September, 1986.

‑vspapers:

‑eland *Gazette*

‑eland *Morning Leader*

‑eland *News*

‑eland *Plain Dealer*

‑eland *Press*

‑ewood *Citizen*

‑ewood *Courier*

‑ewood *Press*

‑ewood *Post (Sun Post)*

‑ewood *Suburban News*

‑ple's Penny Weekly

ABOUT THE AUTHORS

Jim Borchert is a Lakewood native and 1959 graduate of Lakewood High School where he lettered in wrestling and sang in the choir. A student of urban and community life, Jim holds degrees from Miami University, Indiana University, University of Cincinnati, and the University of Maryland. For eleven years he taught community studies and history at the University of California, Santa Cruz. A product of "middle Lakewood," Jim lived in "the Village" for two years while doing research on the neighborhood. In 1984, Jim and Susan returned to Lakewood to live on the Gold Coast. An associate professor of history at Cleveland State University, Jim has written widely on urban-ethnic life and visual history; his published works include a book on *Alley Life in Washington* published by the University of Illinois Press.

Photograph by Chuck Humel, Cleveland State University

Susan Borchert is an Ohio native and a graduate of Cincinnati's Woodward High School where she was act on the debate team. Susan holds three degrees in socio ogy from Ohio State University and has taught at Adrian College, San Jose State University, and Youngstown State University. In addition to her academic life, Susan has served as program director and director of the Associate Neighborhood Centers in Youngstown as well as direct of the Volunteer Center of Santa Clara County, Californi She has written articles on singles, pay-equity, and community history. Susan is currently an assistant professor social science at Lake Erie College in Painesville.

Photograph by Jim Borchert

Block B

Clifton Park Association 67.98

J.F.Rhodes & F.Sims

VISTA ST.

R

J.P.Rhodes & F.Sims 17.15

Phil.P. Miner 4

100 39/100

Clifton Park Association

L. Schlather 12.19

M.F.Wager 12

Francis Wager 10

12

John Zuske 10

A.A.Oviatt (et al) 950

Walter Phelps 20

Sophia Schupp 66

Walter Phelps 40.65

Elizabeth Dippel 41.04

6¾

47

Ebeles Webb 21

H.Osborn Sanderson

2.55

Augusta Hanna 10½ 44

Augusta Hanna 10½ 43

45

46 10.40

47 10½

48 6.94 John Webb 49

42

22 4.55

23

24

25

26

27

28

29

30

31 Geo. A. Beebe 10½ 33

J.C.Alber 8 32

2 F.M. Sherwood

Harriet Jackson

Seldon Beckwith 1342

6 Wm. Scholke

38

37

36

35

34

23

GRANGER ST.

R.Atwell

G.C.Atwell

C.R.Atwell John

50

51 52

Matthew C. Hall

53

8¾ 10½

10½ 54

10½ 55

10½ 56

10½ 57

10½ 58

10½ 59

John C. Hull 10½

2½ Matthew Thomas 2½

2½ Thomas C. Hall

¾

8

10½

10½

10½

Israel D. Wagar

10½

60

61

62

63

64 65

66

Frederick F. Hall 68 Alfred W. Hall

16.28

W. R. Maile 20

Wm. Maile

7.1

DETROIT

Mary Mullaly 26.37

A. M. Wagar 15.54

SUMMIT AVE.

Joseph Stanley 41.09

LA

John Mullaly 16.71

B. Farrell 7.88 S. Murphy 7.58

Jac. Clevring 13.14

Wallace & Julia Gleason 18.78

Israel D. Wagar 2.13

Israel D. Wagar 5

I.D.Wagar

AVE.

A.M.Wagar

A. M. Wagar 32.77

Nettie F. Wager 13.37

Olive M.Wagar 12.19

Caroline I. Wagar 11.74

Stella A. Backert 10.90

2.30

Sarah M. Day 6

Fred. Cook 9.43

F. Day 13.16

M.C. Hall 6

8

Archer Webb 7.87

Wm. Schifke 28.59

Emily McCreary

Hilliard

43.08

18

Reuben Hall 28.81

A. M. Wagar 10

2.70

Louis Gabel 18.27

Sarah Barnum 5

Magdalena Schmidt 18.69

A.Hahn 12.53

Martin Haering 13

Jennie M. Brooks

48